Mastering Unreal Engine 5 Game Development with C++ Scripting

Build efficient, scalable gameplay systems using advanced C++ in UE5

Marco Secchi

<packt>

Mastering Unreal Engine 5 Game Development with C++ Scripting

Portfolio Director: Rohit Rajkumar
Relationship Lead: Nivedita Pandey
Project Manager: Sandip Tadge
Content Engineer: Rohan Datta
Technical Editor: Tejas Vijay Mhasvekar
Indexer: Pratik Shirodkar
Production Designer: Shantanu Zagade
Growth Lead: Namita Velgekar

Production reference: 2080726

Published by Packt Publishing Ltd.
Grosvenor House
11 St Paul's Square
Birmingham
B3 1RB, UK.

ISBN 978-1-80666-593-8
`www.packtpub.com`

To my lovely wife Ambra, for those crazy laughs we share when I need them most.

– Marco Secchi

Foreword

Some time ago, I came across a GitHub page that referenced my blog, Romero Blueprints, as a useful resource for Unreal Engine. That page belonged to lecturer Marco Secchi.

Since then, I have followed his work, and it quickly became clear how dedicated he is to teaching game development to his students, and how much genuine passion he brings to it.

Marco chose to share his extensive knowledge of Unreal Engine with a broader audience through books. In 2023, he authored Multiplayer Game Development with Unreal Engine 5. In 2024, he followed it with Artificial Intelligence in Unreal Engine 5.

Now, we have *Mastering Unreal Engine 5 Game Development with C++ Scripting*, completing this trilogy.

This book is intended for C++ programmers who want to go beyond the fundamentals of Unreal Engine and stand out as professionals. Marco dives deep into the engine's architecture and explores advanced concepts that are essential for building complex projects. This is valuable knowledge for developing scalable, high-performance systems.

Throughout the book, the author uses the development of a game as a practical foundation, allowing readers to see how these concepts are applied in real scenarios and to use the project as a true experimentation lab.

It is rewarding to see that Marco has been able to create this guide for us: a carefully structured path that would be difficult and time-consuming to follow independently.

Marcos Romero

Author of the official Unreal Engine 4 Blueprints Instructor's Guide and Blueprints Visual Scripting for Unreal Engine 5

Contributors

About the author

Marco Secchi is a freelance game programmer with over 20 years of experience, working with game studios to develop custom tools and robust gameplay frameworks. He teaches at NABA (Nuova Accademia di Belle Arti) and Politecnico di Bari, where he mentors students and supports their transition into the game development industry. He is also the author of *Multiplayer Game Development with Unreal Engine 5* and *Artificial Intelligence in Unreal Engine 5*, published by Packt.

About the reviewers

Punya Aachman is a gameplay programmer with over six years of experience in the gaming industry. His work spans game titles, digital twin simulations, and immersive experiences across platforms including PC, PlayStation, Sony's Spatial Reality Display, and various VR headsets. With expertise in gameplay mechanics and building interactive worlds using tools such as Unreal Engine and Blender, along with programming in C++ and Python, Aachman enjoys researching game technology, pushing the boundaries of virtual worlds and exploring new ways to build engaging games.

Wanderson Lopes is a Brazilian software engineer and game developer specializing in Unreal Engine, C++, and gameplay and systems engineering. He has contributed to several game titles, both shipped and in development, working across gameplay features, AI, tools, technical systems, and production debugging. Based in the scenic mountain region of Rio de Janeiro, Brazil, Wanderson collaborates with international teams and is passionate about building reliable game systems, improving development workflows, and connecting technical design with practical implementation. As a technical reviewer, he focuses on clarity, accuracy, and real-world applicability for developers.

Table of Contents

Chapter 4: Getting the Best out of Pointers 59

Chapter 7: Improving Your Code with Subsystems 129

Chapter 8: Understanding Multithreading and Concurrency 149

Chapter 10: Developing Plugins and Modules 191

Chapter 11: Testing Your Application 209

Preface

Over the past decades, game development has evolved dramatically, with Unreal Engine standing at the forefront as one of the most powerful and versatile platforms available to creators. In the last few years, the engine has introduced groundbreaking technologies and tools that redefine the boundaries of what is possible in interactive entertainment, simulation, and real-time visualization. Central to harnessing the full potential of this engine is a deep understanding of C++, the programming language that underpins the engine's architecture and performance capabilities.

This book has been designed to serve as a guide for game developers who aspire to improve their skills and understand the true power of Unreal Engine through expert-level C++ programming. If you are an intermediate programmer seeking to deepen your knowledge, this volume offers a structured and detailed approach to mastering the intricacies of C++ within this dynamic environment.

Unreal Engine 5 is not merely a software, but a complex ecosystem that demands a grasp of both programming fundamentals and engine-specific paradigms. The engine's architecture, with its extensive use of object-oriented programming, memory management, and real-time systems, requires developers to think critically and write efficient, maintainable code. This book addresses these challenges by blending theoretical concepts with practical examples, ensuring readers not only learn the syntax and semantics of C++ but also understand how to apply them effectively within the engine framework.

Throughout the chapters, you will encounter a carefully curated progression of topics, starting from the essentials of the engine build pipeline and moving toward advanced subjects such as pointers, delegates, and multithreading. Emphasis is placed on best practices through practical examples, which are crucial for creating high-quality, scalable projects.

The journey to mastering C++ in Unreal Engine 5 will be both demanding and rewarding. It will require a lot of patience, and the willingness to explore complex concepts. This book aims to be a trusted companion on that journey, providing clarity, insight, and practical knowledge to empower you, as a developer, to create immersive experiences that push the boundaries of technology and creativity.

Welcome to the world of Unreal Engine 5 and the mastery of C++ programming. Your adventure begins here.

Who this book is for

This book has been written for game developers who possess a solid foundation in Unreal Engine and seek to improve their C++ programming skills to an advanced level. If you are proficient with the engine but wish to deepen your understanding of its C++ framework, this book will serve as an essential resource. Additionally, technical designers and gameplay programmers with experience in Unreal Engine who aim to master advanced principles and techniques for developing more robust and maintainable code will find significant value within its contents. Ideal readers should have a genuine passion for programming and game development, which will enable them to take advantage of the practical examples and comprehensive explanations provided. Whether you are an aspiring developer looking to enhance your skills or an intermediate programmer looking to refine your expertise, this book offers the insights and tools necessary to advance your career and create immersive, high-quality gaming experiences.

What this book covers

Chapter 1, Analyzing the Unreal Engine Build Pipeline, serves as an introductory overview of the core engine tools, providing readers with the fundamental concepts necessary to effectively work with the engine.

Chapter 2, Understanding the Engine Reflection System, offers a detailed explanation of the robust mechanism for exposing C++ classes, functions, and properties to the engine and its associated tools, including Blueprints, serialization, and the editor.

Chapter 3, Mastering Macros, explores the purpose, syntax, and best practices for using macros to leverage the full range of features available within the engine system.

Chapter 4, Getting the Best out of Pointers, guides readers through the complexities of safely managing pointers within the Unreal Engine environment.

Chapter 5, Handling Event-Driven Architectures, introduces the principles of event-driven design in Unreal Engine, showing how delegates and event dispatchers facilitate modular and responsive game systems.

Chapter 6, Working with Data Structures, explains the unique aspects of managing data structures in Unreal Engine, highlighting the advantages of using structs and how to expose their properties to the Unreal Editor.

Chapter 7, Improving Your Code with Subsystems, delves into the use of Subsystems to organize game logic and functionality in a modular and efficient manner.

Chapter 8, Understanding Multithreading and Concurrency, presents advanced techniques in multithreading aimed at enhancing game performance and efficiency when required.

Chapter 9, Working with the Log System, outlines common logging methods within the engine and provides guidance on maximizing their effectiveness.

Chapter 10, Developing Plugins and Modules, covers the essential steps for creating scalable features through the engine's module and plugin systems.

Chapter 11, Testing Your Application, introduces readers to the capabilities of the Unreal Engine testing framework, demonstrating how to use its features to maintain clean and reliable code.

To Get the Most Out of This Book

To maximize the benefits of this book, it is important to approach it with a solid foundation in Unreal Engine and a genuine enthusiasm for game programming. This book is aimed at developers who already have proficiency with Unreal Engine and are eager to elevate their C++ programming skills to an advanced level.

Additionally, to get the most out of the material, it is highly recommended to actively engage with the practical code examples and exercises, experimenting by modifying and extending them to fit your own projects. Focus on understanding not just the "how," but the "why" behind Unreal Engine's architecture and techniques presented in every chapter. This book assumes familiarity with core concepts, so be prepared to challenge yourself with complex topics such as memory management, performance optimization, and scalable code design.

Additionally, integrating the lessons learned here into your daily development workflow will reinforce your skills and help you write cleaner, more maintainable code. Use this book as a reference to solve real-world problems and as a guide to architecting gameplay systems. By combining theory with hands-on practice, you will transform your existing knowledge into expert-level proficiency, and you will be subsequently able to work on high-quality projects that stand out in the game development industry.

Download the example code files

This book includes a complete downloadable code bundle containing all the example projects and files used throughout the chapters. We recommend downloading the bundle so you can follow along smoothly and experiment with the examples.

Use the bundle as a practical starting point. Modify it, extend it, and apply what you learn by creating your own variations as you progress through the chapters.

Get the code bundle

If you bought the book directly from Packt:

1. Go to `packtpub.com`
2. Click your **profile picture** and select **Your Orders**
3. Find this book and click **Download Code**

If you bought this book from Amazon or any other channel partner:

1. Go to `packtpub.com/unlock` or scan the following QR code:
2. Search for this book
3. Sign up or log in to your free Packt account
4. Upload your proof of purchase and download the code bundle locally

> Note
>
> **Usage note:** You're free to use and modify this code for personal learning and non-commercial projects.

Download the color images

Your purchase includes a color, DRM-free PDF copy of this book, ideal for viewing color images, screenshots, and diagrams. Refer to *Free benefits with your book section* at the end of the *Preface* to unlock your PDF copy.

Conventions used

There are a number of text conventions used throughout this book.

`CodeInText`: Indicates code words in text, database table names, folder names, filenames, file extensions, pathnames, dummy URLs, user input, and Twitter handles. For example: " Each reflected class will use the `UCLASS()` macro declaration that will define `UE`-specific metadata."

A block of code is set as follows:

```
{
    GENERATED_BODY()

public:
    UFUNCTION(BlueprintPure)
    float GetCurrentHitPoints() const;

private:
    UPROPERTY(EditAnywhere)
    float HitPoints = 100.0f;
};
```

Bold: Indicates a new term, an important word, or words that you see on the screen. For instance, words in menus or dialog boxes appear in the text like this. For example: "The second file to consider is the **build file**."

Note

Warnings or important notes appear like this.

Tip

Tips and tricks appear like this.

Get in touch

Feedback from our readers is always welcome.

General feedback: If you have questions about any aspect of this book or have any general feedback, please email us at customercare@packt.com and mention the book's title in the subject of your message.

Errata: Although we have taken every care to ensure the accuracy of our content, mistakes do happen. If you have found a mistake in this book, we would be grateful if you reported this to us. Please visit http://www.packt.com/submit-errata, click **Submit Errata**, and fill in the form.

Piracy: If you come across any illegal copies of our works in any form on the internet, we would be grateful if you would provide us with the location address or website name. Please contact us at copyright@packt.com with a link to the material.

If you are interested in becoming an author: If there is a topic that you have expertise in and you are interested in either writing or contributing to a book, please visit `http://authors.packt.com/`.

Subscribe to Game Dev Assembly Newsletter!

We are excited to introduce **Game Dev Assembly**, our brand-new newsletter dedicated to everything game development. Whether you're a programmer, designer, artist, animator, or studio lead, you'll get exclusive insights, industry trends, and expert tips to help you build better games and grow your skills. Sign up today and become part of a growing community of creators, innovators, and game changers.

Scan the QR code to join instantly!

https://packt.link/gamedev-newsletter

Share your thoughts

Once you've read *Mastering Unreal Engine 5 Game Development with C++ Scripting*, we'd love to hear your thoughts! Scan the QR code below to go straight to the Amazon review page for this book and share your feedback.

https://packt.link/r/180666593X

Your review is important to us and the tech community and will help us make sure we're delivering excellent quality content.

Free benefits with your book

This book includes free benefits designed to support your learning and help you apply what you learn effectively. Activate them now for instant access (see the *How to unlock* section for instructions).

Here's a quick overview of what you can instantly unlock with your purchase:

Complete Code Bundle

Download the full source code for this book's examples and projects.

DRM-Free PDF Version

Download DRM-free PDF and ePub copies of this book.

7-Day Packt Library Access

Get 7-day unlimited access to 8,000+ books and videos. No credit card required.

Available for first-time Packt+ trial users only.

Next-Gen Reader Access

Read this book on Packt Reader with progress sync, dark mode and note-taking.

How to unlock

Scan the QR code (or go to `packtpub.com/unlock`). Search for this book by name, confirm the edition, and then follow the steps on the page.

UNLOCK NOW

Note: Have your invoice handy. Purchases made directly from the Packt website don't require an invoice.

Part 1

Delving Deep into the Unreal Engine Architecture

In the very first part of this book, you will explore the complexities of a game engine from the perspective of a game programmer. Beginning with a comprehensive analysis of the engine pipeline, you will progress to advanced topics such as Reflection System, macros, and the challenging concept of pointers. Once you have developed a solid understanding of these subjects, you will be well-prepared to advance to the subsequent stages.

This part of the book includes the following chapters:

- *Chapter 1: Analyzing the Unreal Engine Build Pipeline*
- *Chapter 2: Understanding the Engine Reflection System*
- *Chapter 3: Mastering Macros*
- *Chapter 4: Getting the Best out of Pointers*

1

Analyzing the Unreal Engine Build Pipeline

Welcome to the exciting world of C++ programming in Unreal Engine 5! I'm absolutely delighted that you have chosen this book as your guide as you begin what can sometimes be a daunting journey to C++ mastery. Using C++ in Unreal Engine opens up incredible possibilities for game development, and I'm committed to making this learning experience both accessible and enjoyable for you, my dear reader.

Throughout the book, I'll be presenting advanced core concepts, delving into practical examples, and equipping you with the skills to build truly impressive games. We will start by understanding how the engine builds a project, and then we will take a closer look at more advanced concepts, such as how the Reflection System works or how the engine handles the dreaded pointers. As we progress with this journey, you will start learning how to take advantage of your newly acquired skills and how to put them to good use. By the end of this book, you will be proficient in crafting advanced game experiences that will make you a professional in the video game industry.

But first things first! In this chapter, I will introduce you to how the engine build pipeline works and how it handles your project files. In particular, we will be covering the following topics:

- Understanding the Unreal Engine build pipeline
- Presenting Unreal Build Tool
- Presenting Unreal Header Tool
- Presenting Unreal Automation Tool

> Note
>
> **Your purchase includes a free PDF copy + code bundle**
>
> Your purchase includes a DRM-free PDF copy of this book, the code bundle, and additional exclusive extras. See the *Free benefits with your book* section in the *Preface* to unlock them instantly and maximize your learning.

Technical requirements

In this section, we'll be discussing some prerequisite knowledge that will be beneficial during your journey into game engine C++ programming.

Prerequisite knowledge

To ensure you get the most from this book on game programming, I'd like to establish some sort of baseline; all the topics presented require some strong existing UE knowledge. Therefore, to fully leverage the concepts presented in this book, I highly recommend that you are already familiar with the following:

- **UE proficiency**: A working knowledge of the editor interface and core workflows is crucial. You should be comfortable navigating the editor and utilizing its primary features.
- **Game development fundamentals**: A strong understanding of game development principles applied to the engine, including common terminology, design patterns, and core concepts, will significantly enhance your ability to grasp the material. In particular, you should have a good grasp of the UE **Gameplay Framework** (**GF**) and its main components.
- **Programming expertise**: This book assumes a degree of programming fluency. A foundational understanding of C++ is essential, and prior experience with C++ will greatly accelerate your learning and allow you to delve deeper into the advanced topics covered. Additionally, some familiarity with the UE visual scripting system (**Blueprints**) is expected.

> **Note**
>
> If you're relatively new to Unreal Engine C++ programming, I highly recommend starting with some introductory resources to build your foundation. A great place to begin is *Unreal Engine 5 Game Development with C++ Scripting* by *Z. G. Li* (*Packt Publishing*). Another great resource is *Elevating Game Experiences with Unreal Engine 5* by *G. Marques, D. Sherry, D. Pereira,* and *H. Fozi* (*Packt Publishing*). Both of them are excellent guides to the core features of the engine, C++, and Blueprint features.

Hardware requirements

You are most probably aware that the UE editor can indeed be resource-intensive, requiring robust hardware, most notably during the rendering phase.

Luckily enough, this book prioritizes C++ programming fundamentals, and we'll be focusing on the core coding aspects, rather than complex real-time visual effects; this means hardware demands will be less daunting.

To further ease your experience, 3D assets from the companion project use low-poly models that are both aesthetically pleasing and efficient. This means you shouldn't encounter performance issues, even if you don't have the latest high-end computer.

The project presented in this book has been developed with the following hardware:

Desktop:

- **Operating system**: Windows 10 64-bit version
- **Processor**: Intel Core i9 9900K
- **Memory**: 64 GB RAM
- **Graphics card**: NVIDIA GeForce RTX 3090ti

Laptop:

- **Operating system**: Windows 11 64-bit version
- **Processor**: Intel Core i7 13650HX
- **Memory**: 8 GB RAM
- **Graphics card**: NVIDIA GeForce RTX 4060

Software requirements

This book assumes you have the **Epic Games Launcher** and **Unreal Engine 5** installed and fully working on your computer.

> **Note**
>
> At the time of writing this book, the latest version of Unreal Engine is 5.7, but you will be able to follow along with any version more recent than 5.7.

Additionally, as we will mainly be working with C++, you'll need an IDE supporting this language and Unreal Engine, such as **Visual Studio 2019/2022** – available with a free Community Edition – or **JetBrains Rider**.

Now that we have reviewed the necessary background to start reading this book, let's start diving into some of the inner workings of the engine: how the build pipeline works. Understanding how the engine processes information is of paramount importance to becoming a top-level game programmer. So, let's get started!

Understanding the Unreal Engine build pipeline

UE gives developers robust production pipelines, enabling collaboration with professionals from diverse backgrounds. The engine offers a wide range of tools and features to support various workflows, ensuring a consistent stream of content and feature development.

So, the first question that may come to your mind is: what happens behind the scenes when you hit the **Build** button? This section will try to unravel the Unreal Engine (**UE** from now on) build pipeline. We'll explore its tools and the crucial process that transforms your work into a playable game.

If you are an experienced non-engine-related C++ developer, you will find many similarities – it's the C++ programming language, after all! – but you will see that things are not exactly the same; UE has its own peculiarities, and it's best to have a strong grip on them.

In the following sections, we will be exploring the main tools involved during the build project. In particular, we will be focusing on how the engine handles header files during the build phase and how complex projects can be managed and automated by a development team.

The first thing that you will need to understand is how the engine copes with the build phase, something we are going to explore in the next section.

Presenting Unreal Build Tool

Unreal Build Tool (**UBT**) is more than just a mere utility; it's the main actor orchestrating how your UE project is managed and prepared to ship; it will take your source code, assets, and configurations and will transform them into a playable, distributable game or application. In this section, we'll pull back the curtain and explore the inner workings of UBT, uncovering how it handles the compilation, linking, and packaging of your project. We'll delve into its key functionalities, understand its role in the build process, and learn how you can leverage its power to optimize your development workflow.

Exploring UBT core operations

The core operations executed by the UBT are **Dependency Analysis**, **Header Processing**, **Configuration Generation** and **Platform-specific Compilation**.

Let's analyze them one by one, in order to fully understand how they are involved in the build process:

- **Dependency Analysis**: During this phase, UBT begins by examining the project's structure, including all modules, plugins, and their dependencies. Additionally, it will analyze the timestamps of source and header files to determine whether they have changed, and subsequently, a rebuild is necessary. This clever system avoids unnecessary recompilation, saving valuable development time by only rebuilding what has changed.
- **Header Processing**: Once it has determined whether new dependencies have been introduced and whether a new compilation is necessary, UBT invokes an external tool – more on this in the next section – to scan the project C++ header files, identifying engine-specific metadata, such as `UCLASS`, `UPROPERTY`, and `UFUNCTION` macros. This metadata is crucial for the engine's Reflection System, which will be covered in *Chapter 2, Understanding the Engine Reflection System*, which enables features such as serialization, garbage collection, and Blueprint integration. During this phase, the system generates the necessary intermediate code and data structures that the engine will be using at runtime.
- **Configuration Generation**: During this step, UBT leverages the project's build scripts, primarily the `.Build.cs` and `.Target.cs` files, to generate the appropriate compiler and linker options. These files define the modules, dependencies, include paths, preprocessor definitions, and other settings required to build your project for specific

platforms. UBT parses these scripts and creates the command-line arguments that will be passed to the compiler and linker.

- **Platform-specific Compilation**: During this last phase, UBT launches the compiler for the target platforms specified in your build configuration. This involves invoking the compiler with the generated options, passing the source files to be compiled, and finally managing the compilation process. UBT handles the complexities of cross-compilation, platform-specific optimizations, and error handling, ensuring that your project is built correctly for each target platform. The final output is made of compiled object files and libraries, which are passed to the linker in order to create the final executable or package.

If you come from a traditional C++ background, you're likely already familiar with concepts such as dependency analysis and platform-specific compilation. However, you may find header processing and configuration generation somewhat less familiar. That's why I'll be focusing on these two topics; as header processing will be thoroughly examined in the subsequent section, let's first begin by analyzing the configuration generation process.

Understanding the main UBT configuration files

In this subsection, I'll be presenting some of the crucial files that are used by UBT to complete its tasks.

Introducing target files

The first one is going to be the **target file**, whose main task is to declare the target types for your game.

UBT will let you declare the following build targets:

- **Game**: Used for standalone games.
- **Client**: Similar to **Game** but used in networked games. It will exclude all server-specific code.
- **Server**: Similar to **Game** but used in networked games. It will exclude all client-specific code.
- **Editor**: Used to extend the Unreal editor itself.
- **Program**: Used to create standalone tools built on top of Unreal Engine.

Target files are located in the project root directory and are written in C# with a `.Target.cs` extension, and the filename matches the project name.

> **Note**
>
> It's probably worth noting that Unreal Engine configuration files are typically written in C#. This is why you'll frequently come across files with the `.cs` extension.

As an example, a UE project named *MyAmazingGame* will have a file named `MyAmazingGame.Target.cs` in the root directory. The file will declare a class deriving from the `TargetRules` base class and will set build properties in its constructor. Following our example, the target file will be pretty similar to the following block of code:

```
using UnrealBuildTool;

public class MyAmazingGameTarget: TargetRules
{
    public MyAmazingGameTarget (TargetInfo Target) : base(Target)
    {
        Type = TargetType.Game;
        DefaultBuildSettings = BuildSettingsVersion.V6;
        IncludeOrderVersion = EngineIncludeOrderVersion.Unreal5_7;
        ExtraModuleNames.Add(" MyAmazingGame ");
        // Add additional properties here
    }
}
```

Target properties are quite extensive; to delve into the full range of possibilities, I highly recommend taking a peek at the official Epic Games documentation that can be found at the following link: `https://dev.epicgames.com/documentation/en-us/unreal-engine/unreal-engine-build-tool-target-reference`.

Introducing build files

The second file to consider is the **build file**. As your project grows, you'll most likely end up having more than one of these files, as each module you create will have one of its own. We'll explore modules in detail during *Chapter 10, Developing Plugins and Modules*, so you can set those aside for now.

Each build file will define dependencies, libraries, and include paths. By default, each module is compiled into **dynamic-link libraries** (**DLLs**) and loaded by a single executable.

The main build file will be located in the `Source/[ProjectName]` folder and will have a `.build.cs` extension; the file name will be the same as the project name. In the example used earlier, this would be `MyAmazingGame.Build.cs`. The file will declare a class derived from the `ModuleRules` base class and set build properties in its constructor. Following this example, `MyAmazingGame.Build.cs` will look somewhat similar to the following block of code:

```
using UnrealBuildTool;

public class MyAmazingGame: ModuleRules
{
    public MyAmazingGame (ReadOnlyTargetRules Target) : base(Target)
    {
        PCHUsage = PCHUsageMode.UseExplicitOrSharedPCHs;

        PublicDependencyModuleNames.AddRange(new string[] { "Core",
"CoreUObject", "Engine", "InputCore", "EnhancedInput" });

        PrivateDependencyModuleNames.AddRange(new string[] {  });
    }
}
```

The `PublicDependencyModuleNames.AddRange()` function call is a crucial part of managing module dependencies in UE and will ensure that the necessary modules are compiled and linked when your module is built. This helps avoid issues related to missing references during compilation.

The difference between the `PublicDependencyModuleNames.AddRange()` and `PrivateDependencyModuleNames.AddRange()` functions primarily revolves around the visibility and accessibility of the modules you are declaring as dependencies; public dependencies will be available to any other module that includes this module, while private dependencies simply won't.

To have a clear understanding of the build file properties, I encourage you to get a look at the official Epic Games documentation, which can be found here: `https://dev.epicgames.com/documentation/en-us/unreal-engine/module-properties-in-unreal-engine`.

Using Clang

If you come from a Windows C++ background, chances are you are used to using the **Clang** compiler. The good news is that you can integrate Clang into your UE pipeline to compile your projects. To set up Clang, you can configure your build settings through the engine editor or specify command-line arguments during the build process. As Clang is compatible with the UE build system – including UBT – you will be assured of a seamless experience when compiling C++ code for your projects.

If you are interested in getting more information about the Clang and UE setup, I highly recommend checking out the official Epic Games documentation, which can be found at the following link: `https://dev.epicgames.com/documentation/en-us/unreal-engine/use-clang-to-build-microsoft-platforms-in-unreal-engine`.

Common UBT pitfalls

Given the complexity of the tool, it is not surprising that issues may arise during its execution. Setting aside C++ syntax errors, typical issues encountered when using UBT include missing or incomplete Visual Studio components. When required C++ workloads or SDKs are not installed, errors such as format exceptions or missing references may occur; these are typically resolved by installing the necessary components and SDKs.

Another common problem involves failures during project file generation. Such errors are often caused by outdated or corrupted files and can usually be fixed by regenerating the project files.

File access or permission-related issues may also arise; "access denied" errors may occur due to locked files or incorrect permissions. Resolving these issues often involves deleting user configuration files and resetting file or directory permissions.

Incorrect or missing build configuration XML files can further lead to unexpected UBT behavior; invalid configuration files located in user, application, or project directories are a frequent source of such problems.

Finally, static code analysis failures may occur when incorrect or incomplete flags are used. For example, omitting the `-DisableUnity` flag during Clang analysis can lead to suppressed diagnostics or misleading analysis results.

In this section, we have uncovered some of the core files used by UBT to start and manage the build process. In the next section, I will present how the build pipeline handles file headers and why it is so important to understand what's happening during this phase.

Presenting Unreal Header Tool

A crucial part of the build process involves using header files to manage declarations, streamline compilation, and ensure your code is well-structured and error-free. In UE, **Unreal Header Tool** (**UHT**) will manage this fundamental phase. UHT is a custom tool that processes C++ header files of `UObject` derived classes, generating the extra code needed for the engine's Reflection System, garbage collection, serialization, network replication, and editor integration.

This tool operates during the build process by parsing header files containing UE macros – such as `UCLASS()`, `UFUNCTION()`, and `UPROPERTY()` – and subsequently generating engine-specific code that enables UE to manage the lifecycle of `UObject` instances, reflect class metadata at runtime, and provide support for Blueprints.

> **Note**
>
> As a developer, you won't need to invoke UHT manually, unless you are working on custom extensions or debugging. UBT will handle its execution during the build phase.

UHT will also enforce coding conventions and metadata usage, which are essential for features such as Blueprint exposure or network replication. This means that having a proper header file structure is crucial, including the well-known `#include "[YourClass].generated.h"` statement as the final include in the header file.

Checking the .generated.h file

As previously mentioned, the `.generated.h` file enables essential features within the engine – including Reflection, serialization, garbage collection, and so on – and it is important to note that you should never manually edit this file, as it is regenerated each time you build your project. To achieve this, UHT parses your class headers, gathers the necessary metadata, and produces this `.generated.h` file along with the corresponding source one, that will have a `.gen.cpp` extension, before the compilation process begins. Without including this file, classes based on `UObject` would lack the necessary boilerplate code required to function properly within Unreal Engine systems.

> **Note**
>
> Generated files can be found in the `Intermediate` folder of your project. The exact location will depend on your operating system; for example, on a Windows computer, the location may be `/Intermediate/Build/Win64/UnrealEditor/Inc/[YourProjectName]/UHT`.

While you'll hopefully rarely need to examine the generated code, you might be curious about the reasons for even considering it. Firstly, generated functions can appear in the call stack during debugging. Secondly, you might encounter compilation errors that reference generated code. Therefore, understanding this code can significantly aid in resolving any issues.

Extending UHT

One last thing to mention about UHT is that it is completely extensible and will let you customize the process to suit your project needs.

The process begins with creating a plugin within your UE project that will serve as the container for your custom UHT extensions. Within the plugin, you'll develop the code that interacts with UHT, creating new classes or functions to introduce your desired features.

If your extension needs C# integration, you'll need to set up a C# project to facilitate communication with UHT. This can be beneficial for automating tasks or adding new capabilities. Additionally, you'll need to create an exporter to manage the output of your extended functionalities. This might involve generating additional code or modifying existing code based on your custom requirements.

Extending UHT is out of the scope of this book, but knowing that it can be done will open many possibilities for advanced customization and project-specific tooling.

Common UHT pitfalls

Typical issues encountered during the UHT phase of the build often stem from missing or incorrect use of reflection macros. Omitting required macros such as `UCLASS()`, `USTRUCT()`, `UENUM()`, `UPROPERTY()`, or `UFUNCTION()` will result in incomplete metadata and subsequent UHT failure.

Errors may also arise from syntax or formatting problems in header files. Invalid C++ syntax, misplaced macros, or missing semicolons can prevent UHT from successfully parsing headers.

Problems related to metadata or specifiers are another common source of failure. Using invalid, unsupported, or conflicting specifiers within `UPROPERTY()` or `UFUNCTION()` declarations may generate warnings or errors, which are treated as fatal by the tool.

Include issues can further disrupt UHT processing; circular includes, missing forward declarations, or improperly structured header dependencies may lead to incorrect parsing or outright failures.

It is also important to note that UHT runs with warnings treated as errors. As a result, any warnings, such as those related to deprecated features or potential issues, will cause the build to fail.

Incorrect or incomplete module configuration can likewise trigger errors; missing entries in `ModuleRules` or improperly defined `PublicDependencyModuleNames` often result in unresolved dependencies during header processing.

Finally, build configuration or synchronization problems, such as outdated or corrupted project files, can lead to failures during the parsing stage.

In this section, you've been introduced to UHT and its core features, highlighting its critical role in building Unreal Engine projects. In the next section of this chapter, you will be introduced to another actor that will make your life easier as your project grows in complexity.

Presenting Unreal Automation Tool

Unreal Automation Tool (**UAT**) is a command-line tool that includes a set of utility libraries designed to script and automate various UE processes. It is usually executed by UBT during the build process – that is, you won't usually need to execute it by yourself – and it will let you streamline unattended operations such as building, cooking, packaging, deploying, and running games, as well as executing automation tests and other custom scripted tasks.

What's more, as a key part of the UE build pipeline, it will allow you and your development team to integrate automation into **Continuous Integration** (**CI**) systems and ensure consistent, reliable project builds across environments.

UAT will use C# projects with the `.Automation.csproj` extension to define commands that are implemented as classes derived from `BuildCommand`. The system runs on any supported operating system – Windows, macOS, and Linux – either through the command line or the Visual Studio debugger.

> **Note**
>
> If you are curious and want to check out a UAT project, Epic Games provides the full source code with UE. It can be found under the `[UE Version]/Engine/Source/Programs/AutomationTool` folder.

Probably the most important operation in UAT is the `BuildCookRun` command, which will execute the following operations:

- **Build**: Compile the source code of your project
- **Cook**: Process your project assets – such as texture, models, and so on – to be prepared for the target platform
- **Package**: Gather all the needed files in a single distributable format
- **Run**: Execute the packaged project so that it can be tested

As you can imagine, taking advantage of this process will really help you save a lot of time and effort!

Finally, UAT integrates with a variety of systems, including script-based tools. A key component of this integration will be discussed in the next subsection.

Understanding the Build Graph

A key aspect of working with UAT is **BuildGraph**, a script-based build automation system that will organize build processes using common building blocks found in a project.

BuildGraph is a declarative system written in XML that combines elements of makefile-style scripting languages with the features of a build farm configuration script. A BuildGraph operation structure is defined mainly by **tasks** and **nodes**. A task is an action that can be executed during the build process, for instance, compiling or cooking, while a node is a sequence of such tasks that can be executed in sequence. Nodes can be grouped together and identified as a single entity. Additionally, you can define **agents** inside a graph that will perform actions or operations as part of the build process. Finally, elements can be conditionally executed – basically, with an `if` condition – so you will be able to implement your own branching system depending on conditions and build events.

This system allows you to define operation dependencies with highly configurable settings. Furthermore, you can extend it with custom elements.

As a quick example, consider the example depicted in *Figure 1.1*:

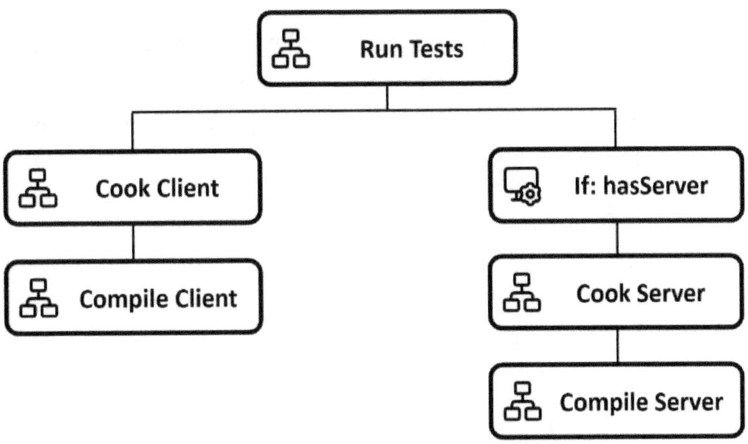

Figure 1.1 – BuildGraph example

As you can see from this quite simple example, BuildGraph will start by running all tests and then cook and compile the client. If needed, the server will also be cooked and compiled.

The last thing to mention is to have a basic understanding of how to take advantage of UAT to test your games before shipping, something I'm going to present right now.

Testing your game

One of the cool things you can do with UAT is test your game features. UAT allows you to automate a wide range of testing procedures, from simple functionality checks to complex performance evaluations. You can set up automated tests that run regularly, ensuring that new changes don't break existing functionality. This includes testing on different platforms, simulating various network conditions, and even running stress tests to identify potential bottlenecks.

There are two main types of tests you can run during the automation phase:

- **Functional tests**
- **Automation tests**

Functional tests are Blueprint-driven tests that are usually run to check gameplay logic; for example, you may use them to check whether your player can pick up some dropped item or whether a weapon does indeed spawn bullets.

A functional test is created as a regular Blueprint extending the `FunctionalTest` class, and it will provide dedicated nodes, such as `Event Start Test` or `Finish Test`, to let you check whether your logic still works as your project progresses. *Figure 1.2* depicts a functional test placed into a game level from this book's companion project:

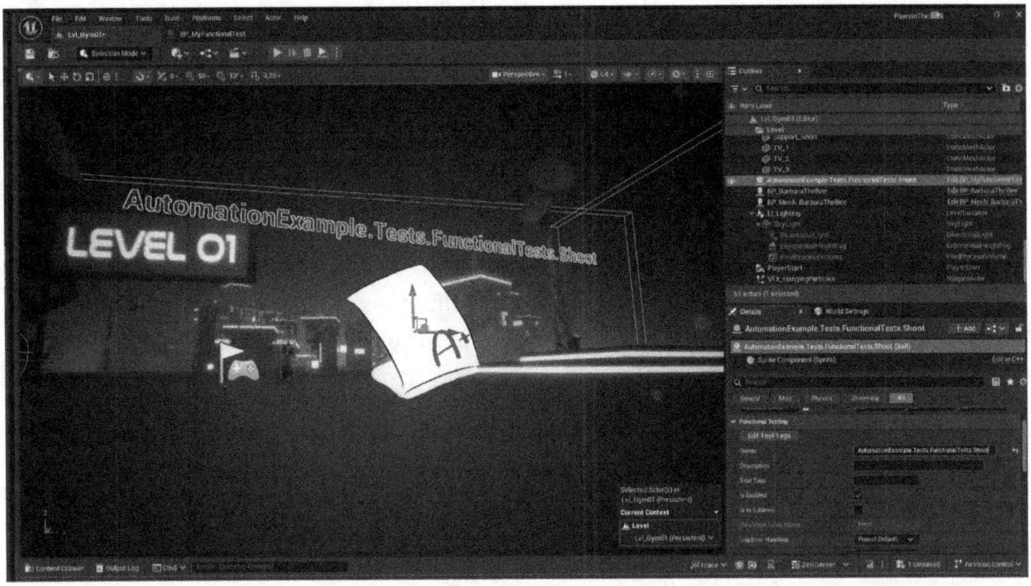

Figure 1.2 – A functional test in the level

On the other hand, automation tests are C++ tests that run outside of the `UObject` system to perform low-level functionality checks within the engine, such as unit tests. They are implemented by deriving from the `FAutomationTestBase` class.

Tests can be grouped into categories to organize and manage them effectively.

If, at the moment, things seem a bit too abstract, fear not! In *Chapter 11, Testing your Application*, I will present a practical example on how to take full advantage of these engine features.

As a final note, UE provides an automation framework named **Gauntlet** designed to run sessions of projects that perform tests and validate results across multiple platforms. Gauntlet manages the execution of game sessions (such as multiplayer clients and servers) and handles testing workflows without requiring specific game-side automation code.

Common UAT pitfalls

Typical issues encountered during the UAT phase are often related to synchronization and configuration problems. One common cause is misconfigured sync filters, where essential directories such as Win64 platform files or source code are unintentionally excluded. This can lead to errors such as `Failed to find command BuildCookRun`.

Another frequent issue occurs when the engine source folder is missing. Even when using precompiled engine binaries, the source directory is still required for cooking and packaging operations, and excluding it will result in UAT failures.

Compiler memory limitations can also disrupt the UAT phase. Errors such as `Fatal Error C1060` or `Fatal Error C1076` indicate insufficient heap space for the compiler; restarting the machine or increasing the system page file size is often an effective workaround.

Problems with Perforce workspaces are another common source of failure. Sync conflicts or incomplete synchronizations, particularly missing engine source files, can cause UAT commands to fail. These issues are typically resolved by performing a force sync or creating a new workspace.

Project file generation errors may also surface during this phase. Exceptions such as `UnrealBuildTool Exception: System.FormatException` often point to corrupted or malformed project files that need to be regenerated.

Additionally, misconfiguration within automation projects can lead to UAT command failures; incorrect settings in custom automation scripts or missing references frequently prevent successful execution.

Finally, errors may occur within the **BuildCookRun** pipeline itself; failures can arise at any stage of the process, including building, cooking, staging, packaging, deploying, or running, and usually indicate underlying configuration or dependency issues within the project or environment.

Summary

In this chapter, you were presented with how the build process works in UE. Starting from UBT, the major orchestrator of all things happening, we explored why UHT is so important and how it handles the header processing phase. Finally, you were introduced to UAT, a tool that will help you in automating the more repetitive tasks of game development. In the upcoming chapter, we'll explore the incredible capabilities of the engine's Reflection System. Brace yourself, as we have just ignited the engine; this is going to be an exciting and rewarding journey!

Credits

The examples in this chapter were created with the help of *Assetwave Black Outline* icons from Flaticon (`https://www.flaticon.com/`).

Get this book's PDF copy, code bundle, and more

Scan the QR code (or go to `packtpub.com/unlock`). Search for this book by name, confirm the edition, and then follow the steps on the page.

UNLOCK NOW

Note: Have your invoice handy. Purchases made directly from the Packt website don't require an invoice.

2

Understanding the Engine Reflection System

In this chapter, I will be presenting a comprehensive examination of the UE **Reflection System**, a fundamental mechanism within the engine architecture. We will explore the theoretical underpinnings of this feature, including its role in metadata management and runtime introspection. Next, we will examine how UE copes with Reflection and the engine core functionalities, analyzing the system's impact on code maintainability and extensibility. After that, I will be presenting you with UE interfaces that heavily use the engine Reflection System. Finally, I will be introducing this book's companion project, which will help us throughout the book in understanding all the presented techniques.

In particular, in this chapter, we will be focusing on the following topics:

- Introducing the UE Reflection System
- Explaining the header file format
- Working with interfaces
- Presenting this book's companion project

Technical requirements

You can download the companion project and code for this book by following the instructions in the *Download the example code files* section in the Preface of this book.

The full source code for this book is included in the downloadable code bundle as a single project.

Visit this link to check out the video of the code being run: `https://packt.link/nHZd2`

Introducing the UE Reflection System

As you may already know, **reflection** is a powerful feature in programming languages and frameworks, allowing your application to inspect and manipulate its own structure and behavior at runtime. This capability is particularly useful in complex software systems – and a game engine such as UE is obviously no exception – as it enables dynamic interactions with objects and their properties without needing to know their types at compile time.

A reflection system presents a range of benefits but also has certain limitations. The decision to use it depends on careful consideration of its advantages relative to its costs, but in many scenarios, the advantages are worth the cost. So, let's start by examining the main advantages of using Reflection when developing an application.

Getting to know Reflection advantages

Whenever talking about reflection, the main feature that comes to mind is **introspection**, which will allow a program to inspect its own types, methods, and properties at runtime. This means you will be able to query information about instantiated objects, such as their class – or interface, type, or available methods.

The second feature you should be aware of is **dynamic instantiation**; this will let you create objects dynamically without the need to know the class name. This will enhance your project's flexibility, allowing you to improve modularity and work with much more decoupled components. This feature comes hand in hand with **dynamic invocation**, which will let you call methods at runtime without hardcoding them when the code is written.

Reflection also gives you supercharged **metadata access** powers; this means you will be able to inspect annotations, decorators, or attributes that describe classes, properties, and methods.

The combined effect of these features is significant extensibility, which allows for the addition of new types or properties. This is particularly advantageous in game engines, where it facilitates the incorporation of new gameplay elements (or even plugins!).

With all this power available, a word of warning should be given about access control, as Reflection will let you bypass visibility rules, such as `private` or `protected`, so it's essential to proceed with extreme caution when dealing with it. Additionally, all these features obviously come with a performance cost, as reflection is slower than using direct calls.

So, let's check why UE makes heavy use of reflection and how it works directly in-engine.

Unveiling the power of Reflection in Unreal Engine

Unreal Engine is widely known for its robust features and flexibility. However, the critical role played by the **Reflection System,** a powerful mechanism at the engine's core, may be less well-known. This framework acts as the engine's internal mirror, allowing it to introspect, manipulate, and manage classes, properties, and functions both at runtime and within the editor. This capability is of paramount importance to many of the engine's key features, contributing to its ease of use and versatility.

At the core of the system are `UObject` and `UClass`; the first one is the base class for all reflected classes, while the second one is a meta-object that describes a class type derived from `UObject`. For each `UClass`, the system will automatically create a special instance, called **Class Default Object** (**CDO**), that will act as a template containing the default values for all properties.

The primary task of the Reflection System is to reflect `UObject` classes, which are the fundamental engine game objects, and their members. By inspecting into these objects, the engine can expose them to various critical systems, including serialization, garbage collection, networking, and the editor user interface. The benefits of the Reflection System are so many that they can't be listed easily.

Here, I will be presenting some of the most important ones in order to better understand why they are so critical. First, serialization is greatly simplified, as properties marked with the `UPROPERTY()` macro are automatically saved and loaded. This means that garbage collection will be highly enhanced, as references tracked by the aforementioned macro will be automatically nulled if the target object is destroyed, preventing much-dreaded memory leaks. Next, the Reflection System provides direct editor and Blueprint support, exposing properties and functions for editing and scripting without requiring manual bindings or complex setup; this is something your game designer and level designers will highly appreciate. Finally, the system enables **Run-Time Type Information** (**RTTI**), a C++ built-in system that allows your program to query the actual type of an object at runtime, rather than just at compile time, allowing developers to query class and type information dynamically. This means you will be able to use type-safe casting and type checking while your game runs.

Now that you have a basic understanding, it's time to explore how a C++ header file is organized, in order to see where some of the most important macros that make the Reflection System so powerful are declared.

Explaining the header file format

Now that you've got a handle on the engine's Reflection System, it's time to switch gears and refresh your understanding of how a UE class header is declared and structured. Perfecting your knowledge about the header file format is essential to becoming a professional UE developer, so in this chapter, we'll break down the format, revealing the secrets behind the macros, specifiers, and other elements that make your code work. As you already know, a header's purpose is to declare classes, functions, and variables that will serve as an interface for the implementation that will usually be coded in a .cpp file; in this section, we will be focusing on reflection-enabled declarations for classes, structures, and enumerations.

Analyzing a class header

When declaring a class header in UE, you will first add the #pragma once directive, which will prevent multiple inclusions of the header during compilation; Epic Games suggests using this directive instead of manual include guards as a best practice.

Next, you will add the needed includes and then the .generated.h declaration; this one needs to be the last directive, as including it earlier will break the ordering of assumptions of UHT and will lead to compilation errors due to missing declarations or unresolved symbols, and will generate issues in reflection serialization and garbage collection systems.

> **Note**
>
> As a good practice, you should try to use forward declarations instead of include directives where possible, in order to minimize coupling. Forward declarations will obviously be written after the .generated.h declaration.

Each reflected class will use the UCLASS() macro declaration that will define UE-specific metadata. A class definition will specify the **module export macro**, for instance, MYAWESOMEGAME_API, that will control symbol export when compiling code into DLLs. As an example, a declaration for a class named AMyAwesomeActor extending AActor that can be used in Blueprints will be pretty similar to the following block of code:

```
UCLASS(Blueprintable)
class MYAWESOMEGAME_API AMyAwesomeActor: public AActor
```

Inside the class, you will find the GENERATED_BODY() macro at the very beginning. This macro is used to inject boilerplate code generated by UHT. Without it, the class won't take part in the Reflection System and will lose all its benefits.

Inside the usual access specifiers – public, protected, and private – you will add functions decorated with UFUNCTION(); this is obviously not mandatory, and you can omit the macro if it is not needed. Similarly, variables will be marked with UPROPERTY(); in this case, you should be aware that not adding the macro will expose your variable to the garbage collection system, and usually the compiler will complain and send you a warning. As for UCLASS(), both UFUNCTION() and UPROPERTY() macros can include specifiers.

Following the previous example, you may have a class body similar to the following piece of code to handle hit points in your actor:

```
{
    GENERATED_BODY()

public:
    UFUNCTION(BlueprintPure)
    float GetCurrentHitPoints() const;

private:
    UPROPERTY(EditAnywhere)
    float HitPoints = 100.0f;
};
```

In *Chapter 3, Mastering Macros*, we will be exploring specifiers in detail, providing a comprehensive view of how macros operate. Let's now get to structures, in order to see how they are declared.

Analyzing a struct header

In UE, a **struct** is a lightweight data structure that is used to group related variables together; their main difference from a class is that they are recognized by the Reflection System, but they are not garbage collected. They can be used in Blueprints and are generally faster to create than `UObject` classes. Finally, they are value types and not pointers. In *Chapter 6, Working with Data Structures*, I will be presenting you with some examples on how to use structures to organize data in your game. For the moment, let's focus on how to declare their headers. To declare a structure, you will use the `USTRUCT()` macro instead of `UCLASS()` and, obviously, the `struct` keyword instead of the `class` one. A typical example may be a set of data for weapons, just like the following piece of code:

```
USTRUCT(BlueprintType)
struct FWeaponData
{
    GENERATED_BODY()

    UPROPERTY(EditAnywhere, BlueprintReadOnly)
    FName WeaponID;

    UPROPERTY(EditAnywhere, BlueprintReadOnly)
    float Damage;
```

```
    UPROPERTY(EditAnywhere, BlueprintReadOnly)
    float FireRate;
};
```

The last thing to mention is how we declare enumerations in the Reflection System.

Analyzing an enum header

In UE, an **enumeration (enum)** is a user-defined type made of a set of named constant values that are called **enumerators**. As you may already know, enums are typically used for categorizing states, flags, types, and so on. To declare an enum, you will use the `UENUM()` macro to expose it to the Reflection System and the `enum` keyword. As an example, consider the following enum for a list of weapon options:

```
UENUM(BlueprintType)
enum class EWeaponType : uint8
{
    Dagger UMETA(DisplayName="Dagger"),
    Sword UMETA(DisplayName="Sword"),
    TwoHandedWeapon   UMETA(DisplayName="TwoHandedSword")
};
```

The optional `UMETA()` macro will let you use a human-readable display name when showing enumerators in Blueprints. Please note the `uint8` declaration, in order to use only one byte per enum value, reducing memory usage. Additionally, a `unit8` type is expected in order to have property serialization and work properly with the Blueprints system.

In this section, I have presented how a UE C++ header file is organized in classes, structs, and enums. It's now time to present you with another crucial component of the Reflection System, that is, interfaces; as they are slightly trickier to understand, I will be presenting them in their own dedicated section.

Working with interfaces

In programming, an **interface** is a structure that defines a set of functions – essentially, a contract – without providing their implementation. In UE, an interface will let you implement this contract with some notable differences from regular C++.

First of all, they are fully integrated with the UE Reflection System and are also fully implementable in Blueprints. Next, while an interface in regular C++ will typically be an abstract class with pure virtual functions, in UE it is composed of two main parts:

- A class with the `U` prefix decorated by the `UINTERFACE()` macro that will be primarily used for reflection
- A class with the `I` prefix that will include all implementable functions

For instance, to create an `EquippableInterface` interface for your game with an `Equip()` function, you will declare something pretty similar to the following piece of code:

```
UINTERFACE()
class UEquippableInterface : public UInterface
{
    GENERATED_BODY()
};

class MYAWESOMEGAME_API IEquippableInterface
{
    GENERATED_BODY()

public:
    UFUNCTION()
    virtual void Equip(FString InventoryId);
};
```

To declare a function as implementable only in Blueprints, you will add `BlueprintImplementableEvent`; on the other hand, to declare a function that can also have a native C++ implementation, you will add the `BlueprintNativeEvent` specifier. In this second case, you will need to add the `_Implementation` suffix to the implementing function. In the previous example, you will be coding something similar to the following piece of code:

```
void Equip_Implementation(FString InventoryId)
{
    // Your code
}
```

This declaration is needed in order for the engine to generate a wrapper function with the interface method's original name. When executed, UE will call the interface wrapper that will route to either the Blueprint override or your `_Implementation` method.

It should be noted that, for regular virtual interface methods – that is, without `BlueprintNativeEvent` – you can override the function without the suffix. One such example can be found in the *First Person* template (*Variant Shooter*) available in UE since version 5.6, where the `ShooterWeaponHolder` interface declares functions such as the following line of code:

```
virtual void PlayFiringMontage(UAnimMontage* Montage) = 0;
```

To check if an instance implements an interface, you will use the `ImplementsInterface()` method, just like the following line of code:

```
if (AnActorInstance->GetClass()->
    ImplementsInterface(UEquippableInterface::StaticClass()))
{
    // Code Logic
}
```

Finally, to call a function implementing an interface, you will use the prefix `_Execute`, like the following code:

```
IEquippableInterface::Execute_Equip(AnActorInstance, InventoryId);
```

In this section, I have presented you with one of the main actors of the engine's Reflection System: interfaces. In the next section, we will get practical and explore a real-world scenario in detail.

Presenting this book's companion project

Let's say you've just landed a new project, and here's what the pitch sounds like:

Welcome to Holo District, where the rain tastes like battery acid, secrets are whispered in the digital wind, and neon signs are brighter than your future! Here, the line between man and machine blurs, and the corporations hold the keys to true power. At the heart of it all lies OmniSight Industries, a corporation that sees everything, knows everything, and most likely judges everything you do; a dark web of influence that touches every corner of the city. But even in this chrome-plated clown show, justice has a chance. Meet Team 33 – also known as The Pack – a team of elite fuzzballs, trained and augmented to sniff out the truth, even if it smells like stale synth-sushi. They're the only ones who can track down OmniSight's machinations, mostly because they're probably the only ones who can still smell them! Prepare to follow them down a rabbit hole that will uncover conspiracies that could shatter the very foundations of Holo District!

That sounds either like the best project ever or, alternatively, something we will lose our minds over, doesn't it? Luckily enough, I have been working on this project while writing this book, so all you will need to do is fire up the project and start checking the code with me. Well, sort of... every now and then, I'll throw in a little exercise, such as improving code or adding a small feature. This will be a great way to check your understanding of each chapter!

Introducing Paws in the Shell

The project we will be working on is called *Paws in the Shell: The OmniSight Conspiracy*. It has been developed in Unreal Engine 5.7 and is set in a futuristic cyberpunk world where the player manages a task force of cyber-augmented characters. The project is by no means a finished game! There's a lot still to be done, such as game balancing, audio, and cutscenes, but it will be more than enough to showcase all the topics that we will be covering throughout the book.

So, where can you find the project files? Packt provides a companion repository on GitHub where you can download a zipped version. The path to the repository can be found in the Preface of the book.

As I am no 3D modeler or graphic artist, but I love nice, clean projects, I have been using a set of open source (CC0) assets from two of my favourite asset providers on the internet. The first one is *Quaternius* (`https://quaternius.com`), where I have used the **Ultimate Space Kit** for the characters and the **Cyberpunk Game Kit** for the environment.

Figure 2.1 – Quaternius website

Then there's *Kenney* (`https://kenney.nl`), who's basically single-handedly responsible for half the indie game assets out there. You've seen his assets. Everyone's seen his assets. In this case, I've been using his **UI Pack – Sci Fi** for all user interface elements.

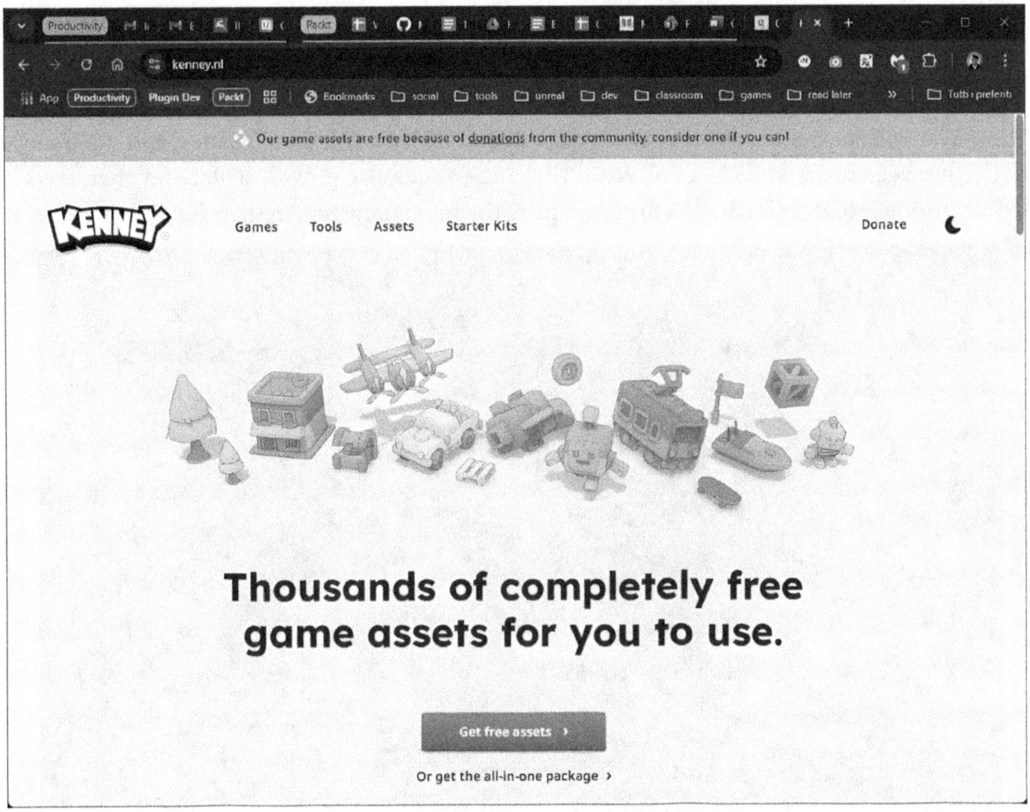

Figure 2.2 – Kenney website

Additionally, I have been using some spare assets from other sources; for a full list of credits, I recommend you check out the GitHub repository. Finally, some assets were modified and edited directly from UE by means of the *Modeling Tools*.

Project organization

So, how is the project organized? Being a book focused on mastering C++, most of the code has been written with this language, leaving Blueprints as a quick way to customize things or for more level design-oriented tasks. Following UE best practices, the source code has been divided into a `Public` folder, where you will find all header files, and a `Private` folder, where you will find all `.cpp` files. Subfolders are used to keep things organized by grouping related files together in a clear and structured way. The majority of the classes have been prefixed with `PITS_` (for *Paws in the Shell*).

On the visual scripting side, you will find all code in the `Blueprints` folder of the engine's editor project. AI code logic for opponents can be found in the `AI` folder.

The Maps folder contains a collection of gym levels that demonstrate most of the features you'll learn about throughout this book. Before continuing, I highly recommend exploring these levels to get an overview of what is ahead.

The player will control a team of characters, each one with its own peculiarities, and can freely switch between them while in a safe zone. These safe zones also provide a place for characters to fully regenerate their health. *Figure 2.3* depicts the four characters in their full glory:

Figure 2.3 – The game characters

> **Note**
>
> Some aspects of the gameplay logic could have been implemented using the **Gameplay Ability System (GAS)**. However, GAS is a large topic by itself, and there was not enough space in this book to cover it in detail. For this reason, I chose to use a more traditional development approach. If you are interested in learning more about GAS, I highly recommend exploring the official Epic Games documentation.

Now that we've reviewed the project at a high level, it's time to dive into the code. We'll begin with one of the concepts introduced in this chapter: interfaces.

Hands-on with interfaces

The *Paws in the Shell* project makes extensive use of interfaces, each designed with its own specific declarations; I will be presenting just some of them, leaving you the task of exploring the remaining. So, let's start by firing up the C++ project with your favorite IDE and navigating to the `Source/PawsInTheShell/Public/Interfaces` folder.

Exploring PITS_SafeZoneEligibleInterface

Once the project is ready, open the `PITS_SafeZoneEligibleInterface.h` file; this interface is quite simple and is used to declare if an object is in a safe zone – that is, it is immune from enemy damage – or not. There are two function declarations as in the following piece of code:

```
UFUNCTION(BlueprintCallable, BlueprintNativeEvent, Category="PawsInTheShell|
Defence")
void SetIsInSafeZone(const bool bNewInSafeZone);

UFUNCTION(BlueprintCallable, BlueprintNativeEvent, Category="PawsInTheShell|
Defence")
bool IsInSafeZone() const;
```

As you can see, they are both self-explanatory and will be used to set the object in a safe zone and to query if an object is in a safe zone.

Now that you have explored the interface, you may be wondering where it is used. Well, our player characters, the members of Team 33, will need a safe place to regenerate from their battle wounds. That's why we will be implementing it. Open the `PITS_BasePlayerCharacter.h` file located in the `Public` folder and check the class declaration. You will find this piece of code:

```
UCLASS(Abstract, BlueprintType, Blueprintable)
class PAWSINTHESHELL_API APITS_BasePlayerCharacter : public APITS_BaseCharacter,
public IPITS_SafeZoneEligibleInterface, ...
```

Along with other interface declarations – we will skip them for now – you will find `IPITS_SafeZoneEligibleInterface`. This means, somewhere in the deep pits of the code, you should find the function implementations. Let's hunt them down!

Scroll down the header and look for the `SafeZoneEligibleInterface Implementation` region. Here they are! You will find the two method declarations, like the following piece of code:

```
#pragma region SafeZoneEligibleInterface Implementations
public:
    virtual bool IsInSafeZone_Implementation() const override;
    virtual void SetIsInSafeZone_Implementation(const bool bNewInSafeZone)
override;
#pragma endregion
```

Please note the use of the `virtual` keyword, in order to make them overridable by child classes and the `_Implementation` suffix, as explained earlier in this chapter. Finally, notice the absence of the `UFUNCTION()` macros; these have already been declared in the interface and so are not needed anymore. If you're interested in seeing the implementation, you can take a look at the `PITS_BasePlayerCharacter.cpp` file.

To check how to call these two functions from your code, as previously explained in this chapter, open the `PITS_SafeZone.cpp` file and focus on the `HandleActorBeginOverlap()` function. The code implementation will have the following piece of code:

```
if (OtherActor->GetClass()->
    ImplementsInterface(UPITS_DefenceInterface::StaticClass()))
{
    // ...
    IPITS_SafeZoneInterface::Execute_SetIsInSafeZone
        (OtherActor, true);
}
```

First of all, we check if the overlapped actor implements `UPITS_DefenceInterface`, and if this is the case, we call the implementation by means of the function prefixed with `Execute_` and we set the safe zone value to `true`.

The `HandleActorEndOverlap()` function will do exactly the same, but setting the safe zone flag to `false`.

If you're used to working only with C++, some of this might feel confusing or even unnecessary at first. But remember – what you're seeing is the full power of the Reflection System at work. Give it some time, and soon it will feel natural and familiar!

Exploring PITS_HealthInterface

The second interface we are going to consider will declare how a character's health is handled. Open the `PITS_HealthInterface.h` file, and you will be presented with the following declarations:

```
UFUNCTION(BlueprintCallable, BlueprintNativeEvent, Category="PawsInTheShell|
Health")
bool IsDead() const;

UFUNCTION(BlueprintCallable, BlueprintNativeEvent, Category="PawsInTheShell|
Health")
float GetHealthPercentage() const;

UFUNCTION(BlueprintCallable, BlueprintNativeEvent, Category="PawsInTheShell|
Health")
bool CanRegenerate() const;
```

These function declarations are self-explanatory and will let you get information about the current state of health of the character. This time, the interface has been implemented in the `PITS_BaseCharacter` class so that both player characters and enemy AIs will be using its features; after all, they can both get damaged! Open `PITS_BaseCharacter.h` and, in the `HealthInterface Implementations` region, you will find the following code:

```
#pragma region HealthInterface Implementations
public:
    virtual bool IsDead_Implementation() const override;
    virtual float GetHealthPercentage_Implementation() const override;
    virtual bool CanRegenerate_Implementation() const override;
#pragma endregion
```

Things are pretty similar to the previous safe zone interface, aren't they? Just a couple of things worth noting: the interface has been used in a sort of façade pattern to hide the `PITS_HealthComponent` declaration that will handle all the health gameplay logic. Additionally, hit points and regeneration stats have been implemented in a stats table. We will be covering this topic in *Chapter 6, Working with Data Structures*; there's still a lot to learn, so keep breathing; it may take a while!

To check one of these interface usages, you can open the `PITS_RegenerationZone.cpp` file, where we handle actual character regeneration. If you look for the `HandleActorBeginOverlap()` function, you will find where we check if the overlapped actor can actually be regenerated:

```
if (OtherActor->GetClass()->
    ImplementsInterface(UPITS_HealthInterface::StaticClass()))
{
    if (IPITS_HealthInterface::Execute_CanRegenerate(OtherActor))
    {
        // Code Logic
    }
}
```

As you can see, we first verify that the actor implements the interface and subsequently call the `Execute_CanRegenerate()` function. The inner logic will simply add the actor to the list of regenerating elements and handle the regeneration timer.

So, where do we show a visual representation of the regenerating character health? Well, this is going to be managed by the next interface.

Exploring PITS_StatsWidgetInterface

The `PITS_StatsWidgetInterface.h` file, is used to update widgets that should display character stats, including the health. If you open the file, you will see, among other declarations, the following piece of code:

```
UFUNCTION(BlueprintCallable, BlueprintNativeEvent, Category="PawsInTheShell|UI")
void UpdateHealth(const float Value);
```

There are several places where this interface is used, including the main HUD, the characters' and the opponents' in-game health bars. Let's check the character health bar, which will be displayed in-game as shown in *Figure 2.4*:

Figure 2.4 - The in-game health bar

To check its logic, open the UE Editor, head to the `Blueprints/UserInterface` folder and double click on the **UW_PlayerHealth** asset to open it. In the Class Settings window, check the `Interfaces|ImplementedInterfaces` section and you will see that **PITS Stats Widget Interface** is listed, as shown in *Figure 2.5*:

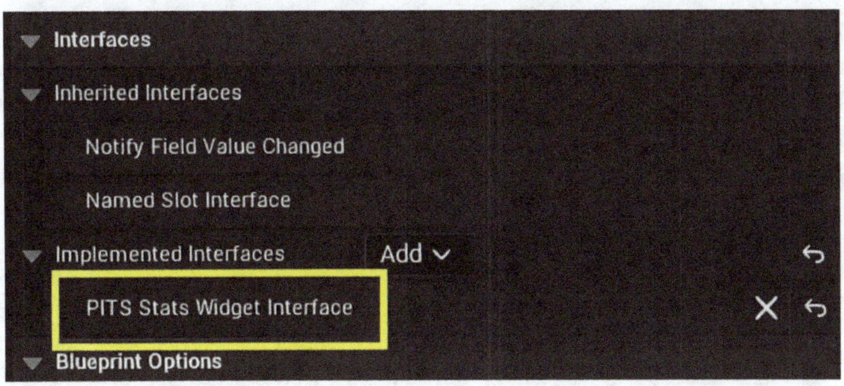

Figure 2.5 - The implemented interfaces section

In this widget Blueprint, we need to implement only the `UpdateHealth` function – in Blueprints, it is not mandatory to implement all interface function declarations – that can be found in the Event Graph, as shown in *Figure 2.6*:

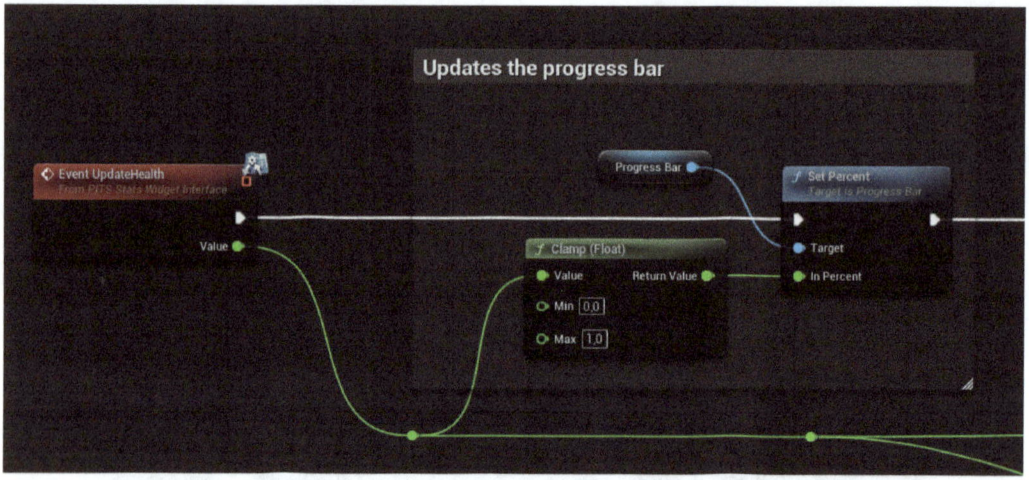

Figure 2.6 – The UpdateHealth function implementation

You can now head over the **BP_BasePlayerCharacter** Blueprint – that can be found in the `Blueprints/PlayerCharacter` folder of the Editor – to look for this function calls in the Event Graph, as shown in *Figure 2.7*:

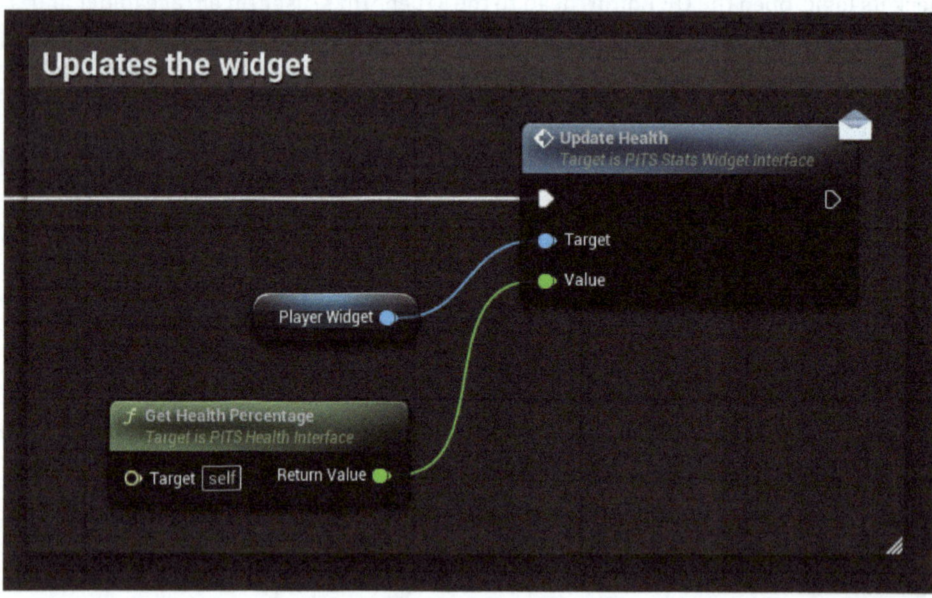

Figure 2.7 – The UpdateHealth function call

This Blueprint uses a reference to the widget. As you can see, we are not using casting to call the function. By using interfaces, we can avoid unnecessary casts, resulting in cleaner and more efficient code.

If you wish to explore more usages of `PITS_StatsWidgetInterface`, I highly recommend heading to the `PITS_CharacterController.cpp` file, where we handle character info for the main widget.

With all of this in mind, it's time to get your hands dirty and start some proper coding!

Develop and self-evaluate

At the end of each chapter, you'll find exercises designed to help you self-evaluate your understanding of the topics covered. Use these exercises at will to reinforce your learning and be more than welcome to add extra features, if you will.

The first exercise consists of creating a `PITS_LevelProgressionInterface` interface – for the `PITS_BasePlayerCharacter` class – with the following function declarations:

- `void AddXp(int Amount)`: To add experience points to the character
- `int GetCurrentXp()`: To get the current value of character experience points
- `int GetCurrentLevel()`: To get the character level of experience

Once you are done, implement the interface inside `PITS_BasePlayerCharacter`; the actual implementation of the gameplay logic is up to you, as long as you are consistent with the game!

The second exercise is to create a `PITS_RepairableInterface` interface for the `PITS_BaseEnemyCharacter` class with the following declarations:

- `bool CanBeRepaired()`: To check if the character can actually be repaired
- `void Repair(float Amount)`: To actually repair the character

Once the interface is complete, implement it in the `PITS_BaseEnemyCharacter` class.

For the moment, don't bother about what happens when a character levels up or what will repair the enemy characters; you'll tackle those topics later when you are feeling more comfortable.

In this section, you were introduced to *Paws in the Shell*, the companion project for this book. After that, you explored how some of the game interfaces have been declared and implemented. This is just the beginning of a full deep dive into the Holo District world and the dark machinations of OmniSight!

Summary

In this chapter, you were introduced to the engine's Reflection System and explored its core features, including how it is used in class, struct, and enum declarations by means of some of the most important engine macros. After that, you were introduced to interfaces and, subsequently, to a real-world scenario where they are declared and implemented. Mastering such a powerful system can significantly improve your ability as a game programmer to create efficient and dynamic games.

In the upcoming chapter, we will take a deep dive into macros to gain a better understanding of how they work behind the scenes. Trust me, you will be amazed by their power!

Get this book's PDF copy, code bundle, and more

Scan the QR code (or go to `packtpub.com/unlock`). Search for this book by name, confirm the edition, and then follow the steps on the page.

UNLOCK NOW

Note: Have your invoice handy. Purchases made directly from the Packt website don't require an invoice.

3

Mastering Macros

Getting the hang of macros in UE is much more than just learning some syntax – it's about improving workflow efficiency and creating cleaner, more maintainable code. In this chapter, I will guide you through the principles, best practices, and practical applications of macros, demonstrating how they can streamline complex logic and enhance project scalability. Additionally, we will explore how applying macro specifiers can elevate the clarity and usability of your Blueprint systems. By intentionally exposing, hiding, or categorizing variables and functions, you ensure that Blueprint users – whether level designers or technical artists – interact with your underlying system intuitively. Proper use of specifiers transforms a Blueprint from simply functional to thoughtfully designed, resulting in faster iteration, reduced confusion, and a more enjoyable development experience overall. By the end of this chapter, you will not only understand how to use and manage macros effectively, but also how to present them in a structured, efficient, and Blueprint-friendly way.

Topics that will be covered in this chapter are the following:

- Understanding core reflection macros
- Using specifiers
- Refining your macros with the metadata specifier
- Presenting a practical example

Technical requirements

To get the best out of the following sections, you should have fully understood the previous chapters.

Understanding core reflection macros

You are likely already familiar with **macros**, an impressive feature provided by the C++ preprocessor that allows the definition of reusable pieces of code before compilation begins. They can be used to create symbolic constants, simplify repetitive expressions, or conditionally include sections of code.

> **Note**
>
> For the sake of clarity, in this section, I will be speaking about C++ macros and not Blueprint macros. Considering that C++ is the main focus of this book, we will stick to this topic.

You will also be aware that, although powerful, macros operate outside the normal rules of the language and can sometimes lead to unexpected behavior if not used carefully. UE is no exception to this; if used wisely, they will improve your code and make it easier to maintain.

In this section, we will be analyzing in detail some of the macros we presented in *Chapter 2, Understanding the Engine Reflection System*, starting from the module export macro.

Understanding the module export macro

The module export macro (such as `MYAWESOMEGAME_API`) that is added to the class declaration is a compiler directive that controls symbol visibility across module boundaries, particularly when modules are built as separate DLLs in Windows.

Windows DLLs require functions, classes, and variables to be explicitly marked with either:

- `__declspec(dllexport)` when building the DLL
- `__declspec(dllimport)` when using the DLL from another module

It goes without saying that manually managing this would be tedious and error-prone, so UE generates a macro for each module that switches between the two declarations automatically depending on whether the code is being built or used.

It is pretty similar to writing the following block of code in your class:

```
#ifdef MYAWESOMEGAME_MODULE
    #define MYAWESOMEGAME_API __declspec(dllexport)
#else
    #define MYAWESOMEGAME_API __declspec(dllimport)
#endif
```

MYAWESOMEGAME_MODULE will typically be defined by the UBT when compiling the module.

When used in your main module – that is, in your UE project – it is typically declared in headers to manage symbol export and import, so you will be controlling its declaration and usage directly.

Understanding the UCLASS() macro

The UCLASS() macro tags a class derived from UObject, and this is a mandatory requirement, in order to be recognized by the Reflection System and to relate to the UE object system. Whenever the engine starts, the system will create a CDO for each UCLASS() macro that will serve as the default template instance for that class and set up the initial default values used by all created instances. This means that, when UE initializes a class, it will construct the CDO only once and before any game instances are created. Every new instance of this class will just need to copy its initial property values from the CDO – quick and simple. This is the reason why you will be using UE factory functions – such as NewObject(), CreateDefaultSubobject(), or SpawnActor() – and not the raw new keyword.

It should be noted that you can retrieve a CDO by using GetDefault<ClassType>() or – if accessing an instance – by using GetClass()->GetDefaultObject(). This access is used internally by Blueprints to get info about the class and show them in the Editor's **Class Defaults** panel.

> **Note**
>
> Once the game starts, the CDO will be read-only.

Let's now take a step further and analyze how functions are decorated by their dedicated macro.

Understanding the UFUNCTION() macro

The UFUNCTION() macro will set up a function so that the Reflection System will recognize it, and the function itself will be able to interact with key engine features such as Blueprint integration, networking, and so on. Once the UHT recognizes a function marked by this macro, it will generate the needed code inside the .generated.h file. This means that, by opening the generated file, you will find all the additional code that will make your system work.

You may remember from *Chapter 2, Understanding the Engine Reflection System*, that, when implementing an interface method, you will need to add the _Implementation suffix. For instance, the PITS_BaseCharacter class, from the *Paws in the Shell* project, has a GetHealthPercentage_Implementation() function to implement the PITS_HealthInterface declaration called `GetHealthPercentage()`. Well, if you take a look at the `PITS_HealthInterface.generated.h` file – located in the `Intermediate/Build/.../UHT` folder, you will find the following line of code inside a macro declaration:

```
virtual float GetHealthPercentage_Implementation() const { return 0; }; \
```

This is the function you will be overriding in your actual class implementation. Additionally, in the same macro declaration, you will also find this line of code:

```
DECLARE_FUNCTION(execGetHealthPercentage); \
```

This declaration will add `execGetHealthPercentage` to a list of virtual functions that can be called by name and will enable runtime systems – such as Blueprints or network RPCs – to dynamically invoke the corresponding functions.

Finally, in the generated file, you will also find the `Execute_` declaration, as shown in the following line of code:

```
static float Execute_GetHealthPercentage(const UObject* O); \
```

That will expose the function to classes implementing this interface.

Although you won't need to write a single line of code inside the generated file, it's still important to understand how it works internally.

Understanding the UPROPERTY() macro

The `UPROPERTY()` macro's main task is to expose class member variables to the UE system, including the editor and Blueprints. Under the hood, it will add the property to the `UClass` class metadata in order to make it discoverable at runtime through the Reflection System. Additionally, it will enable automatic initialization to default values when an object is constructed, and it will ensure automatic reference tracking and nulling for pointers, in order to avoid dangling references and to support proper garbage collection.

You will find all the necessary generated code inside the `.gen.cpp` file for the class. As an example, consider the `PITS_BaseCharacter` class from the *Paws in the Shell* project; if you open its corresponding `.gen.cpp` file, located inside the `Intermediate/Build/.../UHT` folder, you will find this type of declaration for the `CharacterName` property:

```
static const UECodeGen_Private::FTextPropertyParams NewProp_CharacterName;
```

Along with more complex declarations inside the file, this is what makes your property fully functional inside the engine!

Now that you have a stronger grip on the core class macros, let's check how you can get the best out of them with some specifiers.

Using specifiers

In this section, I will be providing an overview of the various specifiers you can use with Unreal Engine's class macros. We'll explore their purpose, functionality, and how they impact the behavior and properties of your classes.

Presenting UCLASS() specifiers

Some of the most important `UCLASS()` specifiers are now presented in a non-specific order.

The `Blueprintable` specifier will allow the class to be a base for Blueprint subclasses. This specifier is inherited by subclasses. The opposite, and default value for `UClass()`, is `NotBlueprintable`, which will prevent Blueprint subclassing. On the other hand, the `BlueprintType` specifier will make the class usable as a Blueprint variable type.

The `Abstract` specifier will mark the class as an abstract base class; this means you will not be able to instantiate it directly in C++ or add it to game levels from the editor or by spawning.

The `HideCategories` specifier will let you list one or more categories that should be hidden in the editor. The opposite specifier is `ShowCategories`, which will come in handy when you want to show categories in a subclass that inherits hidden categories.

One final specifier I'd like to present is `Config`, which will be used to define a configuration file category. You will then mark a class with `UCLASS(Config)` or variables with `UPROPERTY(Config)` to enable automatic loading and saving settings that will be stored in an appropriate `.ini` file – under the `/Script/ModuleName.ClassName` section. UE will load these values at startup, applying them to the marked properties. This way, you will be able to implement a straightforward method for externalizing and adjusting settings without requiring recompilation.

As an example, consider the following class declaration:

```
UCLASS(config=Game)
public MYAWESOMEGAME_API UMyConfigObject : public UObject
{
}
```

If you wish to add a value, named `ConfigurableValue`, in your `Config/DefaultGame.ini` you will add:

```
[/Script/MYAWESOMEGAME.MyConfigObject]
ConfigurableValue=10
```

The `ConfigurableValue` will automatically load to `10` at runtime from the config file and the value will be configurable without recompiling.

Let's now examine some function specifiers.

Presenting UFUNCTION() specifiers

Here are some of the most important specifiers for the `UFUNCTION()` macro.

`BlueprintCallable` will let you call the function from Blueprints. You can also add `BlueprintPure`, which will mark the function as **pure** – this means calling it won't produce effects on the owning object – and will make it callable without execution pins.

The `BlueprintImplementableEvent` specifier will declare a function as implementable only in Blueprints; this means you won't be able to override it in C++. On the other hand, the `BlueprintNativeEvent` specifier will declare a function that can be overridden by a Blueprint, but that can also have a native C++ implementation.

The `CallInEditor` specifier will let you call a function directly from the editor by means of a dedicated button in the **Details** panel; it is usually used for adding helper functions that will let you execute a function for a selected instance in game levels when playing or simulating the level. Pretty similar to this is the `Exec` specifier, which will let you call the function from the editor in-game console.

In addition to the aforementioned elements, there's a lot of additional stuff specifically dedicated to the built-in multiplayer system. This is not in the scope of this book, but if you wish to explore these features, I highly encourage you to check out my *Multiplayer Game Development with Unreal Engine 5* book by Packt, which thoroughly covers all these topics.

As a final step, let's check property specifiers.

Presenting UPROPERTY() specifiers

The most common `UPROPERTY()` specifiers you'll encounter are likely those that control editability. You'll frequently work with `EditDefaultsOnly`, `EditInstanceOnly`, and `EditAnywhere`. These specifiers determine where a property can be edited. `EditDefaultsOnly` restricts editing to the class defaults, `EditInstanceOnly` allows editing only in instances placed on a level, and `EditAnywhere` enables editing in both contexts. Similarly, you will be using `VisibleDefaultsOnly`, `VisibleInstanceOnly`, and `VisibleAnywhere` to control a property's visibility in the editor. To control property exposure in the Blueprint graph, you will be using `BlueprintReadWrite` and `BlueprintReadOnly`.

Having reviewed the most common specifiers, we can now examine one in particular – one that may significantly influence how you will work with UE classes from now on.

Refining your macros with the metadata specifier

Probably one of the most ubiquitous specifiers is `meta`. You will be using it in `UCLASS()`, `UFUNCTION()`, and `UPROPERTY()` macros, and its main role is to provide editor-only metadata that will customize the class, function, or property behavior. There are a lot of metadata keys you can add; for instance, you can use `DisplayName` to change how the name is displayed in Blueprints. As an example, consider a function named `Prefix_MyFunction_Suffix()` where `Prefix_` and `_Suffix` are some texts you are using in your C++ code for some internal naming convention. You do not want to show them in Blueprints, in order to avoid confusion with the user. In this case, you will be adding some metadata pretty similar to the following block of code:

```
UFUNCTION(BlueprintCallable, meta=(DisplayName="MyFunction"))
void Prefix_MyFunction_Suffix();
```

This will make your Blueprint nice and clean for anyone using it.

Another good example is the `Tooltip` key, which will add a useful helper to a property in the editor. As an example, consider the following piece of code for a character stats system in your game:

```
UPROPERTY(EditAnywhere, meta=(Tooltip= "Character defensive amount that reduces
incoming damage"))
float ArmourAmount;
```

Once in the editor, the user will be presented with a descriptive tooltip when hovering on the property, as shown in *Figure 3.1*:

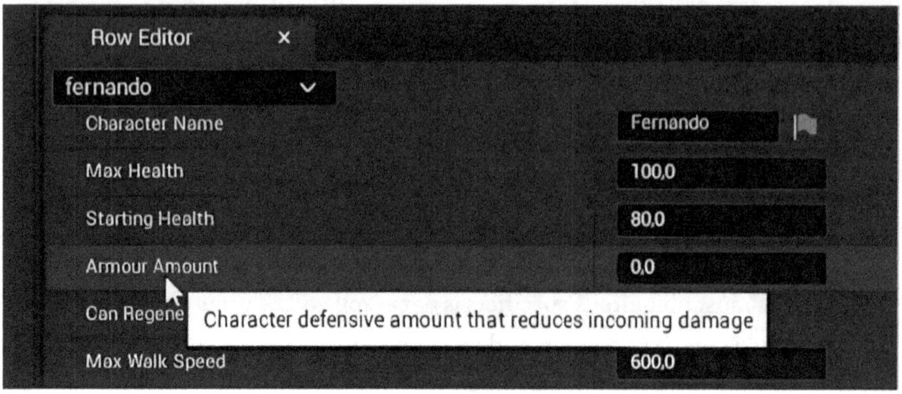

Figure 3.1 – Tooltip metadata in action

A couple of additional metadata keys that will be very useful – and that I'll showcase in the final section of this chapter – are `EditCondition` and `EditConditionHides`, which allow you to control a property's enablement and visibility.

The last metadata key I'd like to mention is `Keywords`, which will improve node searchability in Blueprints by means of a list of space-separated keys. Now you probably understand why typing *if* in the Blueprint graph will immediately pop up the **Branch** node!

In the next section, I will get back to the *Paws in the Shell* project and present an actual implementation of what you have learned so far, along with some other useful specifiers.

Presenting a practical example

It seems the game you are working on has a brand-new chapter:

Commander Finn woke up long before sunrise, his green skin gleaming beneath his training armor. As the leader of The Pack and the only one without cybernetic enhancements, he took every monthly training cycle seriously – no excuses, no shortcuts. While others relied on processors and implants, Finn trusted instinct, grit, and natural talent.

Today's mission: reach the floor top gym, hit every checkpoint, and once again prove he was still the fastest amphibian in the unit. He rolled his shoulders, stretched his powerful legs, and steadied his breathing. Once ready, lights flickered on and a buzzer sounded.

Finn grinned and leaped forward.

In this section, we will continue analyzing the *Paws in the Shell* project and consider the topics we analyzed during this chapter. In particular, we will focus on how to create a trigger system that will be used to create pickups – such as first-aid kits or coin pickups – and other triggerable objects, such as exit points for your level.

So, without further ado, let's start the editor and open the `Gym_03_PointsOfInterest` level located in the `Maps` folder. The level is pretty uncomplicated and contains a group of pickable credits, five **Points of Interest (POI)** elements, and an exit zone. Whenever you play the level, your character will be able to pick up all credits and reach each POI. Once the elements are collected, the exit point will be enabled and visible. The level is displayed in *Figure 3.2*:

Figure 3.2 – The Points of Interest map

All three elements in the level are Blueprints derived from C++ classes, adding just some additional aesthetics and minimal gameplay features. This is obviously a common OOP practice that will let us achieve better consistency and maintainability for the overall project. But how do we achieve this in UE? And most importantly, how do we apply all we have learned so far about macros and the Reflection System? Well... Let's dive into it step by step and start exploring the class hierarchy the Unreal way!

Hands-on with trigger classes

First things first, let's analyze the class structure we have available. The class diagram is displayed in *Figure 3.3*:

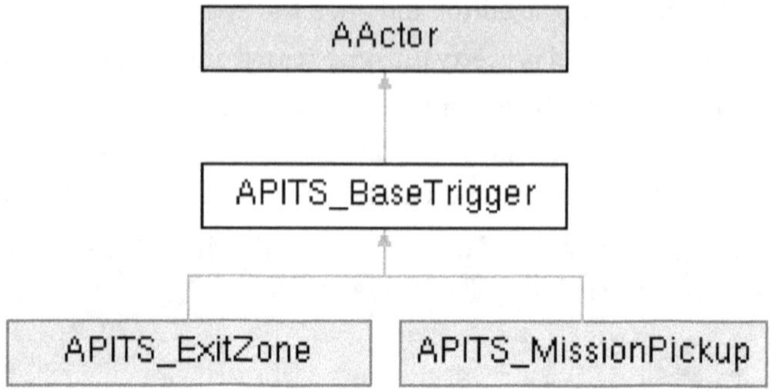

Figure 3.3 – The class diagram

As you can see, we have three classes that derive from the well-known `AActor`:

- `APITS_BaseTrigger`, which can be used as the starting point for any trigger or pickup in the game
- `APITS_ExitZone`, which will be dedicated to managing exit points in the level
- `APITS_MissionPickup`, which can be extended to handle mission achievements

We will start by analyzing the base trigger class.

Exploring the PITS_BaseTrigger class

The `PITS_BaseTrigger` class's responsibility is to create the base gameplay logic for every trigger or pickup zone, including the following:

- Character overlapping management
- Checking that an overlapping character is a player character
- Trigger deactivation on overlap and eventual respawn
- Trigger and respawn handles for subclasses

As we are currently not interested in the actual class implementation, but only in the macro declarations, we will just stick to the header file. Let's start by opening the `PITS_BaseTrigger.h` file. You will immediately notice that the `UCLASS()` macro is using the `Abstract` specifier; as previously mentioned in this chapter, this specifier won't let you instantiate or spawn the class in the level. However, you will be able to create Blueprint subclasses out of it when needed. This type of enforcement clearly shows that this class should be used for inheritance, and you will avoid misuse of its incomplete base functionality.

If you scroll down the class, you will find the following block of code:

```
UPROPERTY(EditAnywhere, Category="PawsInTheShell|Trigger")
bool bWillRespawn = true;

UPROPERTY(EditAnywhere, Category="PawsInTheShell|Trigger",
    meta = (ClampMin = 0, ClampMax = 120, Units = "s", EditCondition =
"bWillRespawn", EditConditionHides))
float RespawnTime = 4.0f;
```

Although we have just a couple of property declarations, they are quite dense and rich with specifiers. First of all, please note the `PawsInTheShell|Trigger` category value for both of them; although I'm pretty sure you are familiar with the `Category` specifier, you are possibly not aware that, by using the pipe character (|), you will be creating subcategories in the **Editor Details** panel.

The second property declares a set of meta values that come together:

```
ClampMin = 0, ClampMax = 120, Units = "s"
```

These three values will clamp the trigger respawn time from a minimum of zero seconds – we do not want to go back in time! – to a maximum of `120` seconds; additionally, we will display a trailing s character to make things clear for anyone editing this value from the editor, as displayed in *Figure 3.4*:

Figure 3.4 – The Respawn Time property in the editor

Lastly, but most importantly, we have this portion of code:

```
EditCondition = "bWillRespawn"
```

That will enable – or disable – the property depending on the `bWillRespawn` value, which is a boolean value.

The additional `EditConditionHides` flag will hide the property when disabled by the previous condition; this is not really mandatory, but hiding unnecessary properties will avoid cluttering in the **Details** panel and make things more readable.

The last thing to analyze in this header file is a way to cope with virtual functions. Head to the following block of code:

```
UFUNCTION(BlueprintNativeEvent, Category="PawsInTheShell|Trigger")
void HandleTrigger(APITS_BasePlayerCharacter* OverlappedCharacter);
virtual void HandleTrigger_Implementation(APITS_BasePlayerCharacter*
OverlappedCharacter)
PURE_VIRTUAL(APITS_BaseTrigger::HandleTrigger_Implementation);
```

`HandleTrigger()` is used to manage trigger functionality after all the overlap logic has been processed. As a first step, we want to let Blueprint subclasses implement this function, and so we have added the `BlueprintNativeEvent` specifier. Implementing an abstract function in Blueprints is not mandatory; however, we want to enforce implementation in C++ subclasses. That's why we have not been using `BlueprintImplementableEvent` – that would have made the function optionally implementable in C++ derived classes – but added a `HandleTrigger_Implementation()` function. As mentioned earlier, we won't examine the actual implementation, but just be aware that this function will simply log an error and crash the game.

Note

The `PURE_VIRTUAL` macro provides a dummy implementation for a function that triggers a runtime error if called, allowing `UObject`-derived classes to remain compatible with UE Reflection System while effectively requiring subclasses to provide an override to avoid program elimination.

As harsh as it may seem, this behavior ensures that derived classes override the function and provide their own proper implementation.

Just after the `HandleTrigger()` function, you will find the `HandleRespawn()` function with the same declaration logic described previously.

Now that we have explored the base trigger class, it's time to analyze its derived classes.

Exploring the PITS_ExitZone class

Let's open the `PITS_ExitZone.h` file and check what's inside. This class will be used as an exit point for completing the level, usually after all missions are completed. As for the previous base trigger class, at the moment, we are not interested in the actual implementation but in macro and specifier usage.

You will notice that the `UCLASS()` macro no longer has an `Abstract` specifier; except for the cosmetic mesh – that will be set in a child Blueprint class – all the code logic lives inside this class, so it is ready to be added to the level.

You will also see that we are overriding the `HandleTrigger_Implementation()` function with the following line of code:

```
virtual void HandleTrigger_Implementation(APITS_BasePlayerCharacter*
OverlappedCharacter) override;
```

Just remember from the previous subsection that the engine will crash when calling this function if it has not been overridden.

As this exit zone will not be respawned, once a character steps in, a new level will be loaded. After all, we simply do not bother with the `HandleRespawn_Implementation()` function, and so, you won't be seeing any sign of it.

A Blueprint implementation for this class is **BP_ExitPoint** and is depicted in *Figure 3.5*:

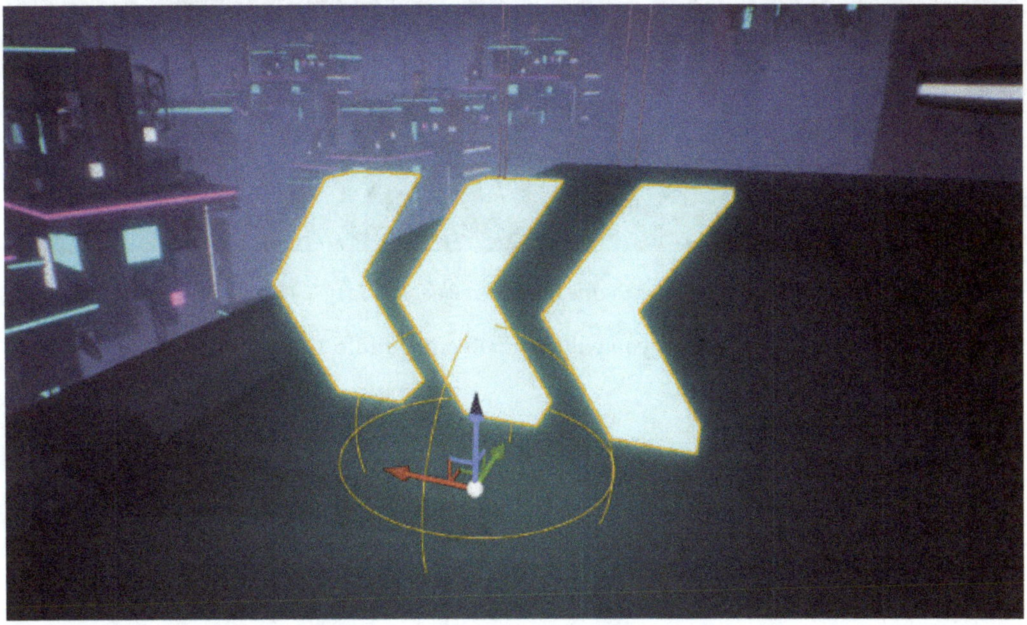

Figure 3.5 – A BP_ExitPoint instance in the level

Now let's go and check out a Blueprint subclass of `PITS_BaseTrigger`.

Exploring the BP_BasePickup Blueprint

The **BP_BasePickup** Blueprint subclasses the `PITS_BaseTrigger` class in order to have a level-spawnable object. It's pretty simple and just adds some cosmetics and an animation timeline for the mesh. It won't be implementing any game logic, leaving children Blueprints with the task. As an example, let's open the **BP_MedkitPickup** asset located in the `Blueprints/Pickups` folder of the UE editor.

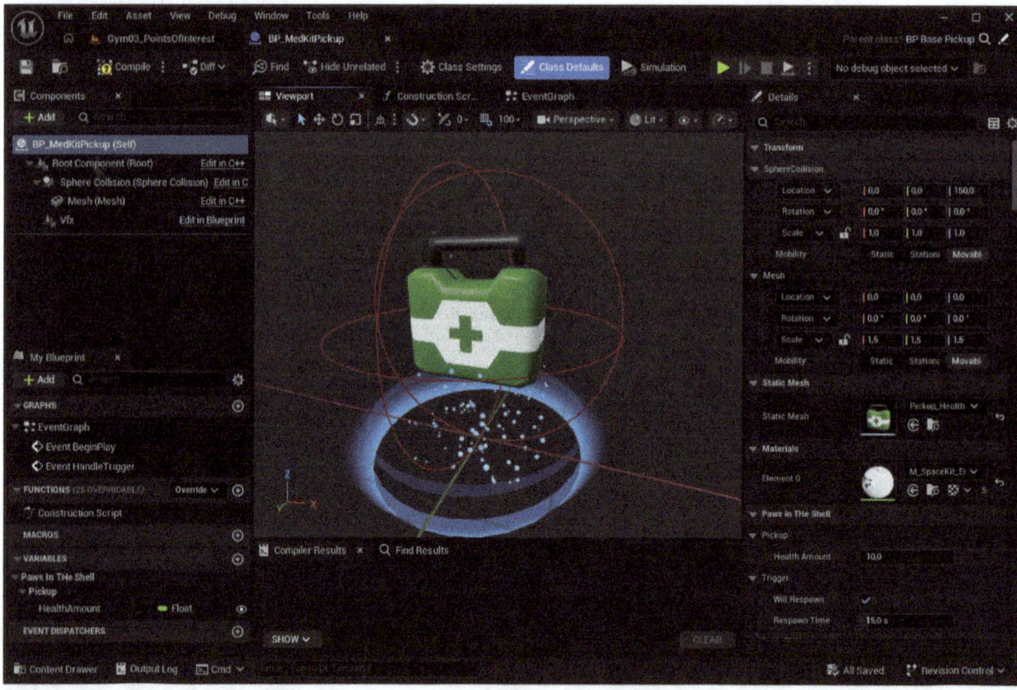

Figure 3.6 – The BP_Medkit Blueprint class

If you open the **EventGraph** panel, you will see an **Event Handle Trigger** node, as depicted in *Figure 3.7*:

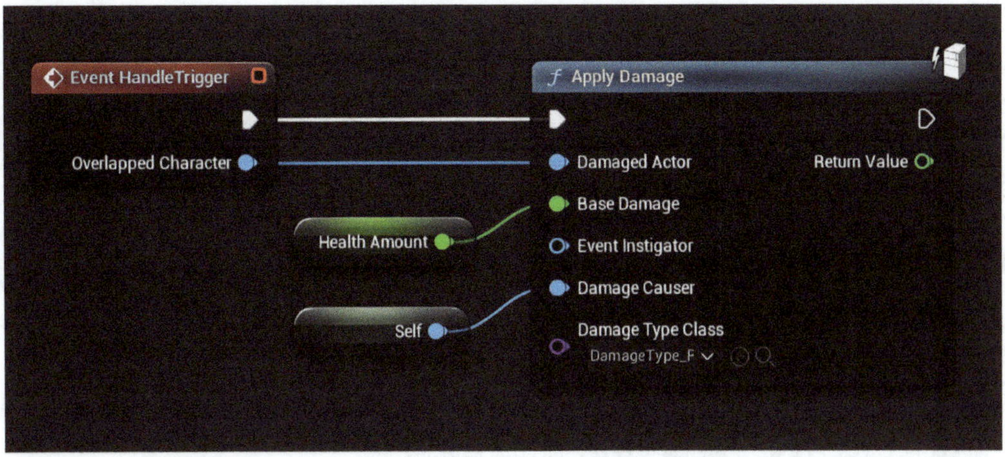

Figure 3.7 – The Event Handle Trigger implementation

This event is the actual implementation of the `HandleTrigger()` function in the `PITS_BaseTrigger` class; as it was decorated with `BlueprintNativeEvent`, you will be able to override it in any child Blueprint class. In this case, the gameplay logic simply adds some damage with the **Damage Type Class** pin set to `DamageType_Regeneration`; this means the overlapping character will treat this special damage differently and will be healed instead of damaged.

Now that you have a strong understanding of how the trigger and pickup system is organized, it's time to write down some code on your own!

Develop and self-evaluate

It's finally time to write down some proper code, so let's get started!

Code refactoring

The first task I am asking of you is a little picky; you may have noticed that `PITS_BaseTrigger` is probably overloaded with features, such as the respawn one, that are not really part of a base trigger but should be added to a base pickup. As an example, the `PITS_ExitZone` class won't make any use of it, will it? Well, that was my fault! I'm the developer here, and I didn't really plan ahead and ended up mixing too many things all at once!

As such, I am requesting some proper refactoring; start by creating a new class named `PITS_BasePickup`, subclassing `PITS_BaseTrigger`. Then, move the respawn capability into it and make sure all pickups will derive from `PITS_BasePickup`.

This will make your code cleaner and easier to understand!

Function overriding

As a second task, I request that you override the `HandleRespawn()` function, which has been intentionally omitted from the implementation. The respawn logic has already been implemented, and it is fully functional; you may add some additional code logic for when a pickup is respawned, such as a visual or sound effect. This will be a fairly simple task, but it will help you become familiar with class abstraction in UE.

Analyzing global functions

The last task is to open the `PITS_Global.h` file that includes some global functions and a set of custom macros that have been used throughout the project. As an example, consider the following block of code:

```
#define CHECK_PTR_WITH_FALLBACK(Ptr, FallbackValue) \
    do \
    { \
        if ((Ptr) == nullptr) \
        { \
            UE_LOG(LogPITS, Warning, TEXT("Null pointer detected: %s [%s:%d]"), \
                TEXT(#Ptr), TEXT(__FILE__), __LINE__); \
            (Ptr) = (FallbackValue); \
        } \
    } while (0)
```

This code checks if a pointer is null and eventually logs a warning and assigns a fallback value.

> **Note**
>
> In case you are wondering what the `do { ... } while (0)` idiom is, it will make a multi-statement macro behave like a single statement, preventing a stray `else` from binding to an inner `if`, and it will scope any local variables declared inside the macro. This ensures safe, predictable use inside `if/else` blocks or other control structures.

Once you have analyzed these macros and if they are used inside the project, try adding your own in order to make your code easier to read and maintain.

Summary

In this chapter, we examined how core macros are used within a class header and why the generated files are essential for your class to function correctly. After that, you were introduced to the most common specifiers for the `UCLASS()`, `UFUNCTION()`, and `UPROPERTY()` macros, including the `meta` specifier, which is essential for customizing how the class is handled in the editor. Finally, you were shown a real-world scenario using the companion project for this book, specifically demonstrating how to handle proper abstraction between C++ and Blueprint classes.

Understanding macros in UE is crucial as they are core to how the engine integrates C++ with the Reflection System; macros are not just syntactic shortcuts – they are part of the engine's architecture.

In the next chapter, we'll dive into one of the most important topics in C++ game development: pointers. Take a break, grab a cup of your favorite drink, and get back as soon as you feel ready – things are about to get quite interesting!

Get this book's PDF copy, code bundle, and more

Scan the QR code (or go to `packtpub.com/unlock`). Search for this book by name, confirm the edition, and then follow the steps on the page.

UNLOCK NOW

Note: Have your invoice handy. Purchases made directly from the Packt website don't require an invoice.

4

Getting the Best out of Pointers

As a game developer, mastering pointers is essential for efficient memory management, performance optimization, and robust gameplay programming. These concepts are obviously of paramount importance if you must cope with such a complex game engine as Unreal.

This chapter delves into the nuanced use of pointers within UE architecture, exploring smart pointers and raw pointers, and their appropriate contexts. By understanding how to leverage pointers effectively, you will be able to ensure safer code, minimize memory leaks, and enhance the responsiveness of your games. Additionally, this chapter will provide practical insights and best practices to harness the power of pointers in a real-world scenario.

The topics we will be covering in this chapter are as follows:

- Introducing pointers in Unreal Engine
- Explaining the Unreal Engine smart pointers library
- Working with raw pointers (when necessary)
- Presenting a practical example

Technical requirements

To get the best out of the following sections, you should have fully understood the previous chapters.

Introducing pointers in Unreal Engine

Pointers can be quite complex, especially when you first encounter them within the UE framework. With concepts such as reference counting, ownership rules, GC, and the engine's unique memory-management patterns, it's easy to feel overwhelmed. UE offers several types of pointers, each designed for specific lifetime and ownership scenarios, so understanding these differences is essential for working effectively with the engine.

If you come from a pure C++ background, you will surely be proficient with **smart pointers** and how they ease your job as a programmer. However, once you enter the realm of C++ in UE, you will be mostly using its dedicated and highly optimized pointer system.

The first thing to mention is that the UE Reflection System primarily handles UObject classes and their properties through macros, such as UCLASS() and UPROPERTY(). This means it will track UObject lifetimes and properties, while smart pointers will manage UObject references.

As a side note, it's still possible to use raw pointers; this means you will need to understand when it's best to use pointers provided by the engine system and when to use a simple raw pointer to achieve better performance. In this section and the next ones, I will cover exactly that; first, I will introduce the smart and specialized pointers provided by UE, and then I will share best practices for using the humble raw pointer.

Presenting TObjectPtr<T>

With the release of UE5, Epic Games introduced TObjectPtr<T>, a template-based system designed as an optional replacement for raw object pointers in editor builds. While maintaining the same performance as raw pointers in non-editor builds, this system provides dynamic resolution and access tracking when used in the editor. Additionally, TObjectPtr<T> variables automatically convert to raw pointers when passed to functions or stored in local variables.

As, during the build process, TObjectPtr<T> will be converted to raw pointers, there won't be any impact on performance once your game is shipped – this means it won't slow down or speed up runtime UObject access or reduce CPU overhead by default. However, your overall experience while developing in-editor will improve most of the time. Even in builds, you will get some improvements.

First of all, TObjectPtr<T> itself is primarily a safer pointer type; as such, it will ensure proper GC tracking. Secondly, TObjectPtr<T> ensures safe and efficient replication and serialization of UObject pointers, supporting stable network play in multiplayer games.

Finally, `TObjectPtr<T>` plays a critical role in **Incremental Garbage Collection**, a brand-new system in UE – still at an experimental stage. Incremental GC will split the process of identifying which `UObject` classes are still in use – called **garbage collector reachability analysis** – across multiple frames instead of doing it in a single frame. During this process, `UPROPERTY()` objects that are exposed through `TObjectPtr<T>` will be marked as reachable, helping maintain accuracy without a full scan in a single frame.

Usually, you will be using a `TObjectPtr<T>` when in need of holding a persistent reference to `UObject` instances within classes or structures that are exposed to the GC, that means `UCLASS`es and `USTRUCT`s.

A typical example involves using `TObjectPtr<T>` to declare components in an `Actor` class header, just like the following piece of code:

```
UPROPERTY(VisibleAnywhere)
TObjectPtr<UStaticMeshComponent> MeshComponent;
```

Afterwards, you will create the object in the `.cpp` file:

```
MeshComponent =
CreateDefaultSubobject<UStaticMeshComponent>(TEXT("MeshComponent"));
```

The `MeshComponent` property will hold a pointer to the component, ensuring proper GC references and cook-time dependency awareness.

Now that you have a clear understanding of `TObjectPtr<T>`, let's examine the next type of pointer.

Presenting TWeakObjectPtr<T>

`TWeakObjectPtr<T>` is a weak pointer to a `UObject`-derived instance; this means it will not keep the referenced object alive and won't affect GC. In other words, whenever the `UObject` is somehow destroyed, the referencing `TWeakObjectPtr<T>` will automatically become null. You will use this pointer whenever you need to use non-owning references, and you want to avoid dangling pointers.

A typical use of `TWeakObjectPtr<T>` involves holding a non-owning reference to a `UObject` without preventing its elimination by the GC; as an example, you may be using it for caching objects or observing other objects while avoiding extending their lifetime. This obviously includes tracking or interacting with objects that may be destroyed independently without forcing them to remain in memory.

As an example of a safe way to hold an Actor reference without preventing elimination, consider the following portion of code from a hypothetical `AMyActor` class:

```
TWeakObjectPtr<AActor> TargetActor;
void CacheTargetActor(AActor* ActorToCache);
void UseTargetActor();
```

Please note that the `TargetActor` declaration won't prevent GC. The `CacheTargetActor()` function will assign a weak pointer without increasing the ref count:

```
void AMyActor::CacheTargetActor(AActor* ActorToCache)
{
    TargetActor = ActorToCache;
}
```

On the other hand, `UseTargetActor()` will check pointer validity – by means of the `IsValid()` function – and obtain a raw pointer safely after validation – by using the `Get()` function – as displayed in the following block of code:

```
void AMyActor::UseTargetActor()
{
    if (TargetActor.IsValid())
    {
        AActor* ValidActor = TargetActor.Get();
        // Safe to use ValidActor here
    }
    else
    {
        // TargetActor is no longer valid (destroyed or GC'd)
    }
}
```

With weak pointers explained, let's consider strong pointers.

Presenting TStrongObjectPtr<T>

Somehow opposite to the weak pointer, `TStrongObjectPtr<T>` is designed to hold strong references to `UObject` instances outside of its ownership system; this means it will enforce ownership by counting references to the target object keeping it alive and preventing it from being garbage collected while the pointer is in scope. One common usage is whenever you need long-lived references in non-`UObject` classes that don't support the `UPROPERTY()` macro and consequently cannot be part of the engine's automatic memory management.

Creating a strong object pointer instance is relatively expensive, so careful usage is recommended, and you should limit its use to cases where it is truly necessary.

> **Note**
>
> `TStrongObjectPtr<T>` cannot be marked with the `UPROPERTY()` macro.

Typical use cases of `TStrongObjectPtr<T>` include strong references inside non-`UObject` owners, for example, standard C++ classes or structures, where there is no automatic `UObject` lifetime tracking.

As an example, consider the following strong pointer to an actor:

```
TStrongObjectPtr<AActor> TargetActor;
```

This strong reference will prevent it from being garbage collected. To access the actor, you will first check if it is valid, by using the `IsValid()` function:

```
if (TargetActor.IsValid())
{
    // Safe to use TargetActor here
}
```

Finally, to release the strong reference and allow GC, you will use the `Reset()` function:

```
TargetActor.Reset();
```

With these concepts firmly in mind, let's now consider soft object pointers.

Presenting TSoftObjectPtr<T>

`TSoftObjectPtr<T>` is a smart pointer that provides an efficient way to reference assets without forcing them to load immediately. Basically, it is implemented as a weak reference that will store the path to an asset on disk rather than holding a direct pointer to the loaded object in memory. This means that an asset referenced in `TSoftObjectPtr<T>` may defer asset loading until it is actually needed; you may have heard about this technique, known as **lazy loading**. It goes without saying that preventing load times upfront will eliminate unnecessary memory usage and lower initialization times when a level is initialized.

Considering the aforementioned topics, such an object pointer will have much less impact on GC, as a non-loaded asset will be marked as pending and will be ignored during the GC phase.

Typical use cases for `TSoftObjectPtr<T>` include mesh, texture, and sound cue references; additionally, any `UObject`-derived assets where you want to avoid hard dependencies and enable asynchronous or on-demand loading are good candidates. Whenever you need to use the asset, you will first check whether the pointer is pending – by using the `IsPending()` function – and then load the asset either synchronously or asynchronously using the engine's streaming systems.

As an example, consider the following declaration:

```
UPROPERTY(EditAnywhere)
TSoftObjectPtr<AActor> TargetActorAsset;
```

To check if the target asset has already been loaded, you will use the `IsValid()` function:

```
if (ActorAsset.IsValid())
{
    // Asset is Loaded, can use directly
}
else
{
    // Asset not Loaded, Load it
}
```

Usually, you will load the asset asynchronously – that means, with a streamable request – and to get the asset path for loading, you will use the `ToSoftObjectPath()` function, like the following piece of code:

```
TargetActorAsset-> ToSoftObjectPath()
```

Now that you have a clear understanding of the main pointer templates, let's check how the engine copes with memory management wrappers such as those available in regular C++.

Explaining the Unreal Engine smart pointer library

Along with the aforementioned pointers, UE provides a custom implementation of C++ smart pointers called the **Unreal Smart Pointer Library,** which present the general idea of automated memory management wrappers in C++. These pointers are not compatible with the `UObject` lifecycle because UE uses a separate GC system for `UObjects`. Additionally, they are thread-safe and performance-wise with constant-time operations (in many cases). Consequently, they are used primarily for managing non-`UObject` data and high-level engine systems, tools, and gameplay code.

The engine provides the following templated smart pointers:

- TSharedPtr<T>
- TWeakPtr<T>
- TUniquePtr<T>

Additionally, TSharedRef<T> has been added as a non-nullable shared pointer variant. In the next subsections, I will present all of them, along with their peculiarities.

Presenting TSharedPtr<T>

A **shared pointer** – implemented by TSharedPtr<T> – owns the object it references, preventing that object from being deleted while it is still in use. The object is deleted only when no shared pointers or shared references refer to it. A shared pointer may be empty, meaning it does not reference any object. Any non-null shared pointer can produce a shared reference to the object it points to.

A common use case for TSharedPtr<T> is lifetime management of non-`UObject` data or custom resource objects that need shared ownership and automatic cleanup. Multiple systems can hold references to the same object through TSharedPtr<T> instances, ensuring the object stays valid as long as at least one owner exists. This approach prevents premature deletion and avoids dangling pointers.

Presenting TWeakPtr<T>

A **weak pointer** – implemented by TWeakPtr<T> – holds a non-owning reference to an object. Unlike shared pointers and references, weak pointers will not prevent the referenced object from being destroyed.

Before accessing the object pointed to by a weak pointer, you should use the `Pin()` function, which will create a shared pointer, ensuring that the object remains alive while it is used. Using weak pointers usually means that you need the system to observe the referenced object without owning it and without managing its lifetime.

Whenever you need to check whether the weak pointer currently references an object, you will compare it to `nullptr`, or you will call the `IsValid()` function.

A typical use case for `TWeakPtr<T>` is observing an object shared by multiple owners; for instance, a UI system might hold a weak pointer to a complex data object managed elsewhere. Before accessing the object, it will pin the weak pointer to get a valid shared reference. If no strong owners remain – that is, the object has been destroyed – the pin will return null, preventing unsafe access. This pattern enables lightweight, non-owning references that avoid dangling pointers and clearly indicate that the object's lifetime is managed externally.

With weak pointers clear in mind, let's consider unique pointers.

Presenting TUniquePtr<T>

A **unique pointer** – implemented by `TUniquePtr<T>` – exclusively and explicitly owns the object it points to. This means only a single pointer will own a particular resource at a time, and if you need to change ownership, you will need to transfer it to the new owner. If you try to copy a unique pointer, you will get a compile-time error. If a unique pointer goes out of scope, it will automatically delete the owned object.

A common use case for `TUniquePtr<T>` in Unreal Engine is when exclusive ownership and automatic destruction of an object within a single owner's scope are required. Typically, you'll use it for managing helper and utility class instances inside another class. As a consequence, you will avoid shared ownership overhead and will automatically destroy the data when the owning object is destroyed or reset; this will obviously prevent memory leaks.

Finally, let me present how shared references are managed.

Presenting TSharedRef<T>

A **shared reference** – implemented by `TSharedRef<T>` – is a strong, non-nullable smart pointer used for data objects outside the engine's `UObject` system; this means you cannot reset a shared reference, create an empty one, or assign it a null object. This means that a shared reference always contains a valid object and does not even provide an `IsValid()` method.

> **Note**
>
> When deciding between shared references and shared pointers, the first option should be preferred unless you specifically need an empty or nullable object. In that case, use the second option instead.

A common use case for `TSharedRef<T>` is when multiple systems need guaranteed, non-null shared ownership of a core data object that must never be null – such as shared data models' in-engine subsystems. As an example, you may be implementing a custom navigation tree structure and use `TSharedRef<T>` for the tree nodes, in order to ensure that each node is always valid while allowing multiple parts of the code to hold references.

> **Note**
>
> Shared-ownership smart pointers – that is, `TSharedPtr<T>` or `TSharedRef<T>` – should not be employed along `TUniquePtr<T>`. Creating shared pointers to an object owned by `TUniquePtr<T>` will break the unique-ownership guarantee and may lead to premature destruction or multiple deletions. Likewise, constructing or assigning `TUniquePtr<T>` from a shared pointer may result in double deletion or dangling pointers. Therefore, you should separate usage contexts and ensure that the same object is never managed by both unique and shared smart pointers.

In this section, you've got plenty of pointer accessors to choose from, haven't you? You might be wondering if it's still worth using the humble raw pointer. Let's find out in the next section!

Working with raw pointers (when necessary)

Knowing when and how to use raw pointers is obviously of paramount importance in order to get the best out of the game engine framework. Generally, you should use raw pointers in the following scenarios:

- When dealing with `UObjects`
- When dealing with non-`UObjects`
- When you're in need of maximum performance

Dealing with UObjects

When declaring a raw pointer to a `UObject`-derived class with `UPROPERTY()`, the engine will treat it as a strong reference. This means the garbage collector will maintain the referenced object alive as long as the pointer exists.

Additionally, `UObjects` and `UPROPERTY()` pointers are auto-zeroed on initialization, preventing unintended invalid pointer values before constructor runs. Finally, if a referenced `AActor` or `UActorComponent` is destroyed during gameplay, raw pointers to it marked with `UPROPERTY()` will be automatically nulled by the engine to prevent dangling references, aiding safer null-checks.

Dealing with non-UObjects

You will most probably be using raw pointers on non-`UObject` types when you need temporary, non-owning references to objects whose lifetime is managed elsewhere and want minimal overhead in performance-critical code or tight loops. Additionally, they may be used when passing pointers to functions or iterating over objects without transferring ownership. Finally, you may stumble on legacy or third-party APIs that require raw pointers, and you need to interface with them.

As a rule of thumb, you should avoid raw pointers when your code is responsible for object ownership or lifetime; in these cases, prefer smart pointers to ensure safe memory management and eliminate risks of leaks or dangling pointers.

Needing maximum performance

As previously stated, raw pointers have less overhead compared with smart pointers and, if not marked with `UPROPERTY()`, will not be tracked by the engine's garbage collector. This means you may take advantage of raw pointers when you need temporary references, or you have performance-critical scenarios where you need to take the maximum out of your PC's computing power.

It is highly recommended to use pointers this way only when you are certain that the lifetime of the referenced object is managed elsewhere and guaranteed to remain valid throughout the pointer usage. Just a small heads-up: treat raw pointers like hot potatoes – drop them, and you're in for some nasty crashes and dangling disasters!

In this section, you have been introduced to some typical scenarios for using raw pointers; now, let's delve deeper into practical examples of in-engine pointer usage.

Presenting a practical example

At this point in the chapter, it seems the right time to present a new character from the *Paws in the Shell* game:

Fernando was no ordinary flamingo. With sleek feathers and cybernetic chromed legs gleaming under the neon lights, he stood tall in the practice arena. Augmented implants weren't just for show – they housed twin blaster guns, perfectly integrated into his limbs.

Every day, Fernando trained relentlessly; the gym buzzed with holographic targets that popped up unpredictably. With a swift, precise kick, his cybernetic leg would pivot, aiming the guns with uncanny accuracy. Pew! Pew! Each shot hit its mark, sending sparks flying.

Flamingo grace combined with cutting-edge technology made him a formidable sharpshooter; cybernetic enhancements amplified natural agility, turning him into a living weapon.

But Fernando wasn't practicing for glory – his sole purpose was to shield with heavy firepower other members of The Pack from the dangers lurking in the Holo District shadows.

In a world where nature collided with technology, he emerged as a symbol of resilience – part bird, part machine, unapologetically pink.

In game development, "weapons" usually mean dealing with lots – and I really mean lots! – of bullets. Handling them effectively often requires diving deep into optimization. As a starting point, in this section, we'll start exploring how to make a shooting system super-fast by using pointers and a widely used design pattern.

Pooling objects

Whenever we need to enhance performance and optimize memory usage, one of the most common techniques is to reuse objects from a fixed pool rather than allocating and freeing them individually. **Object pooling** is a performance optimization strategy that involves pre-creating and allocating a set of objects, which remain disabled or hidden until required, instead of repeatedly creating and destroying them during gameplay. This approach is very useful for expensive-to-create objects, such as Actors, and provides a smoother runtime experience for the player. It goes without saying that pre-allocating objects will use more memory upfront as all objects in the pool reside in memory even when deactivated; a small toll to keep your game super-fast and your players smiling!

In the *Paws in the Shell* project, I have made heavy use of object pooling, starting from the aforementioned bullets, to enemies, and up to object spawning in the level. In the next subsections, I'll be guiding you through some simple object pooling implementation and the best practices applied to make good use of smart pointers. In particular, we will be analyzing a `UObject`-based implementation using `TObjectPtr<T>` for storing pools of actors.

This class is implemented in order to have a fixed pool of objects when initialized – we will get back to this topic by the end of the chapter, as you will have some extra work to do! Additionally, it will be inaccessible from Blueprints, leaving pool creation and management to a dedicated Subsystem.

You might already be familiar with UE Subsystems, but if you aren't, there's no need to worry – we will cover them in detail in *Chapter 7, Improving Your Code with Subsystems*.

Let's dive in and explore some code!

Analyzing the object pooling implementation

We are now exploring how to implement a proper object pooling system – class by class – that can be safely used during gameplay.

Inspecting PITS_FixedActorPool

First things first, open the `PITS_FixedActorPool.h` file located in the project's `Public/Utils` folder. You will notice that the class declaration follows the well-known standards for declaring a `UObject`-derived class:

```
UCLASS()
class PAWSINTHESHELL_API UPITS_FixedActorPool : public UObject
```

Nothing fancy here, but we make sure that this class will participate in the engine's Reflection System and GC.

The actual pool is implemented by using an array container:

```
UPROPERTY(Transient)
TArray<TObjectPtr<AActor>> TheActorPool;
```

As you can see here, we are using a `TObjectPtr<T>` wrapper, which will make our life easier, as explained in the previous sections. Unless there is some unusual behaviour with the pooled objects elsewhere in our code, we can be confident that the pooled objects will not be destroyed, as we maintain a strong pointer to them.

> **Note**
>
> The `Transient` specifier indicates that a property or class should not be saved to disk or loaded from a file, ensuring its value is reset to zero or its default state during initialization to prevent persistent data bloat.

Next, the `public` section will expose the main functions for creating and managing the object pool:

```
void InitializePool(TSubclassOf<AActor> SpawnableClass, const int32 PoolSize =
10);

AActor* GetObjectFromPool();

void ReleaseObjectToPool(AActor* Actor);

bool HasAvailableObjectsInPool() const;
```

```
bool IsObjectPooled(const AActor* Actor) const;
```

The first thing you will notice here is that I have been using raw pointers to actors; I have opted for this solution as I want a simple and clean API.

> **Note**
>
> Returning and accepting raw pointers is idiomatic and efficient, but they risk becoming invalid if the actor is destroyed, so we'll make sure to check their validity every time we are accessing it. An alternative solution would be to replace raw pointers with `TWeakObjectPtr<T>` to make the non-owning nature explicit.

Functions are quite self-explanatory; `InitializePool()` will create a pool of `PoolSize` objects from a subclass of `AActors` – this pool is dedicated to level objects.

`GetObjectFromPool()` and `ReleaseObjectToPool()` will be used during gameplay to activate a pooled instance or to deactivate it, instead of creating and destroying it every time.

Finally, `HasAvailableObjectsInPool()` and `IsObjectPooled()` are utility functions to get information about the pool before requesting an object.

Let's check how these functions are implemented by opening the `.cpp` file. We'll start with the `InitializePool()` function:

```
void UPITS_FixedActorPool::InitializePool(const TSubclassOf<AActor>
SpawnableClass, const int32 PoolSize)
{
    if (!SpawnableClass || PoolSize <= 0)
    {
        return;
    }

    UWorld* World = GetWorld();

    CHECK_PTR_AND_LOG_RETURN(World);

    TheActorPool.Empty();

    for (int32 i = 0; i < PoolSize; ++i)
    {
```

```
        FActorSpawnParameters SpawnParams;
        SpawnParams.SpawnCollisionHandlingOverride =
ESpawnActorCollisionHandlingMethod::AlwaysSpawn;

        if (AActor* NewActor = World->SpawnActor<AActor>(SpawnableClass,
FVector::ZeroVector, FRotator::ZeroRotator, SpawnParams))
        {
            NewActor->SetActorEnableCollision(false);
            NewActor->SetActorHiddenInGame(true);
            NewActor->SetLifeSpan(0.f);
            TheActorPool.Add(NewActor);
        }
    }
}
```

The code is quite straightforward; after validating parameters, we spawn a set of `SpawnableClass`-based instances based on the `PoolSize` value. For each one, before adding it to the `TheActorPool` container, we make sure that they are hidden and won't have any physics collision enabled. After this process, the object pool will be initialized and ready to grant objects on request.

The `GetObjectFromPool()` function will simply cycle through the object pool array and look for the first valid object that is disabled – by checking the `IsHidden()` function – and return it. If no available object is found, it will return `nullptr`:

```
AActor* UPITS_FixedActorPool::GetObjectFromPool()
{
    for (TObjectPtr<AActor>& ActorPtr : TheActorPool)
    {
        if (ActorPtr)
        {
            if (AActor* Actor = ActorPtr.Get(); Actor->IsHidden())
            {
                Actor->SetActorHiddenInGame(false);
                Actor->SetActorEnableCollision(true);
                return Actor;
            }
        }
    }
```

```
        return nullptr;
    }
```

Finally, to release an object back to the pool, we will check that the object is actually in the pool and disable it, as displayed in the following block of code:

```
void UPITS_FixedActorPool::ReleaseObjectToPool(AActor* Actor)
{
    CHECK_PTR_AND_LOG_RETURN(Actor);

    for (TObjectPtr<AActor>& ActorPtr : TheActorPool)
    {
        if (ActorPtr && ActorPtr.Get() == Actor)
        {
            Actor->SetActorHiddenInGame(true);
            Actor->SetActorEnableCollision(false);
            return;
        }
    }
}
```

The remaining functions, `HasAvailableObjectsInPool()` and `IsObjectPool()`, are quite straightforward, so I'll leave it to you to review their implementations.

Before checking how the object pool has been used, I will briefly introduce an interface that will be used to handle the release and acquire phases of each object.

Inspecting PITS_PooledObjectInterface

`PITS_PooledObjectInterface`, which can be found in the `Public/Interfaces` folder, is declared to let pooled objects implement some additional internal code logic when they are acquired or released – such as resetting physics for a bullet or AI behaviors for enemies – that is not implemented in the main pool implementation. The interface has just two declarations:

```
UFUNCTION(BlueprintCallable, BlueprintNativeEvent, Category="PawsInTheShell|
Object Pool")
void HandleAcquire();

UFUNCTION(BlueprintCallable, BlueprintNativeEvent, Category="PawsInTheShell|
Object Pool")
void HandleRelease();
```

Please note that the `BlueprintNativeEvent` specifier will let us implement both C++ and Blueprint pooled objects.

Now that you have a clear understanding of how the object pool has been implemented, let's check how it is used by the game application.

Inspecting PITS_ObjectPoolSubsystem

`PITS_ObjectPoolSubsystem` has been implemented in order to get unified and easy access to object pools, categorized by the pooled object class. To inspect this class, open `PITS_ObjectPoolSubsystem.h`, which can be found in the `Public/Subsystem` folder. Firstly, notice that we are using a map container to store a key/value pair of object classes and object pools, as depicted in the following piece of code:

```
UPROPERTY()
TMap<TSubclassOf<AActor>, TObjectPtr<class UPITS_FixedActorPool>> ActorsPoolMap;
```

As you can see, we are again using the `TObjectPtr<T>` wrapper to follow the engine's best practices and make the actor pool references safer.

Available functions basically act as a *façade* to object pools, and will let you access each pool easily through its class:

```
protected:
    UFUNCTION(Category="PawsInTheShell|Subsystems")
    UPITS_FixedActorPool* GetObjectPool(const TSubclassOf<AActor> SpawnableClass)
const;

public:
    UFUNCTION(BlueprintCallable, Category="PawsInTheShell|Subsystems")
    void CreateObjectPool(TSubclassOf<AActor> SpawnableClass, int32 PoolSize =
20);

    UFUNCTION(BlueprintCallable, Category="PawsInTheShell|Subsystems")
    bool HasObjectPool(TSubclassOf<AActor> SpawnableClass) const;

    UFUNCTION(BlueprintCallable, Category="PawsInTheShell|Subsystems")
    bool HasAvailablePooledObjects(const TSubclassOf<AActor> SpawnableClass)
const;

    UFUNCTION(BlueprintCallable, Category="PawsInTheShell|Subsystems")
    bool IsObjectPooled(const AActor* Actor) const;
```

```
    UFUNCTION(BlueprintCallable, Category="PawsInTheShell|Subsystems")
    AActor* AcquirePooledObject(const TSubclassOf<AActor> SpawnableClass, const
FTransform ObjectTransform);

    UFUNCTION(BlueprintCallable, Category="PawsInTheShell|Subsystems")
    void ReleasePooledObject(AActor* Actor);
```

If you open the corresponding `PITS_ObjectPoolSubsystem.cpp` file, you will notice that the code is quite easy to understand. There is just one thing worth mentioning and it's the extra check we do in the `AcquirePooledObject()` and `ReleasePooledObject()` functions; if pooled object classes implement the aforementioned `PITS_PooledObjectInterface` interface, we make sure to call the corresponding acquire and release functions. In particular, `AcquirePooledObject()` implements this portion of code:

```
if (PooledActor->GetClass()-
>ImplementsInterface(UPITS_PooledObjectInterface::StaticClass()))
{
    IPITS_PooledObjectInterface::Execute_HandleAcquire(
        PooledActor);
}
```

Correspondingly, `ReleasePooledObject()` will implement the following portion of code:

```
if (Actor->GetClass()-
>ImplementsInterface(UPITS_PooledObjectInterface::StaticClass()))
{
    IPITS_PooledObjectInterface::Execute_HandleRelease(
        Actor);
}
```

Since you've already learned about how the Reflection System handles interfaces in *Chapter 2, Understanding the Engine Reflection System*, I won't go over the details again, to keep things simple.

Now that we have a fully developed object pooling system available, let's take a look at a class that will be used to create the pooled objects!

Inspecting PITS_BaseProjectile

Since the *Paws in the Shell* game will use many different types of weapons and bullets, we will need a base projectile class to simplify things; `PITS_BaseProjectile` serves this purpose by exposing the main bullet gameplay logic and, incidentally, by implementing the object pool interface. Let's open the `PITS_BaseProjectile.h` file and check the class declaration:

```
UCLASS(Abstract)
class PAWSINTHESHELL_API APITS_BaseProjectile : public AActor, public
IPITS_PooledObjectInterface
```

As you can see, there is the interface declaration, so you should expect to have its methods implemented somewhere in the code. You will find them at the end of the class, just like the following piece of code:

```
virtual void HandleAcquire_Implementation() override;
virtual void HandleRelease_Implementation() override;
```

Let's open the `.cpp` file to see the actual code. We will start with `HandleAcquire_Implementation()`, which is shown in the following code block:

```
void APITS_BaseProjectile::HandleAcquire_Implementation()
{
    if (ProjectileMovement && CollisionComponent)
    {
        ProjectileMovement->StopMovementImmediately();
        ProjectileMovement->Deactivate();
        ProjectileMovement->SetUpdatedComponent(CollisionComponent);

        const FVector Direction = GetActorForwardVector().GetSafeNormal();
        ProjectileMovement->Velocity = Direction * ProjectileMovement-
>InitialSpeed;

        ProjectileMovement->Activate(true);
        ProjectileMovement->ResetInterpolation();
        ProjectileMovement->SetComponentTickEnabled(true);
    }
}
```

Since game bullets rely on physics and collision detection, we are simply resetting all values that control the gameplay logic. This ensures that no residual data remains from the previous time the object was used before it was returned to the pool.

On the other hand, `HandleRelease_Implementation()` is pretty simple:

```
void APITS_BaseProjectile::HandleRelease_Implementation()
{
    ProjectileMovement->StopMovementImmediately();
}
```

The function call will simply zero the velocity and acceleration – if any.

At this point, you may be wondering when the object is released; in the projectile-based objects, this is handled internally by the `OnHitComplete()` function:

```
void APITS_BaseProjectile::OnHitcomplete()
{
    UPITS_ObjectPoolSubsystem* PoolSubsystem = GetWorld()-
>GetSubsystem<UPITS_ObjectPoolSubsystem>();
    CHECK_PTR_AND_LOG(PoolSubsystem);

    if (PoolSubsystem->IsObjectPooled(this))
    {
        PoolSubsystem->ReleasePooledObject(this);
    }
    else
    {
        Destroy();
    }
}
```

As you can see, we check if the object is pooled in the subsystem; if it is, we release it. If the object is not pooled, we simply destroy it as it has been used as an ordinary object in the level.

So, how do we use these projectile classes in C++ in order to correctly store them in an object pool? Let's check it out in the next subsection.

Inspecting PITS_WeaponSpawnPointComponent

The `PITS_WeaponSpawnPointComponent` class is one of the many using the pool object system; it is used by player characters, enemy AI, and some testing Blueprints. Let's open up the header file located in `Public/Components` to see how it behaves. You will notice that we declare these references:

```
UPROPERTY(EditAnywhere, Category="PawsInTheShell|Weapon")
int32 RequestedPoolSize = 50;

UPROPERTY()
TSubclassOf<APITS_BaseProjectile> CurrentProjectileClass;

UPROPERTY();
TObjectPtr<UPITS_ObjectPoolSubsystem> PoolSubsystem;
```

They will be used during the pool creation process and the projectile shooting phase. There's just one thing to mention; notice we are using the `TObjectPtr<T>` wrapper for the pool subsystem in order to follow the best practices discussed throughout this chapter. If you switch to the `.cpp` implementation, you will notice the object pool creation in the `SetCurrentProjectileClass()` function, as shown in the following line of code:

```
PoolSubsystem->CreateObjectPool(CurrentProjectileClass, RequestedPoolSize);
```

The `Shoot()` function will take care of retrieving the actual spawn location and request a pooled object from the Subsystem:

```
if (CurrentProjectileClass)
{
    FActorSpawnParameters SpawnParams;
    SpawnParams.Owner = GetOwner();
    const FVector SpawnLocation = GetComponentLocation();
    const FRotator SpawnRotation = GetComponentRotation();
    const FTransform SpawnTransform = FTransform(SpawnRotation, SpawnLocation);
    PoolSubsystem->AcquirePooledObject(CurrentProjectileClass, SpawnTransform);
}
```

Just remember that the pooled object will release itself back to the pool upon hitting a target, so the projectile spawner doesn't need to manage it; perfect fire-and-forget logic!

Now that we have gathered all the necessary components, we can switch to the UE Editor and examine how these classes are used in the actual game.

Testing the implementation in-game

Once you have the Paws in the Shell project started in the UE Editor, open the **Gym_05_ObjectPooling** level, located in the `Maps` folder. Once you hit the **Play** button, you will be able to move around the level with Fernando the Flamingo and shoot around with his twin-cannon blasters. Additionally, the level is filled with seemingly dangerous shooting turrets. Fernando and all the turrets at the center of the map use the object pooling implementation presented in this section.

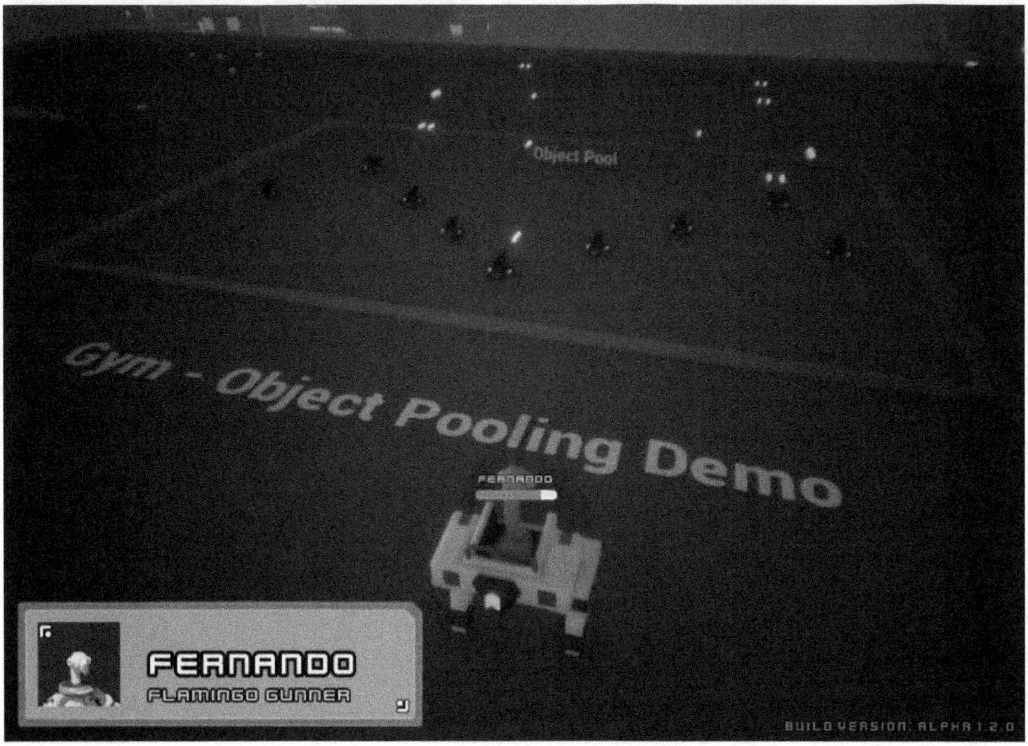

Figure 4.1 – The object pooling system in action

Fernando is provided with four `WeaponSpawnPointComponent` instances, as shown in *Figure 4.2*:

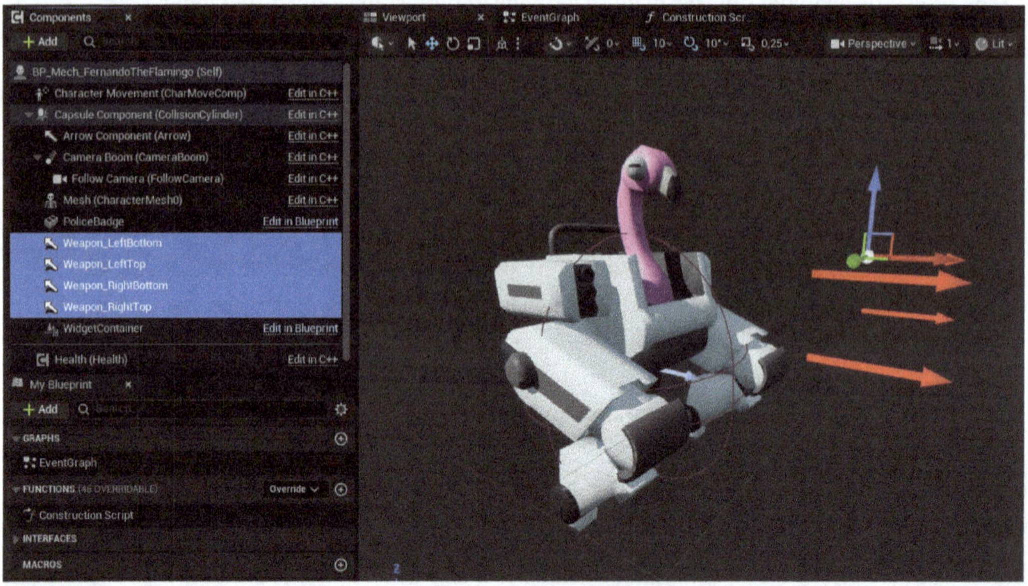

Figure 4.2 – Fernando's shooting points

Each component will shoot a different projectile taken from the same object pool; in *Chapter 6*, *Working with Data Structures*, we will explore in detail how bullet data is retrieved and declared.

Shooting turret objects inside the level use the same object pooling system, but it is implemented directly in Blueprints. Head over to the `Blueprints/Training` folder, open the **BP_AI_TrainingTurret_ObjectPool** Blueprint, and check the Event Graph. Object pool creation is pretty straightforward once you have a class to pool and a pool size, as depicted in *Figure 4.3*:

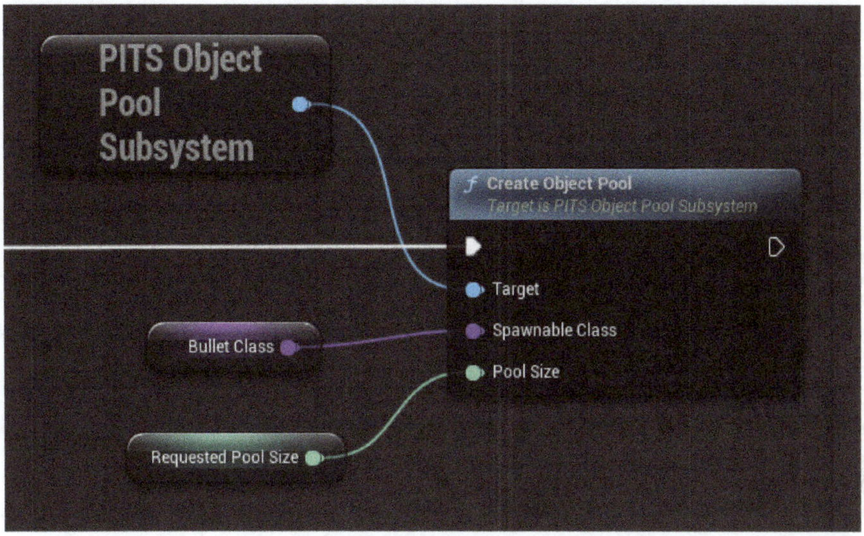

Figure 4.3 – The object pool creation

As you can see, we execute the `BlueprintCallable` **Create Object Pool** node from the subsystem; if the pool is already present, the system will simply ignore this call, so we don't need to take extra checks.

Whenever we need to acquire a pooled object, we will simply execute the **Acquire Pooled Object** node and pass both the object class and the requested transform – in this case, retrieved by a spawn point – as depicted in *Figure 4.4*:

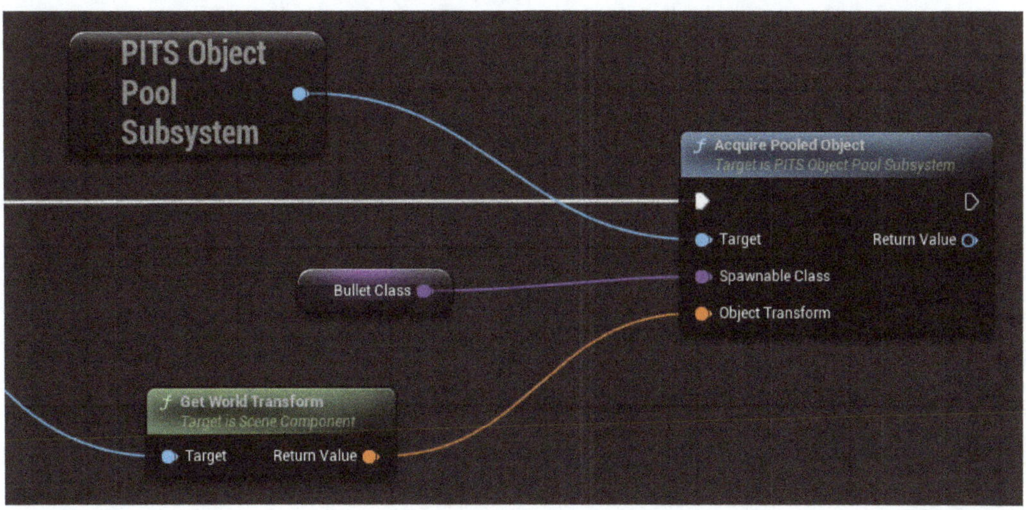

Figure 4.4 – The pooled object request

> **Note**
>
> Keep in mind that, if no object is available, you will get `nullptr`, so if you need to add extra operations to the pooled object, you will need to check its validity before proceeding.

In this subsection, you have seen a full implementation of an object pooling system and how the almost ubiquitous `TObjectPtr<T>` wrapper is used to follow the engine's best practices. Now it's your turn to jump into some coding! I'll be asking you to add a few new features and help track down a sneaky little bug that I may have accidentally introduced.

Develop and self-evaluate

It's now your turn to work on some code; there are a couple of tasks for which I will ask you to improve how things are implemented in the project. We are going to start with non-fixed object pools.

Implementing non-fixed object pools

You may have noticed that my object pool implementation strongly emphasizes a fixed size; once an object pool is created, you cannot add additional pooled objects. This could be either a desired feature or a limitation, depending on your needs. In my case, this is something I want to enforce; as an example, you may wish to explore the **Gym06_TargetSpawner** level shown in *Figure 4.5*:

Figure 4.5 – The target spawner level

This is a training map where the character will be shooting at targets randomly popping up. As I need to have a single target at any time and each spawner works independently, I have created an object pool with a single instantiated object; this means a single target can be active at any time. Any additional request will return `nullptr`, and no target will be shown.

Another use case is enemy spawn control: you might have multiple enemy spawners in a level, but you want to ensure that no more than a fixed number of enemies of the same type are present at any given time.

However, there are some other cases where you may need non-fixed-size object pools; a typical example is a bullet hell game, where you may keep on requesting objects, and the pool itself has none available. In this case, you will be in deep trouble, as bullets won't be generated on request. You may test this scenario yourself in the **Gym05_ObjectPooling** level by lowering the object pool size for the firing turrets and, at the same time, higher the fire rate for each of them. The shooting system will suddenly become erratic and buggy, and bullets will be missing when turrets are shooting!

To improve the object pooling capabilities, try implementing your own with a couple of new features:

- When requesting pool creation, if the object pool already exists and the requested pool size is larger than the original size, increase the pool accordingly
- Whenever an object is requested from the pool, and none are available, create a new object, add it to the pool, and return it to the requester

These new features have the side effect of enabling lazily initialized object pool systems: you can create empty pools and let them grow as requests arrive. This will be useful whenever you need systems that grow slowly but steadily over time!

Analyzing and hunting for bugs

For the second task, I have purposefully and maliciously prepared a nasty little bug for you! First of all, start playing the **Gym05_ObjectPooling** level and focus on the **Weak Object Pool** zone, as shown in *Figure 4.6*:

Figure 4.6 – The weak object pool example

At the start of the game, the turrets appear to behave correctly, but after about a minute, they stop working – no errors and no indication of what's going wrong.

The implementation follows the same gameplay logic as the previous pooling system, but with a different underlying approach. In particular, notice the following:

- The object pool – that is, `PITS_WeakFixedObjectPool` – is implemented as a non-`UObject` derived class
- The actor pool has been implemented as an array of `TWeakObjectPtr<T>` objects
- The object pool map in the `PITS_WeakObjectPoolSubsystem` class has been implemented using a `TUniquePtr<T>` wrapper

One of these elements is the true culprit! The solution is somewhere hidden in the source code comments. But before diving into the actual code, take a moment to think things over and review what we've covered in this chapter. It's all about simple logic and reasoning. Elementary, my dear Watson!

In this section, we have covered a fairly long and, hopefully, illustrative example of how to use pointers effectively, highlighting both their practical advantages and common use cases in real gameplay scenarios.

Summary

This chapter concludes the first part of the book, which focuses on a deep dive into UE core architecture. In particular, we examined how pointers are handled within a game application: starting with pointer wrappers, we then explored Epic Games' implementation of the smart pointer library. We also discussed when it is appropriate to use raw pointers and finally walked through a complete implementation of an object pool system that fully leverages the engine pointers. Mastering these topics will grant you control, safety, and efficiency over your game; all these are essential for professional-level development in UE and in game programming in general.

Get this book's PDF copy, code bundle, and more

Scan the QR code (or go to `packtpub.com/unlock`). Search for this book by name, confirm the edition, and then follow the steps on the page.

UNLOCK NOW

Note: Have your invoice handy. Purchases made directly from the Packt website don't require an invoice.

Part 2

Enhancing your Coding Skills

This second part of the book is dedicated to enhancing your programming skills through the exploration of advanced topics. Once you have achieved a thorough understanding of the material presented, you will be ready to develop games that are both highly scalable and functionally robust.

This part of the book includes the following chapters:

- *Chapter 5: Handling Event-Driven Architectures*
- *Chapter 6: Working with Data Structures*
- *Chapter 7: Improving Your Code with Subsystems*
- *Chapter 8: Understanding Multithreading and Concurrency*

5

Handling Event-Driven Architectures

When developing a game, one of the most critical considerations is the design of communication mechanisms between actors, as these are essential for achieving a robust, modular, and well-decoupled system. UE provides a robust event system that enables the implementation of this type of gameplay logic. In this chapter, we will explore techniques such as delegates, event dispatchers, and event handlers, which will let you send and respond to events. This approach allows efficient real-time reactions by triggering behaviors only when a specific event occurs, while avoiding continuous function calls. For a game programmer, understanding these concepts is of paramount importance, as it enables the development of games that are highly scalable and robust, while also delivering significant performance improvements.

The main topics we will be covering in this chapter are the following:

- Introducing event-driven architectures in Unreal Engine
- Working with delegates
- Understanding event dispatchers in Blueprints
- Presenting a practical example

Technical requirements

To get the best out of the following sections, you should have fully understood the previous chapters.

Introducing event-driven architectures in Unreal Engine

When discussing **event-driven architecture**, we refer to an architectural style in which components communicate by sending and responding to events, thereby enabling modular and decoupled systems. In UE, this approach supports efficient real-time updates by triggering behaviours only when specific events occur, rather than relying on continuous polling. The engine provides a robust event system that propagates and manages events between objects in both C++ and Blueprints. This model promotes a clear separation of concerns, improved performance, and easier maintenance of gameplay and UI systems.

Making good use of event-driven architectures in UE is important because it improves modularity and decoupling by allowing components to communicate through events without direct dependencies, making code easier to manage and extend. It also enhances performance by ensuring that the system reacts only when events occur, reducing CPU overhead instead of relying on continuous polling, such as unnecessary use of the `Tick` function. Additionally, event-driven systems simplify maintenance by isolating logic and reducing overall complexity, which makes debugging, and updates more efficient. This approach enables greater scalability; new features and listeners can be added in the future without modifying existing systems.

The UE Gameplay Framework provides a set of elements to leverage its own event-driven architecture. These elements are the following:

- **Delegates**: Type-safe function pointers in C++ that bind and invoke one or multiple functions dynamically. They enable decoupled callbacks and event handling between objects.
- **Event Dispatchers**: Blueprint-exposed delegates allowing flexible binding to events.
- **Event Handlers**: Objects or components that listen to specific event schemas and process events accordingly.

In addition to the aforementioned elements, there are some inner workings in the engine that should be taken into account. In particular, **Extension Handlers** are delegates that are registered to dynamically modify or extend game objects when game features are activated or when extension events occur. **Scene State** and **Event Streams**, by contrast, are systems that queue and broadcast events within defined contexts, enabling multiple consumers to respond efficiently to gameplay events through the structured management and routing of these event streams.

> **Note**
>
> It should be noted that many core UE systems – most notably Behavior Trees, State Trees and Unreal Motion Graphics (UMG) – are built around event-driven patterns, making mastery of this architecture essential for effective development. Taking all these topics into consideration would require a full book instead of a single chapter; therefore we will primarily concentrate on the main elements of the Gameplay Framework – that means, delegates, event dispatchers and event handlers.

In the following sections, I will demonstrate how to implement fully functional event-driven systems in your games. It is important to note that we will not be focusing solely on pure C++ implementations; leveraging Blueprint exposure is crucial for creating systems that are both easily understandable and extensible by your fellow game designers and technical artists.

Working with delegates

When programming an application, delegates are arguably the unsung heroes of responsive game architecture; they enable object communication in an efficient way – that is, without hard-coupled callbacks. Most notably, they offer type safety, flexibility, and scalability while keeping code clean and maintainable. UE is no exception – it offers a wide range of delegate implementations for most scenarios you'll encounter during development. In this section we will explore these implementations along with their main characteristics.

First off, I want to make sure you have a clear understanding of what a delegate is in UE. A delegate can be described as a type-safe, generic object that stores and invokes one or more functions, enabling flexible event communication between objects.

We can classify delegates into two main categories:

- **Single-cast delegates** are used for simple callbacks; they bind one single function at a time
- **Multicast delegates** enable multiple bindings of functions

Additionally, both single-cast, and multicast delegates can be declared as **dynamic** making them reflection-based and fully serializable. Multicast dynamic delegates are the only ones that can be exposed to the Blueprints event dispatcher system; we will be analyzing them in the next, dedicated, section.

In UE, delegates are implemented as templated C++ objects using macros that will generate classes supporting binding, unbinding, and invocation. Macros are prefixed with `DECLARE_` and followed by descriptive qualifiers – such as `MULTICAST` or `DYNAMIC` – that reflect their implementation. Additionally, they can be given a list of parameters that can be used to send information on bound entities. Finally, some of them can even return a result. Let's begin by examining the aforementioned categories one by one, in order to gain a clear understanding of their differences and use cases.

Analyzing non-dynamic single-cast delegates

Single-cast non-dynamic delegates are designed to be as lightweight and efficient as possible. They are intended for use in situations where you need to create systems with single bindings. This means you can bind exactly one function at a time and invoke it later during gameplay.

Declaring a non-dynamic single-cast delegate

A typical single-cast delegate with no parameters will be pretty similar to the following piece of code:

```
DECLARE_DELEGATE(FMyDelegateSignature);
```

As you can see, the `DECLARE_DELEGATE` macro is used, and the signature is using the `F` prefix that follows the well-known UE conventions. Although not mandatory, adding a `Signature` postfix is a good practice in order to differentiate it from delegate instance variables.

A delegate instance variable will be pretty similar to the following line of code:

```
FMyDelegateSignature MyDelegate;
```

A matching function for this delegate will be like the following:

```
void OnMyDelegate();
```

Adding parameters is pretty straightforward; you'll just need to add the postfix `_OneParam`, `_TwoParams` up to `_EightParams`. Depending on the number of parameters, you will also be adding the parameter types. As an example, consider the following piece of code from the *Paws in the Shell* project:

```
DECLARE_DELEGATE_TwoParams( \
    FShooterPerceptionUpdatedSignature, \
    AActor*, \
    const FAIStimulus&);
```

Please note that, when declaring delegates over multiple lines, you will need to add a backslash character at the end of each line.

Although not mandatory, it is a good practice to add a commented parameter name for extra clarity:

```
DECLARE_DELEGATE_TwoParams( \
    FShooterPerceptionUpdatedSignature, \
    AActor* /* PerceivedActor */, \
    const FAIStimulus& /* Stimulus */);
```

A matching function for this delegate will be like the following:

```
void OnShooterPerceptionUpdated(AActor* PerceivedActor, FAIStimulus Stimulus);
```

A single-cast delegate can also return a value, instead of `void`. The corresponding macro will have an added `_RetVal`, just like the following piece of code:

```
DECLARE_DELEGATE_RetVal_OneParam( \
    bool, \
    FMyDelegateSignature, \
    int32 /* Val */);
```

As you can see, the first parameter declares the returned type. A matching function for this delegate will be like the following:

```
bool OnMyDelegate(int32 Val);
```

Binding to non-dynamic single-cast delegates

To subscribe to a single-cast non-dynamic delegate, you have a list of available functions, each of them with its own use cases. Here, I'll be listing them along with their main characteristics.

The `BindRaw()` method will bind a delegate to a member function of a regular C++ object – that is a non-`UObject` derived class with an externally managed lifetime. Given its pure C++ typology, you will need to ensure the object will outlive the delegate in order to avoid crashes.

On the other hand, the `BindUObject()` method will bind the delegate to a member function of a `UObject`-derived class. In this case, you will be safe to use it within UE GC and, additionally, the bind will be automatically removed once the `UObject` instance is destroyed.

Whenever you bind a delegate to a member function of an object managed by a `TSharedPtr<T>`, you should use the `BindSP()` method. This method safely manages the lifetime of the reference-counted pointer and automatically performs validity checks before execution.

If you need to use a shared-pointer–managed object in a multithreaded environment where delegate execution may cross threads, it is strongly recommended to use `BindThreadSafeSP()` instead of `BindSP()`. This ensures thread-safe reference counting and validity checks when the delegate is executed.

> **Note**
>
> You should prefer `BindUObject()` and `BindSP()` over `BindRaw()` whenever possible to avoid the risk of generating dangling pointers.

The `BindStatic()` method allows you to bind a delegate to a static or global function. This type of binding is always safe to use and should be used whenever you need to bind a delegate to a function that is not associated with any object instance.

Finally, you can bind a delegate to an inline lambda function or functor by using `BindLambda()`; this method will let you handle quick inline callbacks and capture local variables. If you need to bind a delegate to a lambda with a weak reference to an object inside the lambda, you will be using `BindWeakLambda()` instead of `BindLambda()`; this will safely bind lambdas that capture `UObjects` or other pointers without extending their lifetimes. The bound lambda will automatically become unbound once the weak reference is no longer valid. This second option is safer to use when capturing pointers that may be destroyed.

If you later need to remove the binding from the delegate, call the `Unbind()` function. For safety, always verify that the delegate is bound beforehand.

Executing a non-dynamic single-cast delegate

A single-cast, non-dynamic delegate can be executed using the `Execute()` function. Before calling it, it is strongly recommended to verify that the delegate is bound to a function by calling `IsBound()`; executing unbound delegates without checks may cause memory corruption or trigger assertions that will crash your application.

As a shortcut, you can use `ExecuteIfBound()` that(), which will safely execute the delegate only... well, if it is bound. This second method can be called if the delegate has no return value, as output parameters may not be initialized and it can be unsafe to use them.

> **Note**
>
> It is highly recommended to always check `IsBound()` before calling the `Execute()` function.

Let's now check the dynamic counterpart of single-cast delegates.

Analyzing dynamic single-cast delegates

Unlike non-dynamic delegates, **single-cast dynamic delegates** are fully serializable. However, this comes at a cost: they support only `UObject` member functions and incur additional reflection and serialization overhead.

Declaring a dynamic single-cast delegate

A typical single-cast delegate with no parameters will be like the following piece of code:

```
DECLARE_DYNAMIC_DELEGATE(FMyDelegateSignature);
```

As for its non-dynamic counterpart, if you need parameters, you will be adding the following suffixes: `_OneParam`, `_TwoParams` and so on up to `_EightParams`.

Similarly, you will be using `_RetVal` if you need to return a value. This means that a single-cast dynamic delegate with one parameter and a return value will be similar to the following piece of code:

```
DECLARE_DYNAMIC_DELEGATE_RetVal_OneParam( \
    bool, \
    FMyDelegateSignature, \
    int32, Value);
```

Binding to dynamic single-cast delegates

Binding to a single-cast dynamic delegate is pretty straightforward, as you will be using the `BindDynamic()` function. This will bind a `UObject` and its `UFUNCTION()` and will correctly leverage the engine reflection system.

If you need to bind a delegate to a function of a `UObject` by specifying the function name through an `FName`, you can take advantage of the `BindUFunction()` method that will create the binding via the `UObject` Reflection system; this is going to be quite useful in contexts where Blueprints are involved.

If you later need to remove the binding from the delegate, call the `Unbind()` function or use `RemoveDynamic()` to eliminate a specific binding by object and function.

Executing a non-dynamic single-cast delegate

To execute a single-cast dynamic delegate, follow the same rules as non-dynamic delegates: call `Execute()` after performing an `IsBound()` check, or use `ExecuteIfBound()`.

Let's now examine the last C++-only delegate.

Analyzing non-dynamic multicast delegates

Non-dynamic multicast delegates will allow holding and executing multiple bound functions simultaneously. They are designed for high performance and are declared and used without UObject reflection.

Declaring a non-dynamic multicast delegate

Declarations for this type of delegate follow the usual macro syntax explained in the previous subsections. This means that to declare a simple delegate with no parameters, you will be writing a line of code similar to the following:

```
DECLARE_MULTICAST_DELEGATE(FMyDelegateSignature);
```

Parameters can be added, as usual. Unfortunately, if you think about adding a return value, you are out of luck; multicast delegates cannot have _RetVal as they are designed to call multiple bound functions, so a single return value is not supported and not allowed.

Binding to non-dynamic multicast delegates

Subscribing to this type of delegate is pretty similar to single-cast declarations; the only difference is that you will be using Add instead of Bind. This means you will be declaring functions such as AddUObject(), AddRaw() and AddLambda(); it's pretty easy to remember, isn't it?

For multicast non-dynamic delegates, unbinding differs from single-cast delegates. You can remove a specific bound function instance using Remove(), remove all bound functions associated with a particular object pointer using RemoveAll(), or remove all bindings from the multicast delegate entirely using Clear().

Executing a non-dynamic multicast delegate

Execution will be invoked by using the Broadcast() function instead of the Execute() one. Please note that it is safe to call Broadcast() without checking if the delegate is bound; the Broadcast() function will gracefully handle the case when no functions are bound, and you won't get any error. However, if you need to avoid the small overhead of the function call or wish to clarify your intent in code – explicitly skipping the call when nothing is bound – you can use the IsBound() function as usual.

This concludes the overview of non-Blueprintable delegates. As demonstrated, each type has its own characteristics and should be selected based on the specific use case. We will now move on to the final category of delegates, those that can be exposed to Blueprints, which will be covered in the next section.

Understanding event dispatchers in Blueprints

Due to their seamless Blueprint compatibility, **dynamic multicast delegates** are the most commonly used delegate type in UE, particularly in gameplay and UI systems. Compared to standard multicast delegates, they incur additional overhead because of `UObject` safety checks and serialization support; however, this cost is outweighed by the flexibility they provide for Blueprint-driven and persistent event handling.

> **Note**
>
> The ease of use of dynamic multicast delegates in Blueprints often leads to widespread adoption, occasionally beyond what is strictly necessary, so it's wise to evaluate whether a simpler delegate type would suffice before defaulting to them.

Analyzing dynamic multicast delegates

This type of delegate follows the same rules presented in the previous section, with its own peculiarities, so let's start checking them out.

Declaring a dynamic multicast delegate

A typical dynamic multicast delegate will follow the syntax of their single-cast counterparts and will add `_MULTICAST` to identify it, as shown in the following piece of code:

```
DECLARE_DYNAMIC_MULTICAST_DELEGATE(FMyDelegateSignature);
```

As for the other delegates, if you need parameters, you will be adding the following suffixes: `_OneParam`, `_TwoParams` and so on up to `_EightParams`.

Similarly to their non-dynamic counterparts, you are not allowed to add `_RetVal` as multicast delegates are designed for multiple bindings and, as such, a return value is not valid.

Binding to dynamic multicast delegates

Subscribing to this type of delegate, the primary method is `AddDynamic()` and the bound function needs to be a `UFUNCTION()`,with it comes without saying, a matching signature.

> **Note**
>
> Please note that there is no `BindDynamic()` for dynamic multicast delegates; that function is reserved only for dynamic single-cast ones.

To remove a binding, you will use the `RemoveDynamic()` function or `RemoveAll()` to eliminate all bindings associated with a particular object.

Executing a dynamic multicast delegate

As with its non-dynamic counterpart, execution is performed using the `Broadcast()` function. This approach is equally safe, as invoking a broadcast when no functions are bound is gracefully handled internally and will not result in any errors.

Now that you have a clear understanding of how to use dynamic multicast delegates in C++, the next section is dedicated to how they are managed inside Blueprints.

Using multicast dynamic in Blueprints

Dynamic multicast delegates can be seamlessly added to Blueprints and they are referred to as event dispatchers, enabling an event to have multiple bound listeners. As for their C++ counterparts, they facilitate flexible and decoupled communication between Blueprints by broadcasting notifications to all bound functions when triggered. For example, an event dispatcher can be used to notify multiple actors that a game level has been cleared. This may include spawning a pickup, opening the level exit, and displaying a "Level Cleared" message on the HUD.

In order to make a dynamic multicast delegate usable in Blueprints, the delegate variable definition will need to use the `BlueprintAssignable` specifier. As an example, consider the following delegate declaration from the *Paws in the Shell* project:

```
DECLARE_DYNAMIC_MULTICAST_DELEGATE( \
    FOnAllMissionsCompleteSignature);
```

To expose an event dispatcher to Blueprints, you will need to declare the variable definition like the following block of code:

```
UPROPERTY(BlueprintAssignable, BlueprintCallable)
FOnAllMissionsCompleteSignature OnAllMissionsComplete;
```

With this declaration, you will be exposing the following event handlers nodes to Blueprints:

- **Assign On All Missions Complete**, which will unbind all previous event bindings and bind a single new event
- **Bind Event to On All Missions Complete**, which will add a new event binding
- **Unbind Event from On All Missions Complete**, which will unbind a single bound event
- **Unbind all Events from On All Missions Complete**, which will unbind all bound events

As an extension from the previous example, *Figure 5.1* shows a binding registration to the event dispatcher:

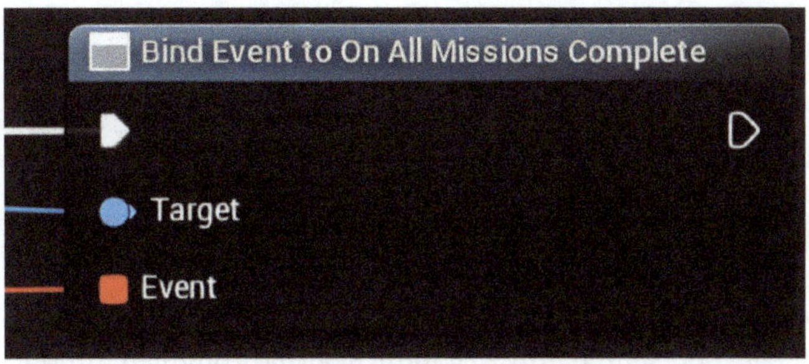

Figure 5.1 – Binding an event

If you need to make the delegate callable from a Blueprint, you will need to add `BlueprintCallable`. This will let you execute it via the **Call** node.

As you can see, using Blueprint-compatible delegates – that is dynamic multicast ones – is absolutely identical to creating event dispatchers directly in the Editor; they both represent the same event-driven mechanism and they are interoperable. Event dispatchers and handlers are essentially the Blueprint-exposed form of C++ dynamic multicast delegates. Now that you've got this new knowledge, it's a great time to go and explore some real-world examples.

Presenting a practical example

Well, it seems about time to present Barbara, from Team 33:

Barbara was no larger than a thumb, the cybernetically augmented bee incursor from The Pack silently walking through the metallic canyons of Holo District. Neon reflections weakened against her carbon-based stealth suit, precisely engineered to minimize visual detection. Around her, steel giants marched in measured paths, their digital eyes hunting intruders far larger than she could ever be.

Her thorax plating was cracked; a Steel Wolf – an OmniSight combat-pattern mecha – had grazed her moments earlier with its lasguns, flooding her systems with warning glyphs and a dull, throbbing pain. One wing faltered, compensating through micro-adjustments learned in a hundred silent missions. Barbara ignored the damage; mission came first.

She slipped through a ventilation seam and perched on a rusted conduit. Two Iron Mantis scout mechas clanked past, unaware. Barbara raised her shuriken pistol – an elegant weapon scaled to her size, its ammunition spinning with encoded malware. She fired.

The shuriken embedded itself in the first mecha's knee joint, blooming into a lattice of blue static energy. Cyber damage rippled through its systems, scrambling targeting protocols. The second turned, too late. Another shot severed its neural bus, and the machine collapsed in a shower of sparks, its fall echoing like distant thunder.

Barbara moved again – a thin blur through the shadows – leaving steel giants motionless behind her.

This scenario – a character taking and reacting to damage in real time – is a perfect case study for event-driven design using delegates.

Handling damage and health is probably one of the most important – and, honestly, one of the most fun – things to program in a video game that involves combat gameplay. In this section we will be exploring how delegates can help you in the process. In *Chapter 2, Understanding the Engine Reflection System*, I presented how to handle health through an interface; in this section we'll explore things a bit deeper, checking out how to handle character health and how to react to incoming damage.

Exploring the PITS_HealthComponent

In the *Paws in the Shell* project, the damage system is implemented as a standalone component that can be added to a character or any destructible actor to manage its health. Since the base character classes were created in C++, I chose to implement this component as non-Blueprintable. As a result, Blueprints won't be able to access or retrieve information from the component but only from the owning character.

Additionally, the design choice was to keep the health logic separate from the character to avoid unnecessary code bloat.

If you open the `PITS_HealthComponent.h` file, you will notice that the gameplay logic will handle the health value, regeneration ability, and so on. At the moment, what we are interested in are obviously delegates; this component has a single one whose sole aim is to communicate to the owning actor the health status for the character.

The health status is identified by a simple `enum class` shown in the following piece of code:

```
UENUM(BlueprintType)
enum class EPITS_HealthStatus : uint8
{
    Update     UMETA(DisplayName="Update"),
    Maximum    UMETA(DisplayName="Maximum"),
    Death      UMETA(DisplayName="Death"),
};
```

Whenever the component takes damage or is healed, it will notify the owning character of any changes. As a consequence, we will need a dedicated delegate, as declared in the following line of code:

```
DECLARE_DELEGATE_OneParam( \
    FHealthUpdateSignature, \
    EPITS_HealthStatus /* HealthStatus */);
```

As you can see, the delegate has a single parameter to communicate the new health status. Additionally, please note that the delegate is non-dynamic and single-cast; the binding logic will be implemented exclusively in C++, and we want to ensure that only a single object can bind to it.

The delegate instance variable is declared as the following line of code:

```
FHealthUpdateSignature OnUpdateHealth;
```

So, how do we execute this delegate? Let's switch to the `PITS_HealthComponent.cpp` file and look for the `AddHealth()` function.

First of all, we check that we actually need to change the health of the owning actor, as shown in the following code snippet:

```
if (IsDead()) return;
if (HealthToAdd == 0.0f) return;
if (HealthToAdd > 0 && CurrentHealth == MaxHealth) return;
```

Then, we execute the following block of code:

```
if (IsDead())
{
```

```
        OnUpdateHealth.ExecuteIfBound(
            EPITS_HealthStatus::Death);
}
else if (GetHealthPercentage() == 1.0f)
{
        OnUpdateHealth.ExecuteIfBound(
            EPITS_HealthStatus::Maximum);
}
OnUpdateHealth.ExecuteIfBound(
        EPITS_HealthStatus::Update);
```

As you can see, the code is self-explanatory. The use of `ExecuteIfBound()` avoids the need to check whether the delegate is bound before executing it, keeping the code cleaner and more readable.

As a side note, the `RemoveHealth()` has been implemented as an `AddHealth()` call with a negated parameter.

With the health component implemented and fully functional, let's see how it is used inside the character.

Analyzing health in PITS_BaseCharacter

The `APITS_BaseCharacter` class has three primary responsibilities related to health:

- Communicate to the health component any damage taken or healing received by the character
- Listen to events from the health component
- Broadcast to any bound function whenever the health status has changed

The first one is not related to delegates, so we will be focusing on the other two.

Listening for health status changes

Open the `PITS_BaseCharacter.cpp` and head to the `BeginPlay()` implementation; you will find the following piece of code:

```
Health->OnUpdateHealth.BindLambda([this](const EPITS_HealthStatus Status)
{
    // Code
});
```

As you can see, we bind the delegate using a lambda function. This approach enhances code conciseness and readability by defining the delegate behavior inline, eliminating the need to declare additional member functions.

Broadcasting health updates

Health updates from the character will need to be broadcast both to C++ and Blueprints listeners; this means we will be using dynamic multicast delegates. Head to the `PITS_BaseCharacter.h` file where you will find, at the very top, the delegate declaration:

```
DECLARE_DYNAMIC_MULTICAST_DELEGATE_OneParam( \
    FCharacterHealthStatusUpdateSignature, \
    float, HealthPercentage);
```

The delegate instance variable is, later, declared as the following piece of code:

```
UPROPERTY(BlueprintAssignable)
FCharacterHealthStatusUpdateSignature OnUpdateHealthStatus;
```

Note the presence of the `BlueprintAssignable` specifier that will expose it to Blueprints as an event dispatcher as shown in *Figure 5.2*:

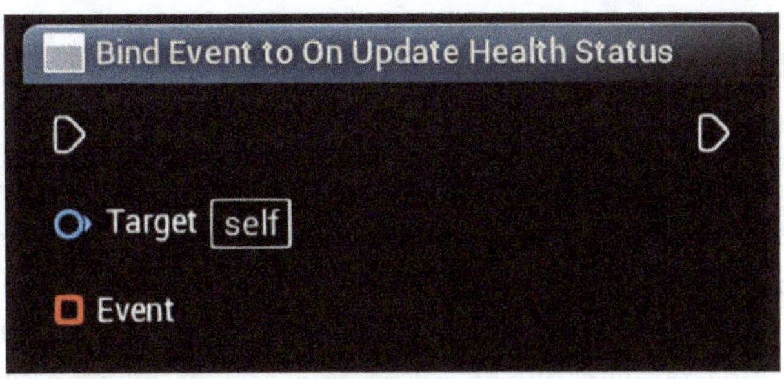

Figure 5.2 – Binding to health update events

It's now time to try this newly acquired knowledge by improving the health system with new features.

Develop and self-evaluate.

You might have spotted that the health gameplay logic conveniently forgets about character death. Yours truly sneakily and mischievously left that part out just for you – consider this your mission for the chapter ahead!

Implementing character death

Although the health component dispatches updates when a character – whether the player or an AI – reaches zero health, the `APITS_BaseCharacter` class simply ignores it. Try implementing your own code logic in order to manage this type of situation. In particular, you should be focusing on creating a dynamic multicast delegate that will dispatch this event to listeners.

First of all, the character should play a death animation – from those available in the project; you may try playing a montage directly from the `APITS_BaseCharacter` class.

Additionally, whenever a player character dies, you should first disable all player input. Next, the controller should be able to handle what's happening after – be it respawning, level reloads or a game over screen.

On the other hand, when an AI enemy character dies, you'll need to take care of its removal. Just a heads-up: since enemy characters are managed by an object pooling system, you should release them back to the pool instead of destroying them for real. This might be a bit challenging, but I'm confident you'll handle it just fine!

In this section, I have presented a practical scenario demonstrating the use of delegates – both single-cast and multicast types. As illustrated, each delegate type serves a distinct purpose, and understanding the appropriate context for their application is critically important.

Summary

In this chapter, a comprehensive overview of all delegates supported by UE was presented; in particular, the concept of delegates as type-safe, flexible function pointers used for event-driven communication within UE were explained. The chapter covered the different types of delegates, including single-cast and multicast, highlighting their distinct roles and appropriate use cases. Understanding delegates and having a strong grip on them is essential for managing gameplay logic and making your code maintainable. Additionally, as a developer, you will be able to leverage the engine event system effectively in both C++ and Blueprints. Finally, with a real-world example of how delegates enable clean, modular, and efficient code by allowing inline behavior definition and event handling without extra member functions were showcased. This chapter was packed with information, so now it's time to take a break, enjoy your favorite drink, and recharge. When you're ready, we'll dive even deeper into the engine's capabilities in the next chapter!

Get this book's PDF copy, code bundle, and more

Scan the QR code (or go to `packtpub.com/unlock`). Search for this book by name, confirm the edition, and then follow the steps on the page.

UNLOCK NOW

Note: Have your invoice handy. Purchases made directly from the Packt website don't require an invoice.

6

Working with Data Structures

Data structures represent an organized format for storing, managing, and accessing related data efficiently within a program. UE is obviously no exception, as it provides specialized types that will help game programmers optimize their development pipeline within this field. Efficient data organization directly impacts gameplay functionality, performance, and especially team workflows.

Throughout this chapter, I will introduce the basic topics on structures before delving into more advanced ones. By the end of the chapter, you will have gained a strong understanding of how structures should be used and what their main pros and cons are. In particular, in this chapter we will be focusing on:

- Explaining structures in Unreal Engine
- Implementing Data Tables
- Implementing Data Assets
- Presenting a practical example

Technical requirements

To get the best out of the following sections, you should have fully understood the previous chapters.

Explaining structures in Unreal Engine

Whenever we discuss **data structures**, we generally refer to specialized methods that facilitate data access and manipulation. This means that a data structure defines how data is organized and the operations that can be performed on it.

If you have a background in C++ programming, you will be aware that the language supports various built-in and user-defined data structures – such as arrays, and through the Standard Template Library (STL), containers like lists, stacks, and queues – designed to optimize data storage and retrieval. Additionally, the STL offers a rich set of predefined, template-based data structures, including vectors, maps, sets, and more. Epic Games consistently adopts a methodology within UE that emphasizes the development of tailored in-engine implementations – that is TArray<T>, TSet<T>, TMap<T> and TMultiMap<T> – that are designed to ensure optimal memory management, performance, and comprehensive support for Reflection mechanisms.

Structures are, of course, considerably more than that. In *Chapter 2, Understanding the Engine Reflection System*, we analyzed the definition of a struct header, and I promised to revisit the subject in this chapter for a more detailed examination. So, let's get started!

Comparing UStruct and UObject

The most important aspect to consider is how a UStruct differs from a UObject. The first thing to be aware of is usage, as a UStruct is, by definition, a lightweight data structure used for grouping variables and data with no independent lifecycle. On the other hand, a UObject is employed for complex objects with a lifecycle integrated within the engine.

Being managed as **plain-old-data** (**POD**), UStructs have a simple and predictable memory layout and are not garbage collected. As a consequence, they have a faster creation and destruction phase, caching contiguous memory layouts. Additionally, you are allowed to use simple constructors, so you won't be using the engine-specific NewObject() and CreateDefaultSubobject() functions.

Next, UStructs do not have UFUNCTION() support, and UPROPERTY() is used just for Reflection. They can be serialized, but just as part of an owning UObject or AActor.

Through the USTRUCT() macro, you can declare three main specifiers:

- BlueprintType that will let you expose structs to Blueprints
- Atomic that declares the struct as a POD-style type safe for copying, serialization and multithreaded access with no custom copy/assignment logic
- NoExport that instructs the UHT not to generate export macros for the struct, isolating it to its defining module

As a final note, as a UStruct is not tracked by the GC, UObject pointers stored as raw pointers inside structs are not automatically tracked or nulled. This means that, inside structs, you should prefer smart pointer types – such as TWeakObjectPtr<T> or TSoftObjectPtr<T> – instead of raw pointers.

If, on the other hand, while using raw pointers you need to inform the GC of `UObject` references inside a `UStruct`, you will need to implement the `AddStructReferencedObjects()` static function inside your struct definition, be it the header or source file, with the following signature:

```
static void AddStructReferencedObjects(
    FYourStruct& Struct,
    FReferenceCollector&Collector);
```

Inside the function, you will need to add each referenced object similarly to the following piece of code:

```
Collector.AddReferencedObject(Struct.MyUObjectPtr);
```

> **Note**
>
> Implementing `AddStructReferencedObjects()` should be done carefully to avoid dangling references and ensure all `UObject` raw pointers are accounted for in the collector.

In this section, we have explored some of the most advanced topics regarding structures in UE, including their main differences with `UObjects`. In the next section, we will be exploring how to get the best out of structures by creating tables with UE built-in support.

Implementing Data Tables

UE provides a robust and efficient solution for organizing extensive structured data within your project. These structures – called **Data Tables** – will let you manage character attributes, item properties, game configurations, and anything you may deem appropriate. One of the best things is that the engine will let you seamlessly import, modify, and reference data from an external source, streamlining development workflows and improving overall project efficiency. In this section, we will be examining how Data Tables are created and how they can improve a game developer's workflow, thereby enhancing a game production pipeline.

As a consequence, you will be able to write your own tables with external software, usually by means of a spreadsheet or a JSON editor, and later import them directly into the UE Editor.

So, let's start by checking how to define a Data Table structure.

Defining Data Tables

To define a Data Table, you will first need to declare how a row is represented; this means creating a `USTRUCT()` inheriting from `FTableRowBase`, whose role is to make sure that what you are defining will be usable inside the Data Table itself. One of the key advantages of this structure is its support for type safety and seamless editor integration with `.csv` and `.json` files. Just think about how much easier this will make things for your game designer friends!

> **Note**
>
> The UE Editor will let you define structures from Blueprints instead of C++; as this is a book about mastering this language, we will just stick to this methodology.

A typical structure for a Data Table will look like the following piece of code:

```
USTRUCT(BlueprintType)
struct FCharacterDataTableRow : public FTableRowBase
{
    GENERATED_BODY()

    UPROPERTY(EditAnywhere)
    FText CharacterName;

    UPROPERTY(EditAnywhere)
    FText CharacterDescription;

    UPROPERTY(EditAnywhere)
    UTexture2D* CharacterIcon;
}
```

As you can see, the declaration is pretty straightforward, you just need to keep in mind that you will be using the `BlueprintType` specifier to make this structure accessible to Blueprints. Additionally, each property should be marked with `EditAnywhere` if you plan to edit tables from the editor. Missing specifiers may cause the Data Table rows to appear empty or uneditable. Finally, please notice that being a struct, properties default to `public`.

Once you have your structure ready, and the project is compiled, you will be able to create your own Data Tables directly from the Editor by choosing **Miscellaneous** | **Data Table** as depicted in *Figure 6.1*:

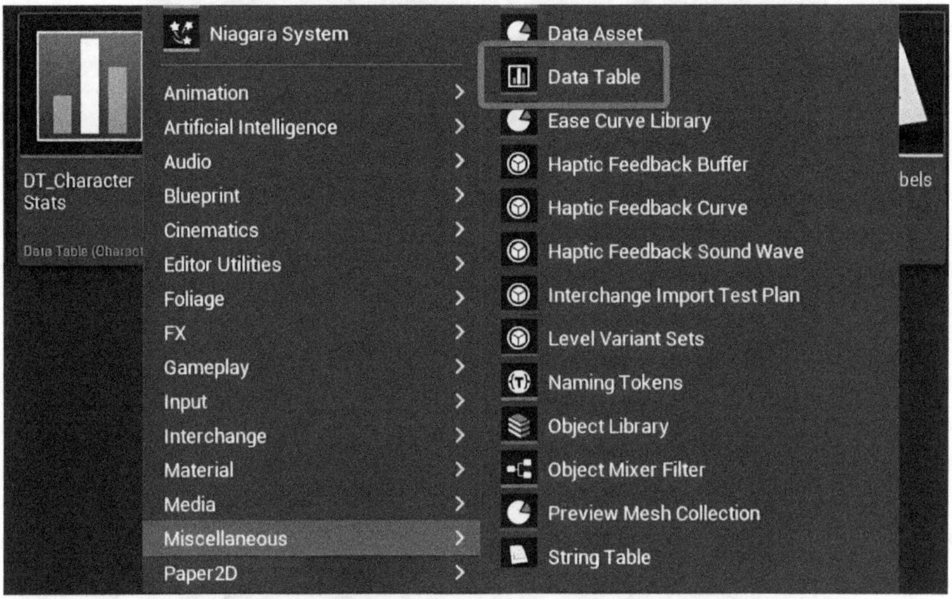

Figure 6.1 – The Data Table creation

After that, you will be presented with the Pick Row Structure panel, where you will be able to choose your own structure.

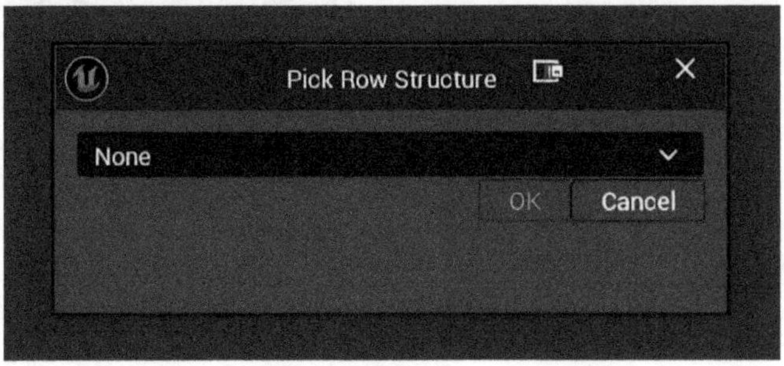

Figure 6.2 – The row type selection

Once the Data Table is created, you will have the ability to customize it to meet your specific requirements.

Exporting it is a straightforward operation as you will just need to right-click on the asset and select **Export as CSV** or **Export as JSON**, as shown in *Figure 6.3*:

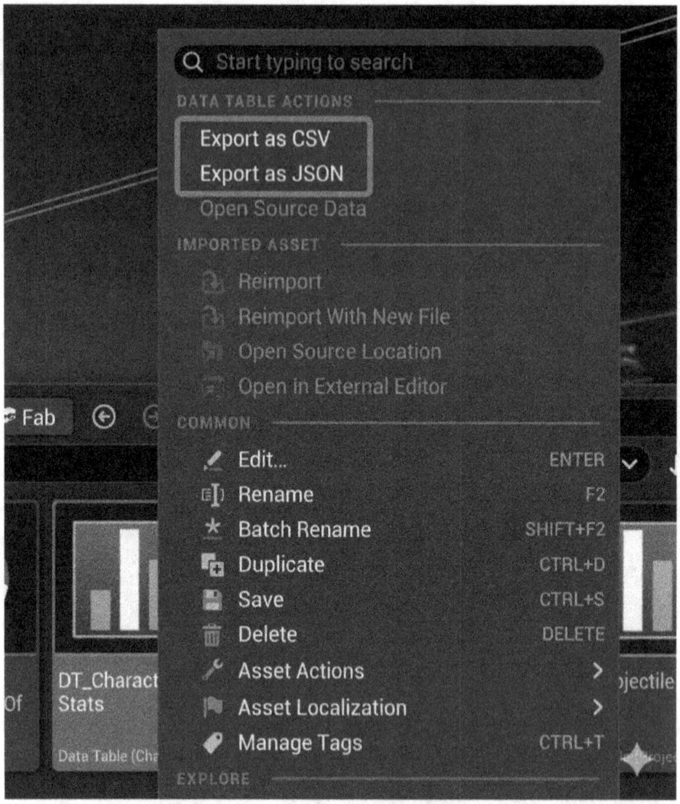

Figure 6.3 – Exporting a Data Table

Similarly, importing a Data Table is quite easy, once you have a `.json` or `.csv` file that respects your structure; simply drag and drop the file from your filesystem into the Content Browser and select the correct row type.

Once your Data Table is prepared, you will only need to implement your code to access the data it contains.

Accessing Data Tables

So, how do we declare and access Data Tables? The process becomes clear once you are familiar with the basics. In general, you will be declaring a Data Table pointer the usual way – that is, with raw or smart pointers – and then you will have access to public methods such as `FindRow()`, `GetRowNames()` or `AddRow()`.

But true power comes with the `FDataTableRowHandle`. This structure cleverly combines a `DataTable` asset pointer and an `FName` to declare the row name you are peeking into. Declaring this row handle will look pretty similar to the following piece of code:

```
UPROPERTY(EditDefaultsOnly)
FDataTableRowHandle CharacterStatsType;
```

Once in the UE Editor, you will be able to access a specific row within the Data Table; this obviously means having a valid selection – only existing row names will be listed – ensuring safe references. *Figure 6.4* depicts a couple of row handles from the *Paws in The Shell* project:

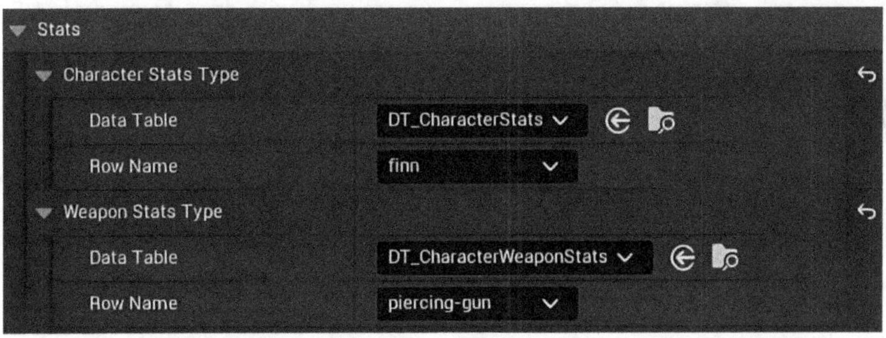

Figure 6.4 – Data Table Row Handles

To retrieve the selected row, you will be using the `GetRow()` templated function. Following the example from this section, you will be using something pretty similar to the following line of code:

```
FCharacterDataTableRow* CharacterData =
    CharacterStatsType
        .GetRow<FCharacterDataTableRow>(FString());
```

By the end of this chapter, I will present you with a real-world example from the *Paws in the Shell* project.

Best practices for using FTableRowBase

When creating and using your own table rows through `FTableRowBase`, there are a few important points you should consider. First of all, ensure that all fields are properly marked with `UPROPERTY()` as missing this macro may cause serialization or data loss issues. What's more, as `FTableRowBase` is a plain `struct`, you will need to be careful when working with complex inheritance or `UObject` pointers. Next, preserve data consistency by avoiding caching pointers or references directly to row data outside local scope; Data Tables can reload or refresh at runtime, and this may cause cached pointer invalidation.

Finally, when working with large Data Tables, it is essential to access their data efficiently by minimizing frequent string-to-name or `enum` conversions; therefore, always prioritize caching row names. By following this short list of tips, you will be ensuring smoother and faster operations when handling your Data Tables.

In this section we have covered how to fully implement Data Tables inside UE; by mastering this skill, you will take full advantage of their powerful data management capabilities to create more efficient, organized, and scalable game systems. In the next section I will be presenting you with another – different, yet very powerful – way to work with data structures in UE.

Implementing Data Asset

A **Data Asset** is defined as an asset, using the `UDataAsset` class, that contains data associated with a specific system within an instance of its class; these assets can be created within the Content Browser by utilizing native classes derived from `UDataAsset`. In other words, Data Assets are `UObject`-based assets designed to store structured, static data that can be easily created, edited, and managed within the Editor.

Typical applications of Data Assets involve the storage of static or configurable data that does not necessitate explicit tracking or manual control over loading and unloading processes. These assets may function as modular containers for various types of data, including individual character or weapon stats, pickup attributes, or configuration presets. This means, they will facilitate editing and updating of data without the need to modify underlying code or Blueprint logic. Additionally, Data Assets offer a structured approach to organizing parameters on a per-instance or per-type basis, independently from Actor or Blueprint classes. As you can probably guess, these assets are easier to use than full Blueprint classes or Data Tables, and this makes them perfect for smaller pieces of data that you want to reuse.

If you need explicit tracking and load management for your asset, you will be using a **Primary Data Asset** through the `UPrimaryDataAsset`, a subclass of `UDataAsset`, that will add integration with the **Asset Manager** system.

The Asset Manager is a Singleton responsible for efficiently managing, tracking, and controlling the loading of game assets, while maintaining game-specific references. It will use a **Primary Asset ID** value to uniquely identify classes of assets for controlled loading and unloading. It exists both in the UE Editor and in packaged games.

It goes without saying that a Primary Data Asset is provided with the aforementioned Primary Asset ID, making it a viable object for manual loading and asset bundle handling through the

Asset Manager. To assign a unique Primary Asset ID to your Primary Data Asset, you must override the `GetPrimaryDataAssetId()` function and return an `FPrimaryAssetId` structure as shown in the following code snippet:

```
virtual FPrimaryAssetId GetPrimaryAssetId() const override
{
    return FPrimaryAssetId( "AssetTypeName", GetName());
}
```

> **Note**
>
> The default implementation of `GetPrimaryAssetId()` uses the class name as the `PrimaryAssetType` and the asset's own name as the `PrimaryAssetName`. You only need to override `GetPrimaryAssetId()` if you want to define a custom asset type string instead of using the class name. Additionally, you might override it to control the asset `PrimaryAssetName` based on some logic other than the asset filename. Another reason to implement a custom version is to establish a specific asset identification scheme that groups or categorizes your assets differently in the Asset Manager or to integrate with custom chunking or loading behaviour.

But why is it called "primary"? Let's find out!

Primary vs Secondary Data Asset

You might be wondering why a Primary Data Asset is designated as "primary". This distinction exists to differentiate it from their "secondary" counterparts. It makes sense when you think about it, doesn't it?

In UE, a **Secondary Data Asset** is an asset not directly managed by the Asset Manager Primary Asset system; as such, they are not provided with Primary Asset IDs. Typical examples include textures, static meshes, materials, and sounds – assets that are typically referenced within primary assets or Actors and not loaded and unloaded independently.

Best practices in using Data Assets

As a rule of thumb, whenever you are creating your own Data Assets, you should derive them from `UPrimaryDataAsset` classes – instead of simple `UDataAsset` ones – to enable Asset Manager integration and asset identification. If you are using a custom Primary Asset ID, always ensure that the name is unique in order to avoid conflicts in asset referencing and loading. Next, try to minimize heavy code logic and keep Data Assets focused on data storage; this will ensure clean separation between data and behavior.

Finally, always plan ahead; most of the time your Data Assets will be used by game designers and technical artists, so ensure they will be able to create Blueprint subclasses out of your C++ classes and that properties and functions are accessible.

Adhering to these simple tips will help you achieve more efficient and quicker management of your Data Assets.

In this section, I have presented you with Data Assets, a powerful feature of the game engine; a correct use will ensure efficient data management and will streamline your development workflow, making your game development easily maintainable and flexible. In the next section, I will provide you with some practical examples on using both Data Tables and Data Assets inside the Paws in the Shell project. Hopefully, you will find them helpful and enjoyable as you continue your journey to mastering C++ in UE!

Presenting a practical example

It's about time to present to you the last – but not least – member from The Pack:

In the neon-lit sprawl of Holo District, where holograms flickered like ghosts and rain slicked the streets with electric hues, Rae strode proudly through the alley. Her red panda fur – never meant for stealth and subtlety – blazed beneath the glow of cybernetic implants that traced sleek lines along her limbs and spine. She was no ordinary creature – Rae was a cyber-gunslinger from The Pack – a lethal fusion of nature and machine. Her eyes, enhanced with infrared and tactical HUD overlays, scanned the alleyways and rooftops with precision.

Tonight, the air buzzed with tension. Reports had come in of a rogue mech gang, the Iron Vultures, planning a heist on the district's energy core. Rae and her team members moved swiftly against the wet pavement. As they reached the core's perimeter, the Iron Vultures unleashed their mechanical beasts – towering, armored monstrosities with their single glowing red eye – revealing their not-so-secret OmniSight Industries affiliation.

Rae's laser gun buzzed through the night, each shot precise and deadly. She darted between cover, her cybernetic enhancements amplifying her reflexes and agility. When a mech lunged, she fired a burst of shots, sparks flying as energy met metal. Her team covered her flank, but it was Rae's fearless charge that turned the tide.

With a final, calculated shot, she disabled a mech core, sending it crashing to the ground. The Iron Vultures retreated into the shadows, defeated but not broken. Rae stood tall, breathing heavily, her eyes glowing faintly in the dark.

A highly capable and well-equipped, character seems like a perfect example for explaining how to implement statistics by using data structures. Likewise, a challenging mission provides an effective context for covering more advanced chapter topics.

In this section I will be presenting you some real-world examples of using Data Tables and Data Asset inside the Paws in the Shell projects. We will be focusing on Data Tables for character and weapon stats and on Data Assets for managing in-game missions. As you will notice, once you have got the hang of it, implementing these data structures is going to be quite easy and, if you are planning things ahead, quite straightforward.

Let's start by checking some good structure and Data Table.

Analyzing character stats

To get the best out of player and AI characters and make them unique, the *Paws in the Shell* project is provided with some stats tables for the characters themselves, weapons, and projectiles. In this subsection, we will be just analyzing the first one; once you have the hang of how things are done, things will be pretty self-explanatory for the other ones.

Inspecting the FPITS_CharacterDataTableRow structure

So, open the `PITS_CharacterDataTableRow.h` file to get a glimpse of how characters can be customized. The full code for the structure is shown in the following piece of code:

```
USTRUCT(BlueprintType,
    meta=(DisplayName="CharacterDataTableRow"))
struct FPITS_CharacterDataTableRow : public FTableRowBase
{
    GENERATED_BODY()

    UPROPERTY(EditAnywhere, meta=(ToolTip="Name of the character displayed in
game"))
    FText CharacterName;

    UPROPERTY(EditAnywhere, meta=(ToolTip="Character description (i.e.:
                                                  speciality)"))
    FText CharacterDescription;

    UPROPERTY(EditAnywhere, meta=(ToolTip="Character icon"))
    UTexture2D* CharacterIcon;

    UPROPERTY(EditAnywhere, meta=(ToolTip="Maximum health reachable by the
character"))
    float MaxHealth = 100.0f;

    UPROPERTY(EditAnywhere, meta=(ToolTip="Character defensive amount that
                                         reduces incoming damage"))
```

```
    float ArmourAmount = 0.0f;

    UPROPERTY(EditAnywhere, meta=(ToolTip="Is the character cybernetic
                                                          or robotic?"))
    bool bCyberAugmented = false;

    UPROPERTY(EditAnywhere, meta=(ToolTip="Can the character regenerate when in a
regeneration zone?"))
    bool bCanRegenerate = false;

    UPROPERTY(EditAnywhere, meta=(ToolTip="Maximum speed of the character when
moving"))
    float MaxWalkSpeed = 600.0f;

    UPROPERTY(EditAnywhere, meta=(ToolTip="Initial velocity (instantaneous force
acceleration) applied when the character jumps"))
    float JumpZVelocity = 500.0f;

    UPROPERTY(EditAnywhere, meta=(ToolTip="Amount of lateral control for the
character while in air (0 = no control, 1 = full control (Max Walk Speed)"))
    float AirControl = 0.35f;

    UPROPERTY(EditAnywhere, meta=(ToolTip="Deceleration applied when walking and
not applying acceleration"))
    float BrakingDecelerationWalking = 2000.f;

    UPROPERTY(EditAnywhere, meta=(ToolTip="Lateral deceleration applied when
falling and not applying acceleration"))
    float BrakingDecelerationFalling = 1500.0f;

    UPROPERTY(EditAnywhere, meta=(ToolTip="Additional notes about this
                                   character (for development purposes)"))
    FString Notes;
};
```

Things are pretty self-explanatory here; the only thing worth mentioning is probably the meta `Tooltip` specifier used to show the user what each property is doing. As we are creating a structure that will most probably be used by fellow game designers – or other people that won't be meddling with your code – it's nice to add a little helper to make things clearer!

Let's now focus on characters in order to check how this data is managed.

Inspecting the APITS_BaseCharacter class

The `APITS_BaseCharacter` class has been used as the parent class for both player characters – declared in the `APITS_BasePlayerCharacter` class – and AI characters – declared in the `APITS_BaseEnemyCharacter.h` class. So, open the `PITS_BaseCharacter.h` class and head to the character stats declaration that looks like the following block of code:

```
UPROPERTY(EditDefaultsOnly)
FDataTableRowHandle CharacterStatsType;
```

As you can see, we are using the `FDataTableRowHandle` structure that will ease data row selection from Blueprints. Now switch to the `PITS_BaseCharacter.cpp` file and head for the `OnContruction()` implementation. You will find the following block of code that handles row data:

```
if (const FPITS_CharacterDataTableRow* CharacterData =
CharacterStatsType.GetRow<FPITS_CharacterDataTableRow>(FString()))
{
    GetCharacterMovement()->JumpZVelocity = CharacterData->JumpZVelocity;
    GetCharacterMovement()->AirControl = CharacterData->AirControl;
    GetCharacterMovement()->MaxWalkSpeed = CharacterData->MaxWalkSpeed;
    GetCharacterMovement()->BrakingDecelerationWalking = CharacterData-
>BrakingDecelerationWalking;
    GetCharacterMovement()->BrakingDecelerationFalling = CharacterData-
>BrakingDecelerationFalling;

    Health->SetMaxHealth(CharacterData->MaxHealth);
    Health->SetCurrentHealth(CharacterData->MaxHealth);
    Health->SetCanRegenerate(CharacterData->bCanRegenerate);

    Armour->SetArmourAmount(CharacterData->ArmourAmount);
    Armour->SetIsCybernetic(CharacterData->bCyberAugmented);

    bIsCybernetic = CharacterData->bCyberAugmented;
    CharacterName = CharacterData->CharacterName;
    CharacterDescription = CharacterData->CharacterDescription;
    CharacterIcon = CharacterData->CharacterIcon;
}
```

As you can see, the `if` statement is retrieving row data through the templated `GetRow()` function; once data has been retrieved and checked for validation, it's just a matter of assigning properties where needed.

As previously mentioned, there are other Data Table row structures inside the project; if you are curious about them, I highly recommend heading to the `PITS_WeaponDataTableRow.h` or `PITS_ProjectileDataTableRow.h` files to see how they are implemented.

Now that you have been introduced to Data Table row declaration, let's head over to the UE Editor to check out some actual assets.

Checking Data Table assets

Once the Editor is open, you can look for the `Content/Data` folder to analyze Data Tables for both player and AI characters. There are two dedicated assets named **DT_CharacterStats** and **DT_EnemyStats**; simply open the first one and you will be presented with the Data Table shown in *Figure 6.5*:

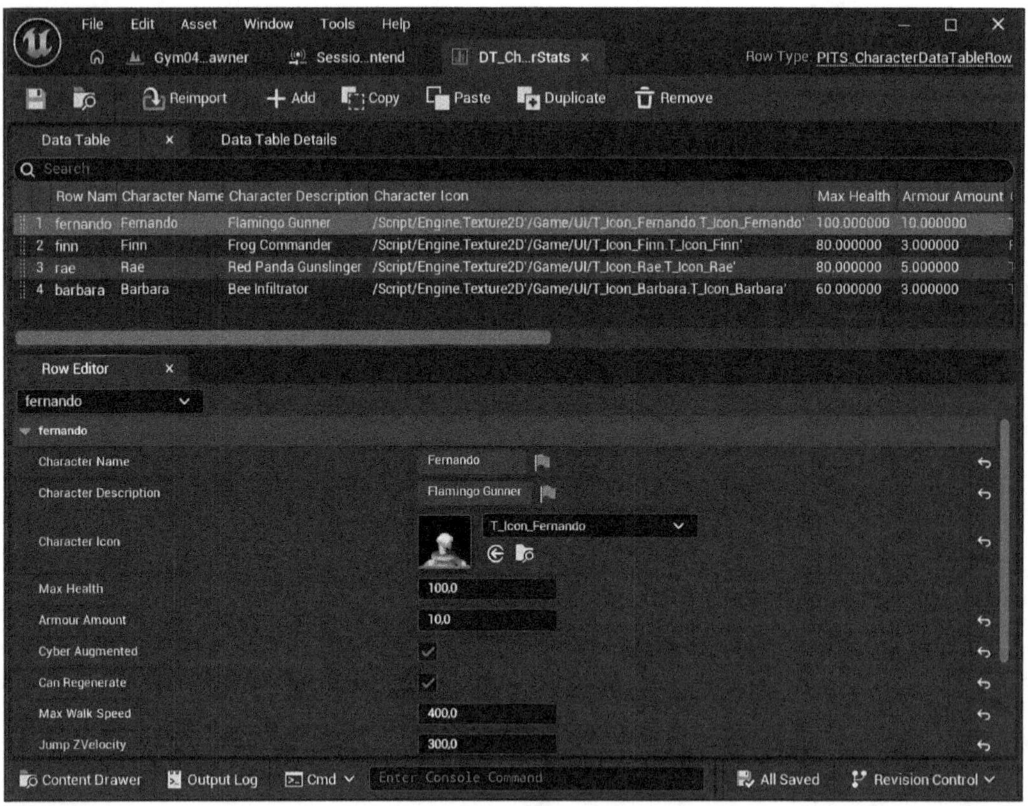

Figure 6.5 – Character stats Data Table

If you try exporting the asset as a `.csv` file, you will get the following result:

```
---,CharacterName,CharacterDescription,CharacterIcon,MaxHealth,ArmourAmount,bCyber
Augmented,bCanRegenerate,MaxWalkSpeed,JumpZVelocity,AirControl,BrakingDeceleration
Walking,BrakingDecelerationFalling,Notes fernando,"LOCTABLE(""/Game/Data/
ST_CharacterLabels.ST_CharacterLabels"", ""fernando"")","LOCTABLE(""/Game/Data/
ST_CharacterLabels.ST_CharacterLabels"", ""fernando_role"")","/Script/
Engine.Texture2D'/Game/UI/
T_Icon_Fernando.T_Icon_Fernando'","100.000000","10.000000","True","True","400.0000
00","300.000000","0.100000","2000.000000","1500.000000","" finn,"LOCTABLE(""/Game/
Data/ST_CharacterLabels.ST_CharacterLabels"", ""finn"")","LOCTABLE(""/Game/Data/
ST_CharacterLabels.ST_CharacterLabels"", ""finn_role"")","/Script/
Engine.Texture2D'/Game/UI/
T_Icon_Finn.T_Icon_Finn'","80.000000","3.000000","False","True","600.000000","800.
000000","0.500000","2000.000000","1500.000000","" rae,"LOCTABLE(""/Game/Data/
ST_CharacterLabels.ST_CharacterLabels"", ""rae"")","LOCTABLE(""/Game/Data/
ST_CharacterLabels.ST_CharacterLabels"", ""rae_role"")","/Script/
Engine.Texture2D'/Game/UI/
T_Icon_Rae.T_Icon_Rae'","80.000000","5.000000","True","True","500.000000","400.000
000","0.350000","2000.000000","1500.000000","" barbara,"LOCTABLE(""/Game/Data/
ST_CharacterLabels.ST_CharacterLabels"", ""barbara"")","LOCTABLE(""/Game/Data/
ST_CharacterLabels.ST_CharacterLabels"", ""barbara_role"")","/Script/
Engine.Texture2D'/Game/UI/
T_Icon_Barbara.T_Icon_Barbara'","60.000000","3.000000","True","True","600.000000",
"750.000000","0.750000","2000.000000","1500.000000",""
```

This file, being a `.csv` one, can be easily shared with your team game designers, who will be able to modify it with any spreadsheet editor. Neat, isn't it?

Now that I have shown a Data Table example, let's head over to Data Assets and check an implementation example.

Analyzing Mission Data

In the *Paws in the Shell* project, Primary Data Assets have been used to organize and create simple mission achievements. This will let designers create their own mission assets and easily assign them to levels and actors.

Inspecting the UPITS_MissionDataAsset class

A mission in the *Paws in the Shell* project is straightforward: a character is given a task to complete a specified number of times. Each task includes a name, a description, and a counter that indicates how many times the task must be completed to earn the achievement. For example, Rae might be assigned the task of hitting ten targets with her gun.

As such, a mission Data Asset is defined by the following class:

```
UCLASS(BlueprintType, Blueprintable)
class PAWSINTHESHELL_API UPITS_MissionDataAsset
    : public UPrimaryDataAsset
{
    GENERATED_BODY()

public:
    UPITS_MissionDataAsset();

    UPROPERTY(EditAnywhere, BlueprintReadOnly)
    FText MissionName;

    UPROPERTY(EditAnywhere, BlueprintReadOnly)
    FText MissionDescription;

    UPROPERTY(EditAnywhere, BlueprintReadOnly)
    int32 CompleteCount;
};
```

The only thing worth mentioning here is the `FText` type for the `MissionName` and `MissionDescription` properties, which will allow us to use String Tables for their values – more on this later.

With this class implemented, it's now time to check how it can be assigned to a level.

Inspecting the APITS_GameModeBase class

To manage achievements in a game level, we will be using a list declared inside a base GameMode that we will be using throughout the game. As such, the project comes with an `APITS_GameModeBase` that will let you assign a list of mission Data Assets. If you open the `PITS_GameModeBase.h` file, you will immediately notice the list declaration, as the following block of code:

```
UPROPERTY(EditDefaultsOnly, BlueprintReadOnly)
TArray<UPITS_MissionDataAsset*> MissionList;
```

At this point, you may be curious about how these missions are actually managed. Please hang tight as I will explain everything in *Chapter 7, Improving your code with Subsystems* – that is, the next chapter.

Inspecting the Data Assets inside the project

It's now time to open the UE Editor and check the `Content/Data` folder, looking for some actual assets. Let's start by opening the `DA_Mission_ReachPointsOfInterest` asset. This asset is shown in *Figure 6.6*:

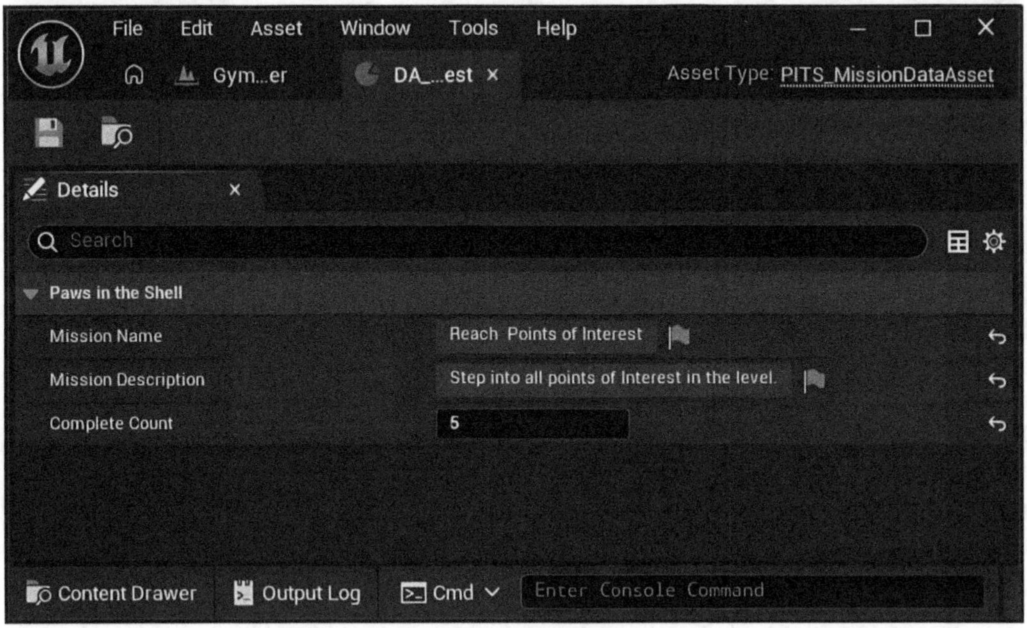

Figure 6.6 – A mission Data Asset

You will notice that the **Mission Name** and **Mission Description** properties have not been edited directly in their corresponding fields but are getting their values from a **String Table** named **ST_MissionLabels**.

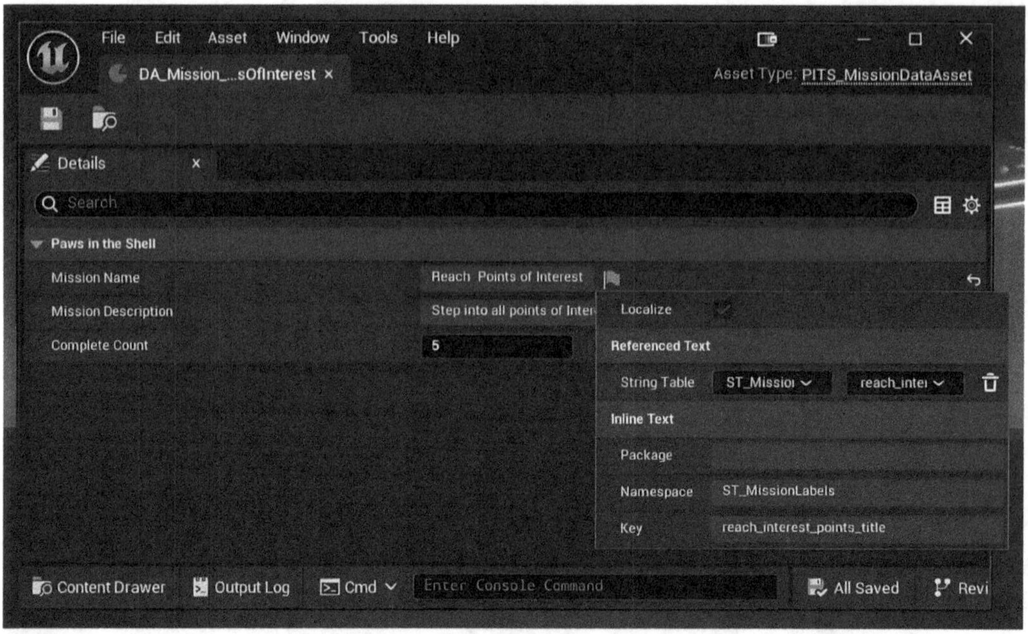

Figure 6.7 – String Table reference

In case you are wondering what a String Table is, it is a centralized asset that stores localized text entries as key-value pairs, allowing robust and easily maintainable localization across a project. Since this chapter is all about data structures, I thought it was worth mentioning this simple but really useful one!

You can now open the **BP_GameMode_Gym03_Missions** Blueprint – located in the `Content/Blueprints` folder – to check the mission list declaration. You will find it in the Paws in the Shell category, as shown in *Figure 6.8*:

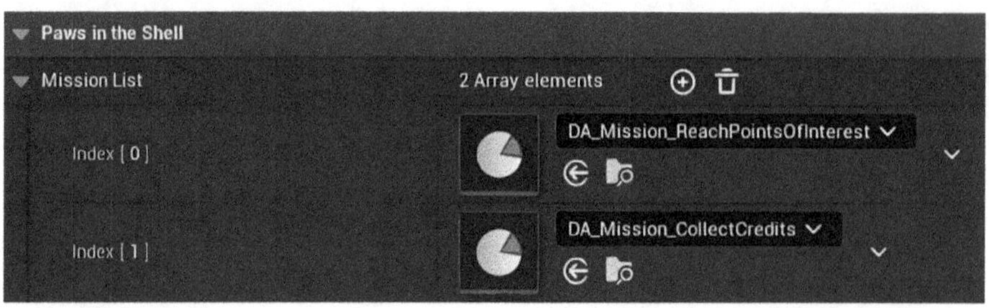

Figure 6.8 – The mission list

To test mission achievements, all you need to do is open the **Gym_03_PointsOfInterest** map and start playing.

Figure 6.9 – The mission map

In the top-left corner of the screen, you will see a list of mission achievements – such as "Reach Points of Interest" and "Collect Eleuterium Credits" – which will update as you collect the corresponding items within the level. The actual implementation of how these achievements are granted will be covered in the next chapter.

As you might have already guessed, it's now time to start coding on your own. So, head to the next subsection for a solo task!

Develop and self-evaluate

By now, you should already be familiar with the Paws in the Shell characters. Each character has strengths and weaknesses, but no one possesses a power that would make a truly unique hero. It's time to amend this by creating a new skill table for your characters.

Implementing a Power Data Table

The `APITS_BasePlayerCharacter.h` class declares a `UsePower()` function that has not been implemented yet. All the input settings are fully functional; each character simply has no skill to use. Let's fix this by giving a unique power to each one, starting with a Data Table that will list powers that can be used during gameplay.

To start with, you will need to define a `FTableRowBase` structure that will include the main features of each power. Here are some examples you may add:

- A `PowerType` enumeration to switch on each power
- A `Duration` value to set how long the power will last
- An `EnergyConsumption` value that will drain character energy when the power is used
- A `Cooldown` value to avoid the character exploiting the power

These are obviously just examples; feel free to add your own properties to the table. You may even develop dedicated components for each power! Once the structure is ready, add an `FDataTableRowHandle` declaration in the `APITS_BasePlayerCharacter` class and manage it in order to add the power gameplay logic. Once you are ready, switch to the UE Editor and create your own Data Table and assign it to each player character.

This is probably the toughest task I've given you so far but trust me – it's definitely going to be worth it!

Summary

In this chapter, we explored data structures in Unreal Engine, with a particular focus on Data Tables and Data Assets. By now, it should be clear why these features are so essential for game programmers: they allow for efficient organization and management of game data. By leveraging them effectively, you can easily update, maintain, and scale your games, resulting in cleaner code and a more streamlined development process. Additionally, this workflow will greatly benefit your game designer teammates, making it easier for them to work within the Editor.

In the next chapter, we will dive into an engine feature that I have mentioned several times throughout the previous chapters. Stay tuned – things are about to get pretty exciting!

Get this book's PDF copy, code bundle, and more

Scan the QR code (or go to `packtpub.com/unlock`). Search for this book by name, confirm the edition, and then follow the steps on the page.

UNLOCK NOW

Note: Have your invoice handy. Purchases made directly from the Packt website don't require an invoice.

7

Improving Your Code with Subsystems

Subsystems are modular, self-contained systems designed to provide global, persistent functionality across a project. As a developer, with Subsystems you will be able to organize and manage efficiently core services such as input handling, audio management, and game state tracking. This means you will be creating scalable, maintainable code architecture that will simplify complex features and improve overall project structure. In this chapter, we will explore the different types of Subsystems in UE, including their roles and best practices for integrating them into your game development workflow. In particular, we will be focusing on the following topics:

- Introducing Subsystems
- Explaining a Subsystem lifecycle
- Presenting a practical example

Technical requirements

To get the best out of the following sections, you should have fully understood the previous chapters.

Introducing Subsystems

If you've started a project with one of the UE templates, chances are you've already come across **Subsystems**. At some point, you'll likely run into this Blueprint node while exploring player characters and controllers, in particular, during input initialization:

Figure 7.1 – The Enhanced Input Local Player Subsystem node

The `UEnhancedInputLocalPlayerSubsystem` depicted in *Figure 7.1* is just one of the many Subsystems available in the engine. If you don't trust me, simply look for the **Engine Subsystems** category in the available Blueprint graphs.

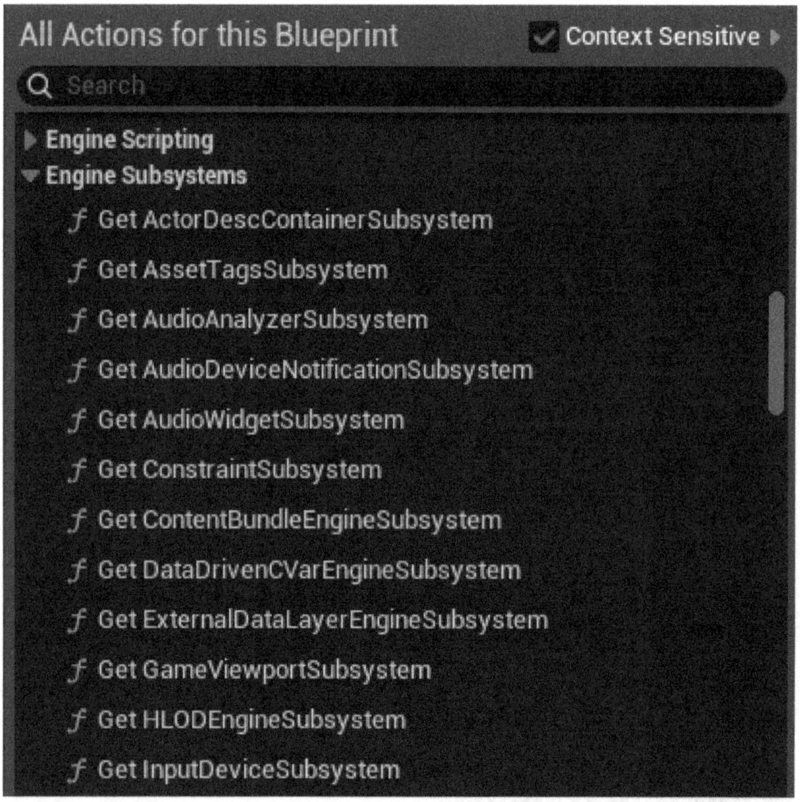

Figure 7.2 – A list of available Subsystems

So, what exactly are Subsystems? Subsystems are modular components managed by the engine that deliver centralized, lifecycle-aware services across different contexts – such as Local Player, Game Instance, and World. They allow developers to neatly encapsulate and organize global functionalities – be it audio management or gameplay statistics – in a way that is both scalable and easy to maintain. As they possess well-standardized initialization and shutdown phases tied to their specific lifecycles, they promote clean architecture and better code separation, making them invaluable for complex projects.

Presenting Subsystem types

Subsystems may vary in type, each characterized by distinct features. Prior to a detailed examination, I present the following quick list:

- **Engine Subsystems** used for global, engine-wide features
- **Editor Subsystems** used for Editor-only features
- **GameInstance Subsystems** used for game session features
- **LocalPlayer Subsystems** used for player-specific features
- **World Subsystems** used for level-specific features

So, let's start analyzing them in detail one by one.

Analyzing Engine Subsystems

An Engine Subsystem is used for low-level or persistent features that should outlive your **Play In Editor** (**PIE**) sessions, such as caching systems and debugging tools. This means that data will persist across PIE sessions.

To create your own Engine Subsystem, you will be inheriting from the `UEngineSubsystem` class and, to access the created instance, you will be taking advantage of the `GEngine` global pointer. For instance, if you have developed an Engine Subsystem named `UMyEngineSubsystem`, you will access it using the following code snippet:

```
UMyEngineSubsystem* MySubsystem =
    GEngine->GetEngineSubsystem<UMyEngineSubsystem>();
```

Access to Engine Subsystems will be granted from the engine module startup until its shutdown.

Analyzing Editor Subsystems

An Editor Subsystem is used for editor-specific workflows, such as asset management and editor tooling. This means it won't be available during gameplay. To create your own Editor Subsystem, you will be inheriting from the `UEditorSubsystem` class and, to access the created instance, you will be using the `GEditor` global pointer. If you have developed an Editor Subsystem named, for example, `UMyEditorSubsystem`, you will access it using the following piece of code:

```
UMyEditorSubsystem* MySubsystem =
    GEditor->GetEditorSubsystem<UMyEditorSubsystem>();
```

Access to Editor Subsystems will be granted during Editor sessions, from module startup until shutdown.

Analyzing GameInstance Subsystems

A GameInstance Subsystem is used for any game-wide manager features requiring access across levels. To create your own GameInstance Subsystem, you will extend the `UGameInstanceSubsystem` class and, to access the instance, you will be using the GameInstance object, that can be retrieved from `UGameplayStatics` or from your Player Controller. For instance, if you have developed a GameInstance Subsystem named `UMyGameInstanceSubsystem`, you will access it using the following piece of code:

```
UGameInstance* GameInstance = UGameplayStatics::GetGameInstance();
UMyGameInstanceSubsystem* MySubsystem =
    GameInstance->GetSubsystem<UMyGameInstanceSubsystem>();
```

Access to GameInstance Subsystems is granted at application start until game end, or PIE stop.

Analyzing LocalPlayer Subsystems

LocalPlayer Subsystems are used whenever you need specific per-player data functionalities; as an example, the previously mentioned `UEnhancedInputLocalPlayerSubsystem` is a LocalPlayer Subsystem. To create a LocalPlayer Subsystem you will be subclassing the `ULocalPlayerSubsystem` class and, to access the created instance, you will need to access the Local Player – usually from the PlayerController. As an example, consider a LocalPlayer Subsystem called `UMyLocalPlayerSubsystem`. You will be accessing it through something similar to the following code:

```
if(PlayerController != nullptr)
{
    ULocalPlayer* LocalPlayer =
        PlayerController->GetLocalPlayer();
    UMyLocalPlayerSubsystem* MySubsystem =
```

```
        LocalPlayer->GetSubsystem<UMyLocalPlayerSubsystem>();
}
```

Being connected to a LocalPlayer object, these Subsystems will exist only on the client side of a multiplayer system and will be used for local player management.

Analyzing World Subsystems

A World Subsystem will be used when you need a system that is scoped to a specific game world. To create a World Subsystem, you will subclass the `UWorldSubsystem` class and, to access it, you will use a valid `UWorld` pointer. As an example, once you have created your `UMyWorldSubsystem`, you will access its instance through the following snippets:

```
UWorld* World = GetWorld();
if(World != nullptr)
{
    UMyWorldSubsystem* MySubsystem =
        World->GetSubsystem<UMyWorldSubsystem>();
}
```

As you might have guessed, World Subsystems exist only during the `UWorld` lifetime.

Having obtained an overview of all Subsystems, one might question whether their use is always appropriate. Obviously, this inquiry needs further examination!

Pros and cons of using Subsystems

Subsystems offer several key benefits that you will need to be aware of, in order to get the best out of them. First of all, they save time by providing an easy-to-use extension system that automatically manages lifecycles; as a consequence, you will be able to concentrate more on functionality rather than lifecycle management. Additionally, Subsystems will let you avoid overriding engine classes such as the Game Mode or Game Instance; this means you will be able to create Subsystems to extend functionality cleanly, instead of modifying existing GF classes. Next, they also come with built-in Blueprint exposure, making it straightforward to integrate with the engine visual scripting system. Additionally, they allow modularity, and consistency by providing a uniform interface for non-actor objects – for instance components – which will make your codebase clearer and easier to maintain. Last, but not least, Subsystems are accessible not only in C++ but also in Blueprints, and this means that they will ease cross-team collaboration a lot!

> **Note**
>
> A bit off topic and still at an experimental stage – yet worth mentioning – Subsystems allow access to Python scripts for editor scripting and for writing test code.

With all this power, it comes as no surprise that they come with some drawbacks to consider. First of all, while they can simplify many tasks, they may also introduce additional complexity if not applied carefully. Overusing Subsystems can create unnecessary layers of abstraction that complicate your codebase. Moreover, Subsystems are primarily designed for non-actor objects, so in certain cases, traditional methods like directly modifying classes might remain the simpler and more practical choice. Once you are aware of these small shortcomings, I'm pretty sure you will be able to get the most out of them!

Let's now consider the Subsystem lifecycle and examine its key stages and behaviors in detail.

Explaining a Subsystem lifecycle

Subsystems have a singleton-like nature by providing a unique, globally accessible instance per scope. However, unlike traditional singletons, Subsystems are automatically managed by the engine according to their lifecycle – that is, they are not lazily initialized – ensuring consistent availability and proper resource management. This means you will have a centralized system, and, at the same time, you will avoid manual instantiation and dependency sprawl. The main phases of a Subsystem lifecycle are the following:

- **Startup**: The containing module loads and performs its startup. Subsystems are not yet initialized.
- **Initialization**: The Subsystem is created and initialized after module startup has finished executing. During this phase, you will set up your logic and resources.
- **Active State**: The Subsystem is running and is providing all its functionalities.
- **Deinitialization**: Called when the Subsystem is being shut down before module shutdown. During this phase, you will clean up resources and detach any bindings.
- **Shutdown**: After Subsystem deinitialization, the containing module will perform its shutdown and subsequently unload.

As mentioned before, Subsystems are not lazily initialized. Instead, they are initialized by the engine during the module's startup lifecycle – that is, after the module's `Startup()` function returns. Next, the engine calls each Subsystem's `Initialize()` method at this time, ensuring they are ready before gameplay or Editor logic begins. When they need to be shut down, Subsystems are properly deinitialized via the `Deinitialize()` function.

Now that you have a clear idea of how a Subsystem lifecycle works, it's time to get back to the *Paws in the Shell* project and get started with some proper coding examples.

Presenting a practical example

It's now time for Team 33 to start a new, ever-dangerous mission:

Beneath the flickering glow of neon, members of Team 33 stood on the brink of a mission that could decide the fate of Holo District. NullVector, a rogue AI twisted by the sinister hands of Omnisight Industries, was puppeteering the city's surveillance system to sow fear and control in harmless citizens.

Finn, the battle-hardened leader with scars etched by countless battles, commanded with unwavering resolve. Barbara, the swift and deadly cyber-bee, darted ahead through the shadows, her sensors piercing the darkness to reveal armed drones patrolling the factory's perimeter – a fortress of steel and death. Rae's eyes never wavered, scanning every corner for hidden threats, every hint of an ambush. Fernando held his position at a distance, ready to unleash devastating firepower if the team was overwhelmed.

Inside the labyrinthine factory, the air thickened with danger. They fought tooth and claw through waves of merciless guards and lethal traps, every step a gamble with death. When they finally reached the NullVector core, Barbara unleashed a pulse of EMP, shattering the AI's defenses like glass. Rae moved in, her laser gun bullets darting with razor precision purging the corrupted intelligence from the system.

With NullVector's reign of terror ended, the city's fractured network flickered back to life, a fragile heartbeat restored.

As dawn's first light bled into the sky, The Pack melted into the shadows – silent, vigilant, and ever ready. Guardians of a fragile peace in a city oblivious to the ever-present danger lurking just beyond its electric-hued streets.

The previous story depicts an example of a typical mission that needs to be managed during gameplay. And what a coincidence – you have just been presented Subsystems! It seems like a perfect match to me!

In this section, we will finalize our analysis of the mission system introduced in *Chapter 6, Working with Data Structures*. This time, the main focus will be, quite obviously, Subsystems.

Inspecting the UPITS_MissionSubsystem class

Let's get started with the Subsystem whose task is to track missions state, the `UPITS_MissionSubsystem` class. This Subsystem is responsible for managing the game's missions, including their progress and completion. It offers functions to initialize missions, update their progress, and send notifications when a mission is completed or when all missions have been finished. Additionally, it provides delegates to alert other systems whenever a mission is updated or completed.

Inspecting the UPITS_MissionSubsystem header

We are going to analyze the header first, so open the `PITS_MissionSubsystem.h` file. You will first notice that this is a World Subsystem, as shown in the class declaration:

```
class PAWSINTHESHELL_API
    UPITS_MissionSubsystem final : public UWorldSubsystem
```

As missions are per-level, opting for this type of Subsystem seems the appropriate decision. This Subsystem uses three main properties:

```
UPROPERTY()
TArray<UPITS_MissionDataAsset*> ActiveMissionList;

UPROPERTY(BlueprintReadOnly)
TArray<UPITS_MissionDataAsset*> MissionList;

UPROPERTY(BlueprintReadOnly)
TMap<UPITS_MissionDataAsset*, int32> MissionMap;
```

The first property is used to keep track of all the missions that need to be completed, the second one keeps a list of all the missions and is used for mission initialization, and the third one will keep track of each mission and its current progress.

To initialize and update missions, we will be using two main functions, listed in the following code snippet:

```
UFUNCTION(BlueprintCallable)
void InitializeMissions
    (const TArray<UPITS_MissionDataAsset*> Missions);

UFUNCTION(BlueprintCallable)
void UpdateMission(
    UPITS_MissionDataAsset* Mission,
    const int32 ProgressIncrement = 1);
```

They are almost self-explanatory, so I won't be bothering you with extra information; just keep in mind we are using a `UPITS_MissionDataAsset` pointer to define missions. For a refresher on these Data Assets, you may wish to go back to the last section, *Chapter 6, Working with Data Structures*, and take a peek at how they were implemented.

You may have noticed we are not taking advantage of the Subsystem lifecycle hooks; this was a design decision as the Subsystem is quite simple and does not need any extra setup and teardown. In a more complex scenario, you may have hooked into the `Initialize()` and `Deinitialize()` functions to properly set up and tear down your system.

The last thing to consider is delegates. At the top of the file, you will find these declarations:

```
DECLARE_DYNAMIC_MULTICAST_DELEGATE_OneParam(
    FOnMissionCompleteSignature,
    UPITS_MissionDataAsset*, Mission);
DECLARE_DYNAMIC_MULTICAST_DELEGATE_TwoParams(
    FOnMissionUpdateSignature,
    UPITS_MissionDataAsset*, Mission,
    int, CurrentProgress);
DECLARE_DYNAMIC_MULTICAST_DELEGATE(
    FOnAllMissionsCompleteSignature);
DECLARE_DYNAMIC_MULTICAST_DELEGATE(
    FOnMissionsInitializeSignature);
```

As you can see, these are all dynamic multicast delegates, so we will be able to bind functions both in C++ and Blueprints. Specifically, these delegates are used to broadcast information about mission completion, update, and initialization. As we are using a World Subsystem, you will be able to bind these delegates from anywhere – be it a UI, a Character or a level Actor. Things are falling into place nicely, aren't they?

To create bindings, we will be using the following functions:

```
UPROPERTY(BlueprintAssignable)
FOnMissionCompleteSignature OnMissionComplete;

UPROPERTY(BlueprintAssignable)
FOnMissionUpdateSignature OnMissionUpdate;

UPROPERTY(BlueprintAssignable)
FOnMissionsInitializeSignature OnMissionsInitialize;

UPROPERTY(BlueprintAssignable)
FOnAllMissionsCompleteSignature OnAllMissionsComplete;
```

We are now going to check how the Subsystem is actually implemented.

Inspecting the UPITS_MissionSubsystem implementation

Let's now focus on the actual implementation of the Subsystem, so open the `PITS_MissionSubsystem.cpp` file. As you will see, the `InitializeMission()` function will just clean up and properly set the mission lists and map. After that, it will broadcast the `OnMissionInitialize` delegate, as shown in the following block of code:

```
MissionList.Empty();
MissionList.Append(Missions);

ActiveMissionList.Empty();
ActiveMissionList.Append(Missions);

MissionMap.Empty();
for (UPITS_MissionDataAsset* Mission : Missions)
{
    if (Mission)
    {
        MissionMap.Add(Mission, 0);
    }
}

OnMissionsInitialize.Broadcast();
```

On the other hand, the `UpdateMission()` is slightly more complex; its tasks include updating the mission map, checking if the mission has been achieved, and then broadcasting the appropriate delegates. The full code is shown in the following snippet:

```
if (MissionMap.Contains(Mission))
{
    MissionMap[Mission] += ProgressIncrement;
    MissionMap[Mission] = FMath::Clamp(
        MissionMap[Mission], 0, Mission->CompleteCount);

    if (MissionMap[Mission] >= Mission->CompleteCount)
    {
        OnMissionComplete.Broadcast(Mission);
        ActiveMissionList.Remove(Mission);
```

```
        if (ActiveMissionList.Num() == 0)
        {
            OnAllMissionsComplete.Broadcast();
        }
    }
    else
    {
        OnMissionUpdate.Broadcast(
            Mission, MissionMap[Mission]);
    }
}
```

Let's now check what is initializing the mission list.

Inspecting the APITS_GameModeBase class

You might remember from *Chapter 6, Working with Data Structures* that mission Data Assets were declared in the APITS_GameModeBase class. I said I'd come back to the Game Mode in this chapter, so go ahead, and open the PITS_GameModeBase.cpp file. You will find this quite simple block of code executed by the BeginPlay() function:

```
MissionSubsystem =
    GetWorld()->GetSubsystem<UPITS_MissionSubsystem>();
if(MissionSubsystem && MissionList.Num() > 0)
{
    MissionSubsystem->InitializeMissions(MissionList);
}
```

As you can see, once we have retrieved the Subsystem, we execute the InitializeMissions() function, which will add all the missions declared in this Game mode.

Let's now explore how we can implement objects that will let the character achieve and complete the missions.

Inspecting the UPITS_MissionHolderComponent class

As we have seen in the previous subsections, mission state can be updated through the Subsystem UpdateMission() function. Obviously, this function can be called from anywhere – it's a World Subsystem after all! – but why not implement a dedicated component to handle all the gameplay logic that will let us update missions without uselessly repeating code?

That's why the `UPITS_MissionHolderComponent` has been created! Once you open the `PITS_MissionHolderComponent.h` file, you will find these two properties:

```
UPROPERTY(EditAnywhere)
UPITS_MissionDataAsset* Mission;

UPROPERTY(EditAnywhere)
int32 MissionIncrement = 1;
```

They will be used to hold the mission Data Asset and the increment value to be applied on request. Excluding some helper functions, you will get the following function, used to dispatch mission updates:

```
UFUNCTION(BlueprintCallable)
void DispatchMissionUpdate();
```

If you switch to the corresponding `.cpp` file, you will find this function's implementation:

```
if (UPITS_MissionSubsystem *MissionSubsystem =
    GetWorld()->GetSubsystem<UPITS_MissionSubsystem>())
{
    MissionSubsystem
        ->UpdateMission(Mission, MissionIncrement);
}
```

As you can see, we are simply retrieving the Subsystem and then executing the mission update. Let's check for some actual usage for this component.

Implementing mission pickup

The `UPITS_MissionHolderComponent` has been used both in C++ and in Blueprints. We will be starting from a C++ class that has been created specifically for mission pickups – that is, pickups that will update missions once collected. Open the `PITS_MissionPickup.h` file – a derived class from the `APITS_BaseTrigger` superclass – and you will find the component declaration:

```
UPROPERTY(
    EditAnywhere, meta = (AllowPrivateAccess = "true"))
TObjectPtr<UPITS_MissionHolderComponent>
    MissionHolderComponent;
```

If you open the corresponding `.cpp` file, you will see the broadcast request when the actor is triggered:

```
MissionHolderComponent->DispatchMissionUpdate();
```

This actor is used as an abstract class you can implement in Blueprints, so let's fire up the UE Editor and head to the `Content/Blueprints/Pickups` folder. Open the **BP_PointOfInterest** asset that is a child of the `APITS_MissionPickup` class.

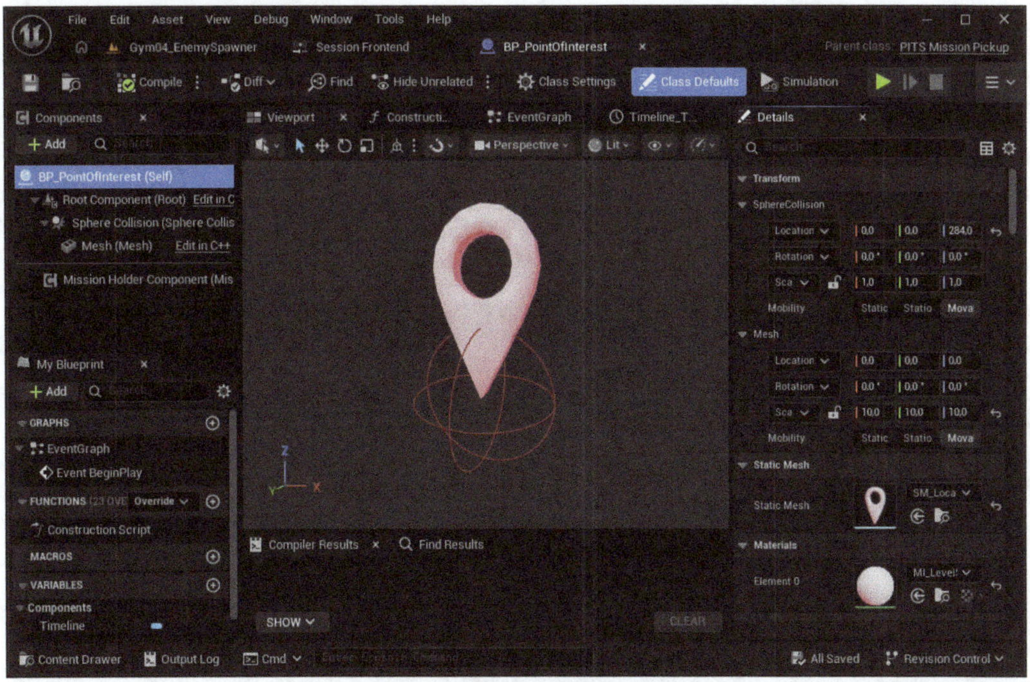

Figure 7.3 – The PB_PointOfInterest asset

In the **Details** panel, look for the **Paws in the Shell** category; you will find the **Mission** and **Mission Increment** properties. The **Mission** property has been set to the **DA_Mission_ReachPointsOfInterest** asset and the Mission Increment has been set to **1**, as depicted in *Figure 7.4*:

Figure 7.4 – The mission data properties

As all gameplay logic is managed internally, setting up the Data Asset is all we need to do to make the pickup work; everything else is pure aesthetics.

On the other hand, if you plan to implement your own mission achievement logic in a Blueprint, you will just need to add the **MissionHolder** component to a Blueprint and communicate with the Mission Subsystem. As an example, open the **BP_MissionAccessCard** located in the `Content/Blueprints/Pickups` folder.

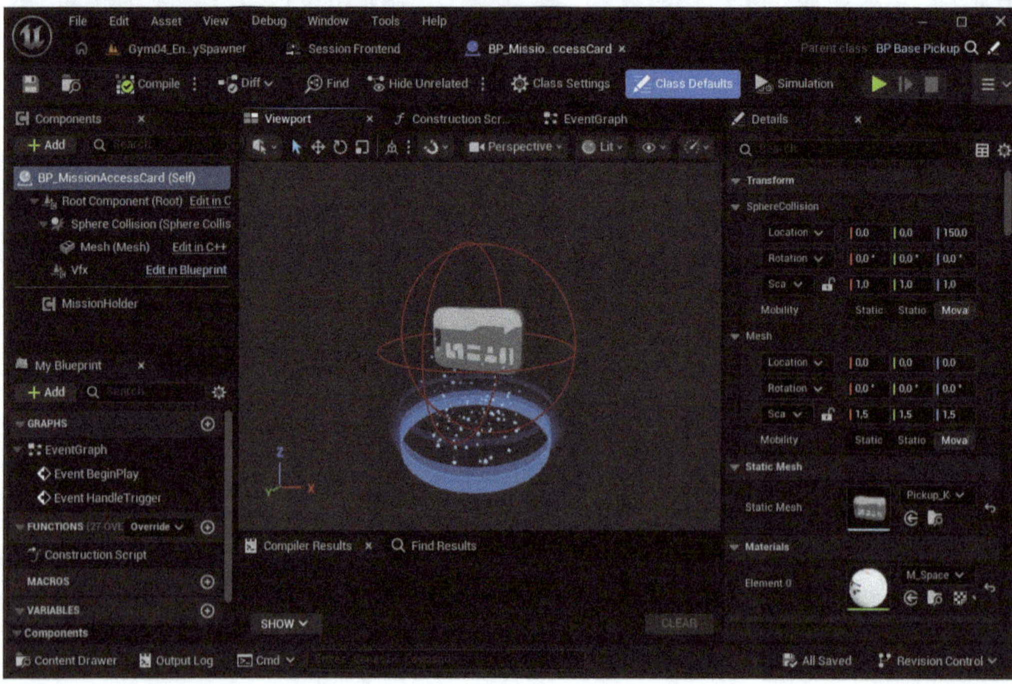

Figure 7.5 – The BP_MissionAccessCard asset

You will notice that, in the **Components** Panel, a **MissionComponent** instance – which is not available in the parent class – has been added. This component has the **Mission** property set to the **DA_Mission_CollectCards** asset, as depicted in *Figure 7.6*:

Figure 7.6 – The mission data properties

If you head over to the Event Graph, you will immediately find the gameplay logic implementing the mission update when the trigger is activated, as shown in *Figure 7.7*:

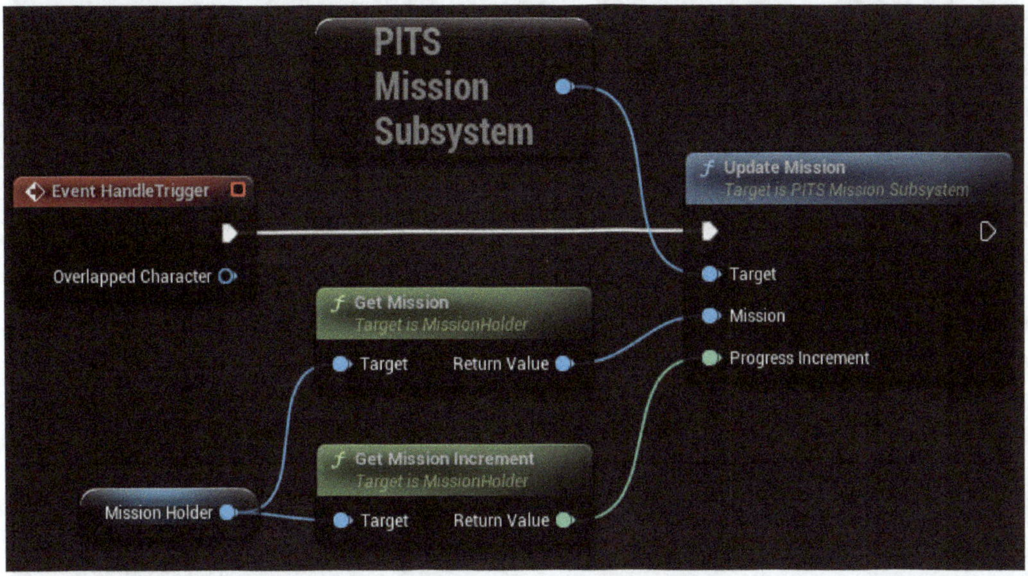

Figure 7.7 – The mission gameplay logic

As you can see, if you plan ahead and set up the basic code logic, everything else will be pretty straightforward. It's something you can easily delegate to junior developers, so you can focus on more important tasks!

Let's now focus on binding delegates in order to update the UI.

Listening to mission events

To show and update missions on the main UI, we will be using two widgets: a mission renderer – that will be showing a single mission's details and progress – and a mission container – that will create a mission renderer widget for each level mission. Let's start examining the mission container.

Inspecting the UW_MissionContainer

As mentioned, the mission container will get information about missions and create a widget for each of them. Let's open the **UW_MissionContainer** located in the `Content/Blueprints/UserInterface` folder. Once the asset is open, switch to the Graph view, locate the **Initialize** function, and open it. You will notice we are retrieving the mission list from the Mission Subsystem through the following portion of the graph:

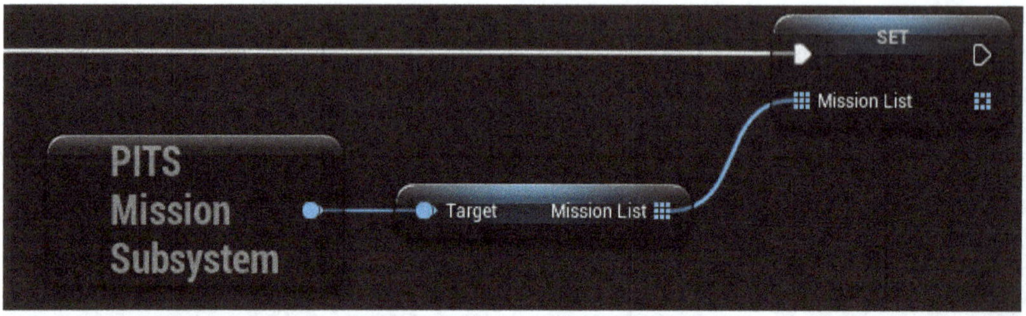

Figure 7.8 – Retrieving the mission list

Once the mission list is stored, we will be looping through each item and creating a renderer, passing the corresponding mission data, as shown in *Figure 7.9*:

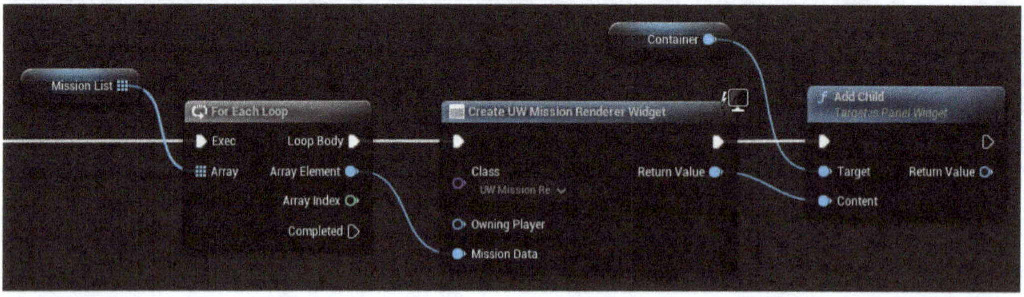

Figure 7.9 – Creating mission widgets

Once the renderer widget has been created, it will take care of binding to Subsystem events, as explained in the next subsection.

Inspecting the UW_MissionRenderer

Open the **UW_MissionRenderer** widget and head over to the Event Graph in the Graph view. In the **Event Construct** event, the first thing we are doing is binding the **On Mission Complete** and **On Mission Update** delegates from the Mission Subsystem.

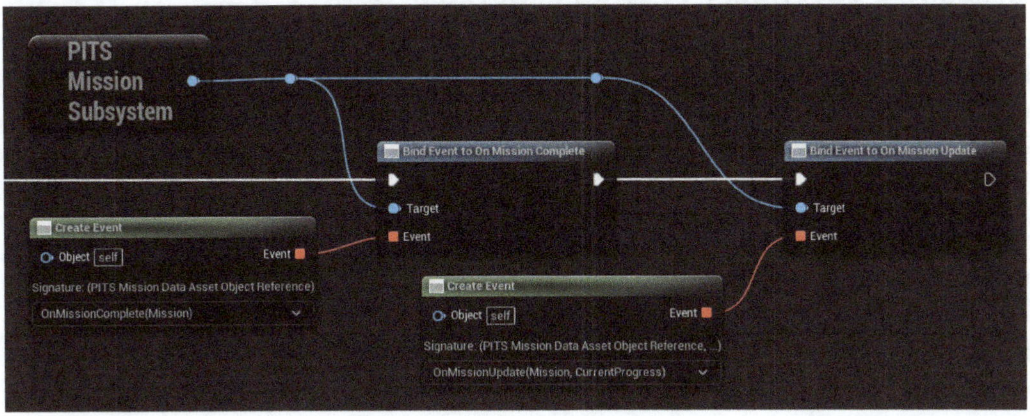

Figure 7.10 – Binding to mission events

Once Subsystem delegates are broadcasted, updating the UI is just a matter of checking if the mission data corresponds and then taking opportune actions. For example, check the **OnMissionUpdate** handler shown in *Figure 7.11*:

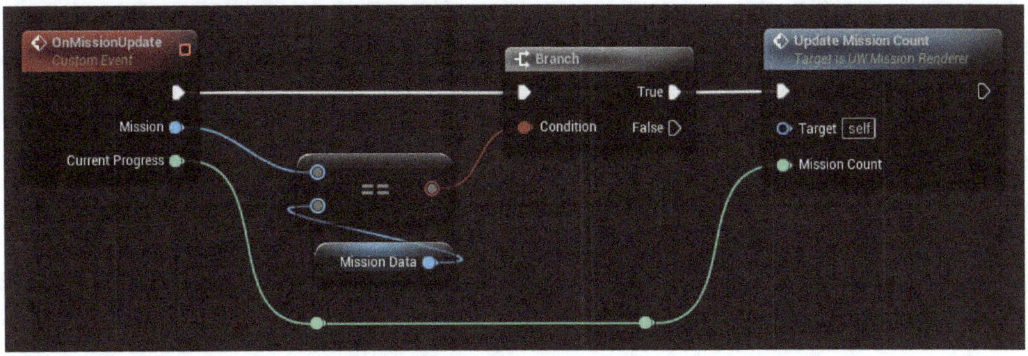

Figure 7.11 – The OnMissionUpdate handler

This concludes the presentation on this game scenario, focusing on Subsystems for in-game mission achievements. Now it's time to get back to work and start writing some code ourselves!

Develop and Self-Evaluate

It is now time to improve the *Paws in the Shell* project by adding some extra code to improve the overall gameplay experience. I will be proposing two tasks, so let's start with the first one.

Creating a secondary mission subsystem

The first exercise is about secondary – or optional – missions. Optional missions are usually side tasks that players can choose to complete but are not required to finish the level in the game. These missions provide extra challenges and allow players to gain additional experience or unlock special items.

What you should create is a subset of missions handled by the `UPITS_MissionSubsystem` that won't take part in the overall level completion, but that may grant some extra prizes. This means the Subsystem will need an extra set of dedicated delegates and containers. What's more, to make things more customizable, submissions won't be declared in the Game Mode, but through dedicated Actors, that will contain a `UPITS_MissionDataAsset` instance. Doesn't it sound easy?

Improving enemy characters

Enemy characters exist to make the player's life gloriously challenging – and a little more intense. What's more, they will probably be the target of your players to complete a level. Why not add a Mission holder component in order to track casualties?

This second exercise starts from the `APITS_BaseEnemyCharacter` class, and requests to add a `UMissionHolderComponent` reference and handle enemy kills from the Mission Subsystem. These kills should be used both in the main mission achievements, but may also be handled separately, in order to keep track of character experience points. Experience points are not implemented in the project – yet – but why not give your player this extra opportunity?

In this section we have explored a real-world case of Subsystem usage; there's some more in the project and I highly recommend checking them out. After all, you may recollect from *Chapter 4, Getting the Best out of Pointers* we explored pooling systems based on Subsystems.

Summary

In this chapter, I have introduced and explained Subsystems. Beginning with their main types, I explored why they are crucial in project development. Additionally, I presented the concept of a Subsystem's lifecycle to maximize its effectiveness. Finally, we examined a real-world example demonstrating how to utilize Subsystems. Understanding Subsystems will simplify your work in most cases and significantly enhance your code's reusability and flexibility.

In the next chapter, we'll take a big step forward and dive into a really exciting topic: multithreading and concurrency. Get ready to take your skills to the next level!

Get this book's PDF copy, code bundle, and more

Scan the QR code (or go to `packtpub.com/unlock`). Search for this book by name, confirm the edition, and then follow the steps on the page.

UNLOCK NOW

Note: Have your invoice handy. Purchases made directly from the Packt website don't require an invoice.

8

Understanding Multithreading and Concurrency

When we speak about multithreading, we refer to the capability of a CPU, or a single software application, to run multiple threads of execution concurrently. Each thread functions autonomously, handling distinct tasks or computations in parallel. In contemporary programming languages, and in particular within a game engine such as UE, implementing multithreading is critical for maximizing the use of multi-core processor architectures at their best. Mastering multithreading and concurrency is an essential skill for game developers as it will allow software performance optimization, scalability, and resource efficiency in modern multi-core computing environments. In this chapter, I will provide you with an extensive analysis of the fundamental concepts behind multithreading, focusing obviously on UE. In particular, we will be covering the following topics:

- Introducing threads and concurrency
- Introducing Task Graph and Task System
- Presenting multithreading techniques
- Presenting a practical example

Technical requirements

To get the best out of the following sections, you should have fully understood the previous chapters.

Introducing threads and concurrency

In modern software engineering, the demand for improved computational performance and system responsiveness has driven widespread adoption of **multithreading** and **concurrency** techniques. These approaches enable simultaneous execution of multiple computational tasks, thereby optimizing the use of multi-core processor architectures and enhancing overall system throughput. It goes without saying that many programming languages, including C++, offer extensive support for multithreading and concurrency.

When referring to a **thread**, we mean a single sequence of executable instructions within a program that can operate independently and concurrently alongside other threads. Multithreading allows multiple threads to run simultaneously, often on separate CPU cores, facilitating parallel task execution to enhance performance and responsiveness. Each thread maintains its own execution context – including its program counter, stack, and registers – while sharing the same memory space with other threads within the same process. Therefore, managing and synchronizing threads effectively is critical for making your game work, and preventing issues such as race conditions and deadlocks is of paramount importance.

It comes as no surprise that a game engine such as UE leverages advanced concurrency and multithreading systems to maximize performance across its diverse subsystems, including gameplay logic, rendering, physics, and asset streaming. At its core, the engine uses an advanced task management framework and – through sophisticated **thread pooling** systems – distributes work across available CPU cores without blocking critical threads like the game or the rendering ones.

> **Note**
>
> Please note that multithreading is not always advantageous, as some tasks must be executed sequentially. Additionally, it introduces complexity in the form of potential data races, synchronization overhead, and an increased risk of bugs.

Multithreading is a key element in game development as it enables a game application to leverage multiple CPU cores, ensuring that it remains responsive for tasks such as rendering, input handling, and actor updates. The system can prevent frame hitches and maintain smooth performance by offloading intensive CPU tasks – such as AI pathfinding, physics simulations and large-scale computations – to other threads.

Presenting the Game Thread

The main engine thread, called **Game Thread,** serves as the central execution thread and is responsible for coordinating all gameplay logic during each frame. It will handle Actor tick execution and operations involving the creation, destruction, or modification of objects. What's more, the Game Thread follows a single, deterministic flow, and this will help avoid data races and ensure stable gameplay. It should be noted that many engine operations are not thread-safe and, consequently, need to be executed on the Game Thread itself. This means that a critical aspect of multithreading strategy in UE involves identifying which tasks must remain on this thread and which can be safely offloaded to other threads.

Presenting the Render Thread

In UE, rendering is managed by the **Render Thread** that generally runs one to two frames behind the game thread. This thread executes rendering commands based on the data generated by the Game Thread with an intentional delay of one to two frames to help maintain optimal performance and ensure thread safety. At the end of each tick, the Game Thread will briefly pause to allow the Render Thread to catch up, but it will not wait for complete synchronization on every frame. The engine provides a low-latency frame synchronization mode that adjusts the synchronization between the Game Thread, Render Thread, and GPU to reduce input latency.

Presenting the RHI Thread

Think about the Render Thread as a frontend that enqueues platform-agnostic graphics commands. These commands are then passed to the **RHI Thread** – that works as an engine backend – that will process them into graphics with API-specific instructions for the GPU. This thread enables parallel processing with the Render Thread. This means that, in supported platforms, such as DirectX 12 and Vulkan, you will get high rendering efficiency.

Beside the Game, Render and RHI threads, the engine includes the **Audio Thread** dedicated to processing sound and music asynchronously and the **Loading Thread** that will manage loading and unloading of assets and data without blocking the Game Thread.

In this section, I provided a concise overview of multithreading and concurrency. This introduction will lay the foundation for the following sections, where I will discuss the main techniques employed by UE to manage multithreading.

Introducing Task Graph and Task System

Now that you have been introduced to multithreading and the main threads in Unreal Engine, let's dive deeper and explore how the engine enables you to work with threads. First of all, let's define the **job manager**, that is basically a system designed to handle and schedule small units of work, known as **jobs** or **tasks**, to run asynchronously across multiple CPU threads. Its primary function is to maximize CPU core usage by distributing workloads away from the main thread, which enhances the overall performance and responsiveness of an application.

A job manager performs several critical roles. First, it schedules tasks by launching and queuing them to run on available worker threads. Next, it manages dependencies to ensure that tasks with prerequisites are executed in the correct sequence. Additionally, it provides synchronization mechanisms that allow waiting for jobs to finish. What's more, it balances the workload dynamically across CPU cores to maintain optimal performance. Finally, it allows prioritization of tasks, managing their execution order.

UE provides two job managers, named **Task Graph** and **Task System,** that are designed to execute gameplay and engine code asynchronously on multiple threads and to improve performance by parallelizing workloads.

The Task Graph is the earlier system that enables running jobs on worker threads with dependencies. On the other hand, the Task System is a newer and improved job manager built on the same backend scheduler and worker threads; it has been developed aiming for a more modern and flexible management of tasks.

At its core, the Task System is built on the backend of the Task Graph with the aim of enhancing usability and adding more features. While the Task Graph is closely integrated with specific engine threads, such as the Game or Render thread, the Task System operates on a set of global pooled worker threads. Sooner or later, the Task System will replace the Task Graph by providing more flexible and versatile APIs. As you may guess, the Task System provides a robust framework for managing tasks efficiently. Some of its main features are:

- **Launching Tasks**: a task can be launched once provided with a unique debug name and a callable – usually a lambda – to execute asynchronously.
- **Task Handles**: A launched task will return a handle to check validity, completion status, wait for completion, or get results.
- **Prerequisites**: A task can specify dependencies on other tasks to ensure the order of execution.
- **Nested Tasks**: A task can launch nested child tasks, and it will be completed only after all nested tasks have finished.
- **Task Priority**: A task can have priorities – for instance high, normal, etc. – that will affect scheduling order.
- **Task Chains**: Tasks can be executed sequentially.
- **Task Events**: Tasks can be coordinated through a set of primitives specifically implemented for synchronization.

A task has its own lifecycle with the following dedicated phases:

- **Creation/Launch**: The task is created asynchronously with a unique name
- **Scheduling**: Once the prerequisites are completed, the task is queued to run.

- **Start**: The task begins its execution on a worker thread.
- **End**: The task body completes execution.
- **Completion**: Any nested tasks finish, ending the lifecycle.

In this section I have presented a brief overview of the Task Graph and Task System: as you have seen, the Task System allows developers to launch asynchronous tasks represented as callable objects, optionally specify dependencies – or prerequisites – between tasks, and handle nested tasks. These tasks are scheduled on worker threads managed within a thread pool, balancing the workload dynamically for optimal CPU utilization. Finally, tasks can be assigned priorities to ensure timely execution of high-importance workloads.

In the next section, I am going to give you an overview of the most important multithreading techniques provided by the engine and based on the Task Graph and Task System themselves.

Presenting in-engine features

In UE, there are two primary approaches to handling asynchronous work: **Runnables** and **Tasks**. A Runnable operates on a dedicated thread that developers have full control over. Such a thread automatically terminates once its assigned tasks are complete. Runnables are particularly well-suited for large computations that require a thread to run almost continuously. On the other hand, a Task runs on the Task Graph that, as previously stated, will distribute workload efficiently across multiple existing threads. This approach is ideal for dispatching small units of work, as it abstracts the complexity of thread management. Queuing Tasks will not typically cause performance issues since the threads are already running. However, the engine may be less responsive at times because it will need to find available slots within a limited thread pool. It is highly recommended to avoid sending long-running tasks to prevent thread congestion.

In the next subsections I am going to present you an overview of the most important in-engine features that deal directly with multithreading or are part of the Task Graph and Task System.

Presenting multithreading techniques

The UE engine provides a set of low-level methods for creating and managing multiple threads directly – for instance manual thread creation, synchronization primitives and atomics. The main multithreading technique is provided by the `FRunnable` class, so let's start examining this one in detail.

Explaining FRunnable

The `FRunnable` class implements a low-level threading API that will give you full control over threads; this means you will be most probably using it when in need of long-running or custom tasks with fine-grained control.

Once you have subclassed the `FRunnable` class, you will implement its `Run()` function that will include the code executed on the new thread. To create a thread, you will be instantiating your `FRunnable`-derived class and then start it with `FRunnableThread::Create()`. As an example, consider a `FRunnable`-derived class named `FMyRunnable` and an `FRunnableThread` pointer declaration similar to the following code snippet:

```
FMyRunnable* Runnable = nullptr;
FRunnableThread* RunnableThread = nullptr;
```

To start the thread, you will be using:

```
Runnable = new FMyRunnable();
RunnableThread = FRunnableThread::Create(
    Runnable, TEXT("The RunnableThread"));
```

You can also implement the `Init()` function in the `FRunnable` class that is going to be called when the `FRunnableThread::Create()` function is executed.

> **Note**
>
> Proper cleanup and management of the Runnable thread are of utmost priority in order to avoid resource issues.

Once the thread is executed, you will be able to perform a cleanup by implementing the `Exit()` function.

Let's now talk about the most common Task Graph and Task System classes and utility functions.

Task Graph and Task System Abstractions

Unreal provides a set of Task Graph and Task System abstractions that provide efficient task management; these tools are meant to simplify launching and scheduling units of work across multiple threads. So, let's get started and analyze the most common ones.

Explaining TFuture and TPromise

`TFuture` is a template class that represents the result of an asynchronous operation. It acts as a handle or placeholder for a value that will be available later when the async task completes. `TFuture` works in combination with `TPromise`, which sets the value that `TFuture` will hold once done.

The setup is usually a two-step process:

1. A `TPromise` is created and then designed to hold the results of a computation
2. From this `TPromise`, a `TFuture` is obtained, enabling the retrieval of the results or the ability to chain further operations once the background computation has been completed

A `TFuture` provides a `Get()` function to wait for and retrieve the operation results. Please note that this function is a blocking call; this means that it will wait until the asynchronous task is complete and then return the result. As an example, consider the following code snippet:

```
TPromise<int32> MyPromise;
TFuture<int32> MyFuture = MyPromise.GetFuture();
Async(
    EAsyncExecution::Thread,
    [Promise = MoveTemp(MyPromise)]() mutable
    {
        int32 ComputedResult;
        // Perform heavy computations...
        Promise.SetValue(ComputedResult);
    });
```

As you can see, we are running the task on a new, dedicated, thread. The `SetValue()` function fulfills the promise on the thread itself. Later in your code, you will be using the following snippet:

```
int32 Result = MyFuture.Get();
```

As mentioned, it will be a blocking call until the `SetValue()` function is called.

On the other hand, if you do not wish to have a blocking call, you may use the `IsReady()` and `IsCompleted()` functions, which can be checked at any time.

Explaining Async

The `Async` is a templated function that will let you run any callable code, such as a function or a lambda, without blocking the current thread. It has been created to execute quick asynchronous tasks with a minimal setup. Internally, it will take advantage of the UE Task System or thread pools to schedule efficiently. Once executed, it will return a handle – actually, a `TFuture` – that will let you check if it's complete and let you retrieve the result. As an example, consider the following code snippet:

```
TFuture<int32> MyFuture =
    Async(EAsyncExecution::ThreadPool, []()
    {
        int32 ComputedResult;
        // Perform heavy computations...
        return ComputedResult;
    });
```

Through the `Async()` we are running a lambda asynchronously on a background thread. Inside the lambda we are performing heavy computations and then we are returning the result.

To get the result, we will use something similar to the following line of code:

```
int32 Result = MyFuture.Get();
```

As you can see, the code is pretty straightforward and easy to set up.

Explaining ParallelFor

The `ParallelFor` is another utility function used as a high-level helper to abstract the complexity of multithreading; in this case it focuses on splitting a large workload into parallel task execution of smaller tasks. Once executed, each task will run in parallel while the Game Thread waits for completion. Whenever you execute a `ParallelFor`, you will usually provide a lambda or a function along with the number of iterations; the engine will internally distribute these iterations to worker threads in parallel. As an example, please check the following piece of code:

```
ParallelFor(Num, [](int32 Index)
{
    // Process data
});
```

The `Num` parameter indicates the number of calls to the function body.

> **Note**
>
> Be aware that `ParallelFor` has been designed for large, independent tasks where the benefits of parallelism outweigh the overhead of threading. Excessive use of `ParallelFor` for small tasks may lead to decreased performance.

A common use case for `ParallelFor` is processing and updating large arrays efficiently. As an example, consider the `ProcessArray()` function in the following block of code:

```
void ProcessArray(TArray<int32>& Values)
{
    ParallelFor(Values.Num(), [&Values](int32 Index)
    {
        // Do some computation on Values[Index]
    });
    // The parallel is finished
    // and we have the final result.
}
```

As you can see, we run a lambda in parallel passing the `Values` array length; this means we will be executing the task that exact number of times. Inside the parallel we will be executing some computation – for instance retrieving the array element at the computed index – that will be safe because each computation will be handled independently. Once all the parallel tasks have finished, you will have the final result for the full computation.

Explaining AsyncTask

The `AsyncTask` is a utility function used to schedule code to run asynchronously on a background thread, allowing heavy or blocking operations to avoid stalling the game thread. It typically executes a lambda or callable function on a worker thread and, upon completion, has the ability to queue another `AsyncTask` on the Game Thread to safely handle results. It has no built-in logic for handling results or waiting; in fact, it has no result value at all. Its main difference with `Async`, is that it is usually used for fire-and-forget background tasks or for code dispatching to specific threads – such as the Game Thread – with no result handling. As a consequence, you will need to implement your own control flags – usually a `bool` variable – to track a task state and avoid overlapping executions. As an example, consider the following code snippet:

```
AsyncTask(ENamedThreads::AnyNormalThreadNormalTask, []()
{
    // Task code logic
});
```

The code is launching an async task, selecting – by means of `AnyNormalThreadNormalTask` – any normal-priority worker thread from the thread pool that is suitable for general background work. If you need to execute one asynchronous task after the other, your code will look something like the following class:

```
class FMyAsyncClass {
public:
    bool bIsRunning = false;
    void RunAsyncSequence()
    {
        if (bIsRunning) return;
        bIsRunning = true;

        AsyncTask(
            ENamedThreads::AnyNormalThreadNormalTask,
            [this]()
            {
                // First AsyncTask is running

                AsyncTask(
                    ENamedThreads::GameThread, [this]()
                    {
                        // Second AsyncTask is running
                        // on Game Thread
                        bIsRunning = false;
                    });
            });
    }
};
```

The `bIsRunning` flag is used to check if the async tasks are being executed; this will avoid running them again if the function is called once more before it has finished executing. The first task is executed selecting any normal-priority worker thread from the thread pool that is suitable for general background work. The second one – nested inside the first one – is executed on the Game Thread. Once tasks have finished execution, the `bIsRunning` flag is set to `false` in order to reset their state.

You may have noticed that, although less powerful, the `AsyncTask` is easier to set up and handle than its `Async` counterpart.

Explaining TGraphTask

The `TGraphTask` is a templated class that can be used to create custom task types with fine control. It is usually used when you need tasks with complex logic where you need high flexibility. To create an asynchronous task execution with the `TGraphTask`, you will need to define a struct or a class with two key requirements: `GetTaskName()` and `DoTask()` function implementations. As an example, consider the following block of code:

```
class FMyGraphTask
{
public:
    static const TCHAR* GetTaskName()
    {
        return TEXT("FMyGraphTask");
    }

    void DoTask(
        ENamedThreads::Type CurrentThread,
        const FGraphEventRef& MyCompletionEvent)
    {
        // Perform heavy computations...
    }
};
```

First of all, this class provides a debug name for the task with the `GetTaskName()` function and then defines the `DoTask()` function that will be executed asynchronously by the task system.

To schedule this task, you will be using the following piece of code:

```
FGraphEventRef TaskRef =
    TGraphTask<FMyGraphTask>::CreateTask()
    .ConstructAndDispatchWhenReady();
```

This line creates, schedules, and dispatches the `FMyGraphTask` task to run asynchronously and, when ready, returns a handle to manage it.

Explaining FFunctionGraphTask

The `FFunctionGraphTask` class is a lightweight task wrapper that can be used for running a simple lambda or function asynchronously. Just like `AsyncTask`, it is ideal for fire-and-forget background work. Compared to `TGraphTask`, it is more lightweight since it requires less setup; however, the downside is that you end up with a less flexible system. When creating a task with this class, you will usually call the `CreateAndDispatchWhenReady()` function that will return an `FGraphEventRef` – a handle to the task completion event in the engine Task Graph system. The `FGraphEventRef` can then be used to track, synchronize, and wait for the task to complete. The following code snippet shows a simple example of how to dispatch a task using the `FFunctionGraphTask` class:

```
FGraphEventRef Task =
    FFunctionGraphTask::CreateAndDispatchWhenReady([]()
    {
        // Execute some computation...
    },
    TStatId(),
    nullptr,
    ENamedThreads::AnyBackgroundThreadNormalTask
    // Run on any background thread
    );
```

As you can see, we are executing a lambda function for some heavy computation. The `TStatId()` call is used for optional debugging or analysis tools, while the `nullptr` indicates that we do not want any prerequisites for this call. Finally, we are setting the thread to run this task as any background thread. As previously stated, through the returned `FGraphEventRef` handle, you will be able to hook and synchronize the task.

Explaining FNonAbandonableTask

The `FNonAbandonableTask` class, as the name suggests, represents a way to define asynchronous tasks that must always be completed and cannot be abandoned once started. This means the engine will complete the task even if it is shutting down. You should use it whenever you are performing critical background operations that require guaranteed execution – such as saving data. As a simple example, please consider the following piece of code:

```
class FMyNonAbandonableTask : public FNonAbandonableTask
{
    FMyNonAbandonableTask()
    {
    }

    void DoWork()
    {
        // Async Logic
    }

    FORCEINLINE TStatId GetStatId() const
    {
        RETURN_QUICK_DECLARE_CYCLE_STAT(
            FMyTask, STATGROUP_ThreadPoolAsyncTasks);
    }
};
```

As you can see, once we extend the `FNonAbandonableTask` class with our own subclass, we implement the `DoWork()` function that will execute the async logic in a thread-safe manner and the `GetStatId()` function that is required to use the engine profiling system.

> **Note**
>
> `RETURN_QUICK_DECLARE_CYCLE_STAT` is a macro used to declare a cycle counter stat and immediately return its unique `TStatId`, typically used to provide a persistent identifier for manual profiling scopes within functions.

To start the task, we will be using something similar to the following code snippet:

```
FAsyncTask<FMyNonAbandonableTask>* Task =
    new FAsyncTask<FMyNonAbandonableTask>();
Task->StartBackgroundTask();
Task->EnsureCompletion();
delete Task;
```

As a first step, we are creating the task, then we are starting it through the `StartBackgroundTask()` function, and lastly we wait for completion with the `EnsureCompletion()` call; just keep in mind that this second call is blocking the current thread. Finally, we manually delete the task, in order to avoid memory leaks.

If, on the other hand, you are planning to have a fire-and-forget pattern for the task and avoid manual memory management, you may use an instance of `FAutoDeleteAsyncTask` as shown in the following example:

```
(new FAutoDeleteAsyncTask<FMyNonAbandonableTask>())
    ->StartBackgroundTask();
```

This option will safely clean up memory when the task is complete, and you will avoid memory leaks.

In this rather extensive section, I have introduced some of the most common multithreading techniques available in Unreal. Hopefully, you now have a well-equipped set of skills to handle various scenarios involving parallelism – from fire-and-forget tasks to executing multiple tasks in parallel. It's just up to you to wisely decide which approach to use and when!

In the next section, I'll walk you through the usual use case in the *Paws in the Shell* project. Get ready to dive into some serious coding!

Presenting a practical example

It looks like the next assessment for the Paws in the Shell story has just landed on these pages.

In the electrically charged maze of Holo District, Team 33 hunted relentlessly for the stolen Eleuterium – a once-promising digital cryptocurrency designed to empower the people and stabilize the Holo District economy. But OmniSight Industries had twisted Eleuterium into a dangerous weapon, scattering corrupted fragments into every shadowed corner of the city, infecting everything from street terminals to core AI systems.

With neural implants firing and reflexes honed to deadly precision, The Pack prowled rain-soaked alleys and breached virtual backdoors, clashing violently with Omnisight's relentless drones and cybernetic mercenaries. Their mission was clear although desperate: recover Eleuterium's pure code before the corruption destroyed the city's fragile balance.

In a brutal final showdown atop Holo District's tallest spire, they harvested the last shards of Eleuterium from the grip of a corrupted, braindead OmniSight CTO – the Spectre Shade – an empty shell consumed by greed and power. As dawn bled over the horizon, The Pack vanished into the sprawling crowd, leaving behind a city forever scarred – where technology and humanity balanced on a razor's edge, and the war for digital dominion raged on without end.

Cryptocurrency sparsely distributed across a level shows a typical example of many objects that should be efficiently added at the start of the game.

In this section, we will analyze a spawn system designed to operate asynchronously. This implementation addresses the requirement to spawn a large number of objects with randomized spawn points.

Implementing an Asynchronous Spawner

Handling spawn processes within the main Game Thread could lead to performance issues; that's why I am showing an alternative version using `Async` and `AsyncTask`. The implementation logic can be summarized as follows:

1. Asynchronously compute a set of random spawn locations inside the bounds of a trigger volume
2. Validate those locations on the Game Thread with line traces
3. Spawn actors on validated locations

This feature has been implemented inside the `UPITS_WorldSubsystem` and it has been marked as `BlueprintCallable`, in order to access it inside Blueprints. If you head to the `PITS_WorldSubsystem.h` declaration, you will find the following function:

```
UFUNCTION(BlueprintCallable)
void SpawnActorsAsync(
    TSubclassOf<AActor> SpawnableActorClass,
    const int32 MinAmount,
    const int32 MaxAmount,
    ATriggerVolume* SpawnArea);
```

To check the actual implementation, open the `PITS_WorldSubsystem.cpp` file and head over to the function implementation. Once the World has been retrieved and validated, we create the bounding box that will be used to check the possible spawn locations, starting from the `SpawnArea` trigger volume:

```
FBox SpawnBox = SpawnArea->GetComponentsBoundingBox(false);
```

We compute this on the Game Thread, so the async lambda executed subsequently won't need to touch the `SpawnArea` object. After this, we launch heavy computations on a dedicated thread with the lambda capturing only plain data, in order to avoid accessing `UObjects` directly on the thread itself:

```
Async(EAsyncExecution::ThreadPool,
    [World,
     SpawnableActorClass,
     SpawnBox, MinAmount, MaxAmount]()
    {
        // Perform computations
    });
```

Inside the thread you will find the following loop that will compute a set of possible spawn locations without calling any `UObject` APIs or doing any traces:

```
for (int32 i = 0; i < SpawnCount; ++i)
{
  FVector Location(
    FMath::FRandRange(SpawnBox.Min.X, SpawnBox.Max.X),
    FMath::FRandRange(SpawnBox.Min.Y, SpawnBox.Max.Y),
    SpawnBox.Max.Z + 100.0f
  );
  SpawnLocations.Add(Location);
}
```

The results are then added to the `SpawnLocations` array.

Once the process is finished, we start performing all needed `UObject` and physics computations inside an `AsyncTask`, as shown in the following code snippet:

```
AsyncTask(ENamedThreads::GameThread,
    [World = World,
     SpawnableActorClass,
     SpawnLocations,
     SpawnBox]()
    {
    }
```

Inside this thread, for each candidate location, we perform a line trace to find a valid surface point; in this case, we need to execute it inside the Game Thread as we are calling `LineTraceSingleByChannel`.

The loop is shown in the following block of code:

```
for (const FVector Location : SpawnLocations)
{
    FHitResult HitResult;
    FVector TraceStart = Location;
    FVector TraceEnd(
        TraceStart.X, TraceStart.Y, SpawnBox.Min.Z);

    if (const bool bHit = World
        ->LineTraceSingleByChannel(
            HitResult, TraceStart, TraceEnd, ECC_Visibility))
    {
        ValidatedLocations.Add(HitResult.Location);
    }
}
```

The result of the traces is then saved inside the `ValidatedLocations` array. Once the process is finished – still in the Game Thread – we execute the `SpawnActorsOnGameThread()` function that will take care of the actual spawn.

This implementation follows recommended best practices for async spawning in UE with clear thread boundaries, safe data capture, and deferred validation and spawning on the Game Thread.

Now that the asynchronous spawner has been implemented, let's check how it works at the project level.

Inspecting the asynchronous spawner in a level

Inside the Paws in the Shell project, the asynchronous spawner feature has been used to randomly generate pickups, for instance *Eleuterium* credits, in large numbers around the level. You can test the feature on your own by opening the **Gym_08_AsyncSpawn** map, depicted in *Figure 8.1*:

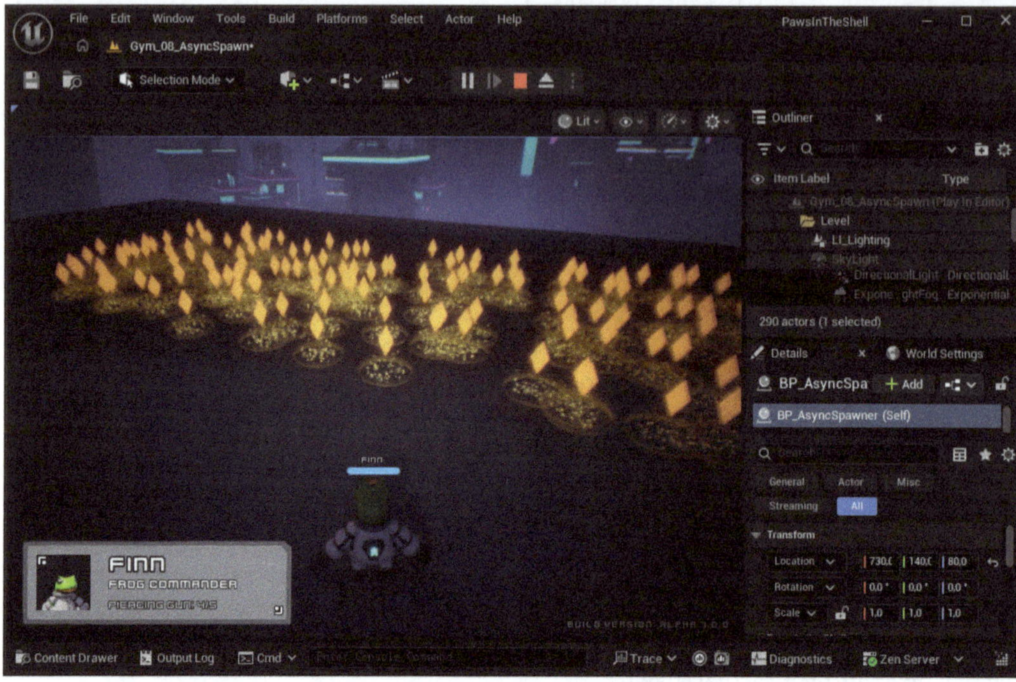

Figure 8.1 – The Gym_08_AsyncSpawn level

The Blueprint implementation for the spawner is quite simple and can be found by opening the **BP_AsyncSpawner** asset. The Event Graph will present the visual scripting code shown in *Figure 8.2*:

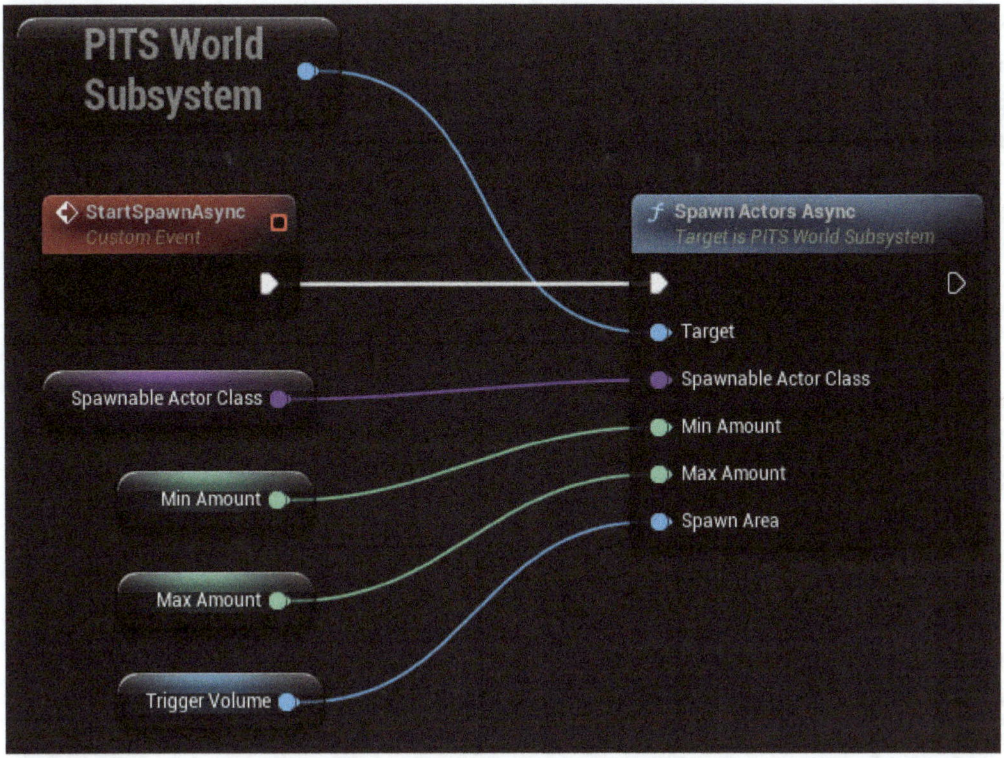

Figure 8.2 – BP_AsyncSpawner code

As you can see, we are just calling the `BlueprintCallable` **Spawn Actor Async** function from the **PITS World Subsystem**, passing the appropriate parameters.

Now that you've seen a real example of how multithreading works, it's your turn to write some code yourself. This is something you're probably already familiar with!

Develop and Self-Evaluate

It is now time to improve the *Paws in the Shell* project again and check your comprehension of the topics covered in this chapter. I will be proposing a couple of tasks, so let's start with the first one.

Improving the async spawner

The first task I am asking you to implement is some much needed improvements on the async spawn feature; at the moment, object spawn is handled through the `SpawnActorsOnGameThread()` function through a loop:

```
for (const FVector& Location : SpawnLocations)
{
    FActorSpawnParameters SpawnParams;
    SpawnParams.SpawnCollisionHandlingOverride =
  ESpawnActorCollisionHandlingMethod::AdjustIfPossibleButAlwaysSpawn;

    World->SpawnActor<AActor>(
        SpawnableActorClass,
        Location,
        FRotator::ZeroRotator,
        SpawnParams);
}
```

This is obviously a computationally intensive action performed on the Game Thread. Why not use an object pool, as explained in *Chapter 4, Getting the Best out of Pointers*? Try creating your spawn implementation, that will create a pool of objects from the `UPITS_ObjectPoolSubsystem`, and use them on demand.

Additionally, for a more advanced implementation on finding spawn points, you may consider using async physics traces – such as `AsyncLineTraceByChannel` – that will offload trace overhead from the main Game Thread. In this case, you will need to pay attention, as the result will be returned on the next frame after the trace.

This augmented approach will help maintain smooth gameplay performance by minimizing frame drops and ensuring that heavy computations do not block the main thread.

Fixing a parallel spawner

The second task is all about fixing some wrong code written by the *Paws in the Shell* developer – yep, that's me! – who has implemented the `SpawnActorsOnNavMesh()` function in the `UPITS_WorldSubsystem` class. The following code snippet shows the code that should be fixed:

```
for (int32 i = 0; i < SpawnCount; ++i)
{
    UWorld* World = GetWorld();
    CHECK_PTR_AND_LOG_RETURN(World);
```

```
    UNavigationSystemV1* NavSys =
        FNavigationSystem::GetCurrent<UNavigationSystemV1>(World);
    CHECK_PTR_AND_LOG_RETURN(NavSys);

    FVector2D RandomOffset =
        FMath::RandPointInCircle(SpawnRadius);
    FVector RandomLocation =
        SpawnCenterLocation +
        FVector(RandomOffset.X, RandomOffset.Y, 0.f);

    FVector Extent = FVector(200.f, 200.f, 100.f);
    if (FNavLocation NavLocation;
        NavSys
            ->ProjectPointToNavigation(
                RandomLocation, NavLocation, Extent))
    {
        FVector SpawnLocation = NavLocation.Location;
        FActorSpawnParameters SpawnParams;
        SpawnParams.SpawnCollisionHandlingOverride =
            ESpawnActorCollisionHandlingMethod::AdjustIfPossibleButAlwaysSpawn;

        World->SpawnActor<AActor>(
            SpawnableActorClass,
            SpawnLocation,
            FRotator::ZeroRotator,
            SpawnParams);
    }
}
```

This function simply loops in the Game Thread and mindlessly spawns actors from a predefined class. What's more, the spawn location is randomized by probing through a nav mesh, if any. No need to mention that all of this is computationally intensive and will probably cause issues for large numbers of objects. Try fixing all this mess by implementing your asynchronous implementation. Just keep in mind which async functions are thread safe and which are not. For instance, you won't be able to use `ParallelFor` to safely call separate nav mesh queries – this is something that needs to be implemented in the main Game Thread. Just try to be creative, but with a pinch of salt!

Summary

In this comprehensive chapter, I have outlined some of the key concepts essential for working with multithreading and parallelism in Unreal. Beginning with an overview of the Task Graph and Task System, I subsequently introduced several of the most used utility functions and classes provided by the engine. Understanding these topics is crucial for game programmers, as efficient multithreading and parallelism can significantly enhance game performance and responsiveness, enabling smoother gameplay and better resource utilization.

This chapter also wraps up this second part of the book, and I hope that by fully understanding the topics covered, you'll become a stronger programmer and an outstanding developer.

In the next chapter – and the last part of the book – we'll begin exploring how to test your applications and how to expand them by creating your own plugins. This will open up new possibilities for customizing your projects and making them amazing!

Get this book's PDF copy, code bundle, and more

Scan the QR code (or go to `packtpub.com/unlock`). Search for this book by name, confirm the edition, and then follow the steps on the page.

UNLOCK NOW

Note: Have your invoice handy. Purchases made directly from the Packt website don't require an invoice.

Part 3

Extending and Testing your Game

In this final part of the book, you will be presented with several topics designed to consolidate and refine your skills as a game programmer. By the end of the book, you will be fully prepared to apply your skills as a game programmer at a professional level, meeting the demands of the competitive game industry.

This part of the book includes the following chapters:

- *Chapter 9: Working with the Log System*
- *Chapter 10: Developing Plugins and Modules*
- *Chapter 11: Testing Your Application*

9

Working with the Log System

Logging is a fundamental practice in software development as it provides critical visibility into the behavior of applications. It helps developers monitor runtime events, diagnose issues, and understand system performance. When using C++ in UE, its effective logging system is essential for debugging complex codebases and facilitating maintenance. Developers will be able to capture detailed runtime information, and so they will be able to identify and remove errors faster and improve software quality and reliability. In this chapter, we will be focusing on the main logging techniques provided by the engine and, as always, by the end of it, we will be checking some real-world examples in order to make things clearer. We will be covering the following topics:

- Introducing the Unreal Engine log systems
- Working with `UE_LOG`
- Using the Visual Logger
- Presenting a practical example

Technical requirements

To get the best out of the following sections, you should have fully understood the previous chapters and have the *Paws in the Shell* project properly set up.

Introducing the Unreal Engine log system

In any development environment, having a log system available is of paramount importance to track, debug, and monitor applications at runtime. It provides a structured way to analyze and record function calls, variable values, and events by means of system messages. These messages help identify issues and verify game logic. UE provides a full set of log features, including some dedicated macros that we will be covering during this section. What's more, the engine system supports customizable log categories and multiple verbosity levels that allow for granular control over information and the way they are recorded and displayed. So, without further ado, let's get started by analyzing the most common log features available.

Understanding logging

Whenever discussing logging messages, it is essential to understand the fundamental components that are used to generate output messages. First of all, output messages are usually displayed in the Output Log window of the UE Editor and saved in the `Saved/Logs` folder of your project.

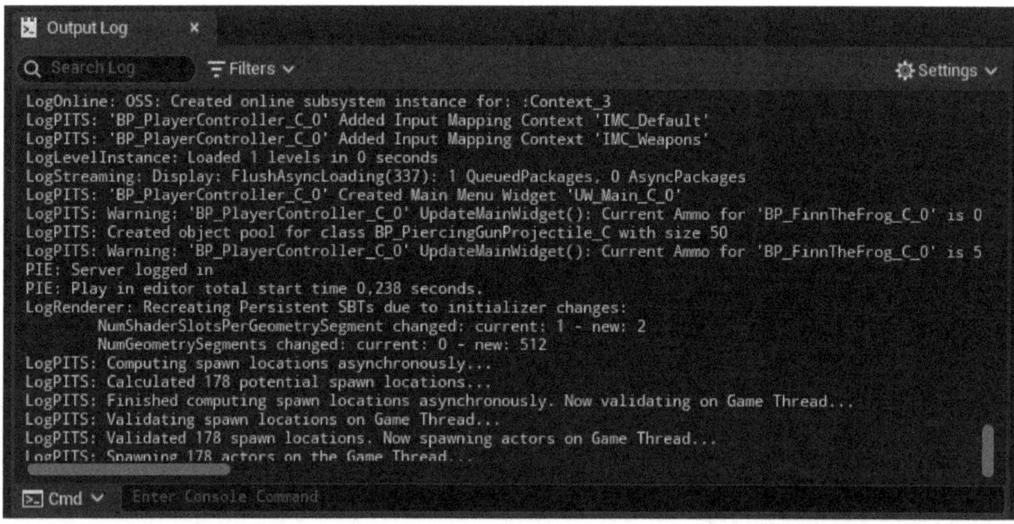

Figure 9.1 – The Log Output window from the Paws in the Shell project

A log message usually has the following properties:

- **LogCategory**: To identify and group related messages
- **Verbosity**: To specify the importance of the message
- **Message**: The actual message you are sending to the output log

The engine system provides some predefined log categories – such as `LogTemp` – but you can create your own, in order to better categorize your messages. Defining a custom category is a straightforward process as you will be using the `DECLARE_LOG_CATEGORY_EXTERN` macro inside a header file. This macro will declare the existence of a category without defining it, allowing you to use the category itself in other files. A typical declaration will be similar to the following code snippet:

```
DECLARE_LOG_CATEGORY_EXTERN(LogMyCategory, Log, All);
```

> **Note**
>
> A strong convention and best practice highly recommends the use of the prefix `Log` when declaring a category. This will clearly identify the category itself as a logging-related identifier.

The `DECLARE_LOG_CATEGORY_EXTERN` macro must be paired with the `DEFINE_LOG_CATEGORY` in the `.cpp` source file. This essential step will bind the declaration to the actual log category.

Additionally, UE provides a list of verbosity levels you can assign to your log messages. These levels can be used to control visibility and filter log messages in the Output Log console.

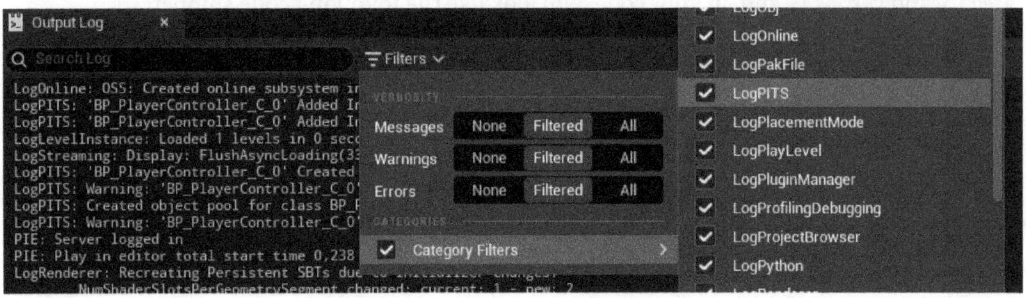

Figure 9.2 – The Log Output filter panel

The engine's available verbosity levels are declared in the `ELogVerbosity::Type` enumeration and are:

- Fatal: Used to define critical errors causing immediate termination
- Error: Used for serious issues requiring attention
- Warning: Used when potential problems or unexpected situations arise
- Display: Used for important messages always shown to users
- Log: Used to display general informational messages
- Verbose: Used for detailed debugging information
- VeryVerbose: Used when in need of extremely detailed, fine-grained logs

Finally, the actual message will be declared as a formatted string by means of the `TEXT()` macro.

Let's now check the macros that will let you output messages to the logging system.

Presenting log macros

UE provides several log functions and macros designed for specific logging scenarios. The first one is `GLog`, which is an internal global logging object responsible for routing log output. It does not support category and verbosity, and you will be using it like the following code snippet:

```
GLog->Log("A log message");
```

This log system is not typically used directly as it is mostly reserved for engine or low-level development, but it is probably worth mentioning that other log systems internally route messages through `GLog`.

The second log macro, and probably the most used one, is `UE_LOG`, which will allow you to output messages both to the Output Log window and in the saved log files. It supports both log category and verbosity and, in your code, will look like the following code snippet:

```
UE_LOG([LogCategory], [Verbosity], TEXT("A log message");
```

Due to its importance, I will present to you its main characteristics in their own dedicated section.

The third log system is pretty similar to `UE_LOG` but it will allow you to log messages only under certain circumstances; the `UE_CLOG` macro represents a conditional message and will prevent unnecessary log spam. The following line of code is showing its syntax:

```
UE_CLOG(bFlag, [LogCategory], [Verbosity], TEXT("A log Message"));
```

As you may have guessed, the message will be logged only if `bFlag` is set to true.

The `UE_VLOG` macro is used for runtime visual debugging and uses the syntax shown in the following code snippet:

```
UE_VLOG([Actor], [LogCategory], [Verbosity], TEXT("A log Message"));
```

Just like `UE_LOG`, it is quite an important macro. I will be presenting its main features in its own dedicated section later in this chapter.

Finally, you can take advantage of the UE_VLOG_UELOG, which will log simultaneously as a UE_LOG and a UE_VLOG:

```
UE_VLOG_UELOG([LogCategory], [Verbosity], TEXT("A log Message"));
```

Let's now quickly consider something that is somewhat related to logging.

Displaying on-screen messages

Although not directly related to logging, it is worth mentioning that you can display on-screen messages in C++, just like the **Print** node available in Blueprints. To do this, you will be using the AddOnScreenDebugMessage() function through the GEngine global pointer. To display an on-screen message, you will be using the following line of code:

```
GEngine->AddOnScreenDebugMessage(
    [Key],
    [TimeToDisplay],
    [Color],
    TEXT("An on-screen message"));
```

As this is not a log message, you should not expect the message to pop in the Output Log window, nor in the log file. The Blueprints **Print** node is usually used to print on-screen messages but, unless disabled, it will also serve as an output logger in Visual Scripting.

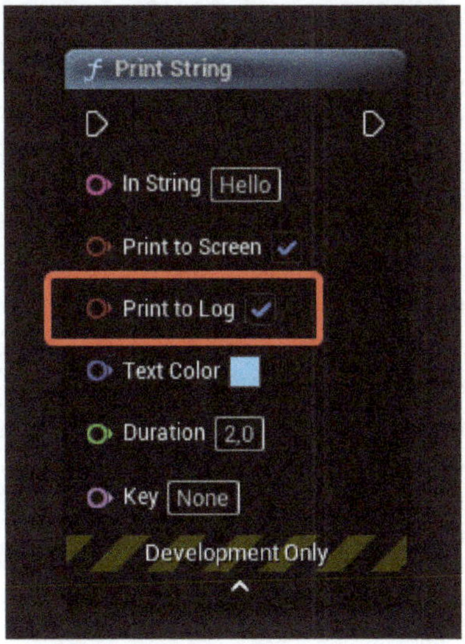

Figure 9.3 – The Print to Log checkbox

In C++ you will have to handle the two features separately.

In this section, I have been presenting a brief overview of the available log system macros along with their syntax. In the following section, we will discuss arguably the most widely used logging tool, the `UE_LOG`. I will provide guidance on how to maximize its effectiveness.

Working with UE_LOG

Central to the log system is the `UE_LOG` macro, which lets you output formatted messages into log files and the Editor Output Log window, categorized by severity, and type. As we have already seen, the category name parameter will let you categorize your messages for filtering. For quick debugging and prototyping, you will usually use the `LogTemp` category as, in these cases, you won't probably need organized and categorized logs. It comes without saying that you should avoid overusing it in larger codebases to keep logs clean! For a well-organized log system, always define your own custom log categories, as explained in the previous section; without proper categorization, important messages may get lost among less relevant messages.

> **Note**
>
> If you are curious about the built-in categories, you will need to head to the engine `CoreGlobals.h` file, where you will be finding all the `DEFINE_LOG_CATEGORY` declarations.

The second `UE_LOG` parameter is the log verbosity; in this case, there is not much to say, except that you should avoid excessive use of high verbosity – such as `Verbose` or `VeryVerbose` – as it may produce overwhelming output and degrade performance. Always try using appropriate verbosity depending on the context.

The third parameter of the `UE_LOG` macro represents the actual message. Proper formatting of the log message, especially using the `TEXT` macro and handling `FString` values, is crucial to avoid errors and produce readable logs.

This means you should always wrap your log format string in the `TEXT` macro to support UE character encoding. `UE_LOG` uses C++ `printf`-style formatting and common specifiers include:

- `%s` for strings
- `%d` or `%i` for integers
- `%f` for floats
- `%u` for unsigned integers

It should be noted that %s expects a `const TCHAR*`, not an `FString` object. To log an `FString` type, you will need to dereference it with * to get its pointer as shown in the following line of code:

```
FString MyStringVal = TEXT("A string val");
UE_LOG(
    LogTemp,
    Log,
    TEXT("String value: %s"), * MyStringVal);
```

Omitting the dereference operator will cause compile errors.

You may have noticed that booleans are omitted. To format a `bool` value, you will need to somehow convert the value to a string, as in the following example:

```
UE_LOG(
    LogTemp,
    Log,
    TEXT("Bool value: %s"),
    bMyValue ? TEXT("true") : TEXT("false"));
```

By default, `UE_LOG` messages are not logged in shipping builds except for `Fatal` errors which always log even before crashing the application. Logging can be enabled in Shipping builds by modifying your project `Target.cs` file and setting the `bUseLoggingInShipping` flag to `true`.

> **Note**
>
> As a rule of thumb, try avoiding shipping builds with logging enabled to ensure that expensive operations are performed or sensitive logs are exposed.

As a final note, it may be worth mentioning that you can make logs even more helpful using the `_ANSI_TO_TCHAR(__FUNCTION__)` macro that will print the function name and make it easier to identify which function is logging it. As an example, consider the following piece of code:

```
UE_LOG(LogTemp, Log, TEXT("Log from %s"), ANSI_TO_TCHAR(__FUNCTION__);
```

If you declare it, for instance, inside a `MyFunction()` function, you will get the following log message:

```
Log from MyClass::MyFunction
```

In this section, I have presented some of the most important features to know about `UE_LOG`, along with its common pitfalls. In the next section, I will be presenting a powerful debug tool that will help create visual representations of the gameplay state. Things will be pretty interesting, I promise!

Using the Visual Logger

The **Visual Logger** has been created to be a robust debugging instrument that can be used to generate and archive visual representations of the gameplay state; this means, it will ease comprehensive post hoc analysis within your development environment. This tool will allow you to observe debug outputs in real-time during active play sessions and, most importantly, retrospectively examine recorded data within the Editor following session completion when needed. This capacity to capture and preserve information for subsequent review is particularly critical when addressing infrequent or elusive bugs.

To open the Visual Logger, you will be selecting **Tools** | **Debug** | **Visual Logger** from the Editor main menu, and you will get the window displayed in *Figure 9.4*:

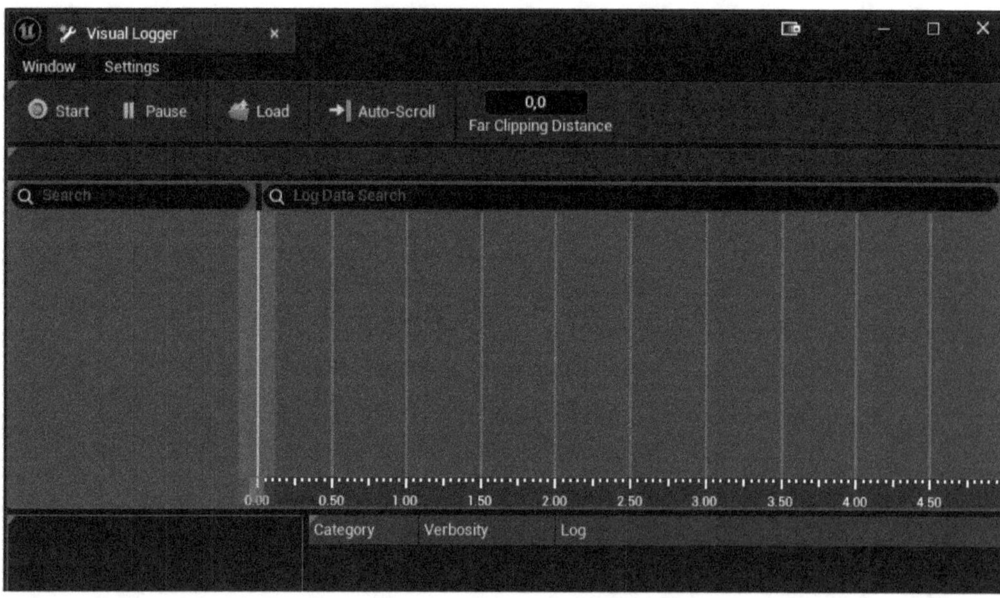

Figure 9.4 – The Visual Logger window

You can initiate logging by clicking the **Start** button. Once the level begins, the viewport will display a list of all Actors that have recorded visualization data, a detailed snapshot of the status of the Actor selected from this list, a text window for presenting debug message output, and a timeline bar that allows scrubbing through the recorded data, as shown in *Figure 9.5*:

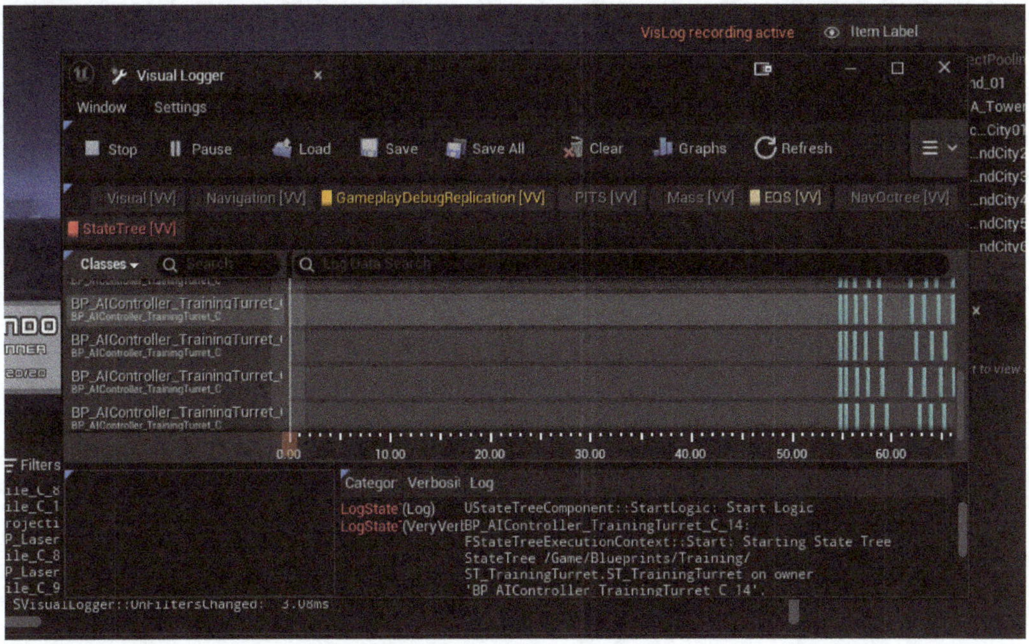

Figure 9.5 – The Visual Logger in action

Log categories can be enabled or disabled at will by clicking their corresponding button. The **Save** button will let you save a recording session and, quite unsurprisingly, the **Load** button will let you reload a recorded one.

Logging with the UE_VLOG macro

Inside this system, the UE_VLOG macro is used to log textual information to the Visual Logger window, which records, and visualizes debugging data within the editor. It works almost identically to UE_LOG but you will need to pass the owning Actor pointer to associate the log entry. This log system is automatically excluded from builds that do not support the Visual Logger, so there will not be any runtime costs. Additionally, as it will just log one frame at a time, you will get per-frame temporal analysis for free.

Taking advantage of shape drawing macros

The Visual Logger system exposes some additional and quite interesting features: **shape-drawing macros** that will let you enhance debugging by visually representing spatial information directly within a level. These macros allow you to draw shapes like boxes, spheres, lines, and points tied to Actors or locations over time, making it easier to track gameplay states, collisions, or movement. If cleverly used, you will be able to quickly identify issues and understand complex interactions in your scene without relying solely on textual logs. The following list enumerates some of the available macros:

- `UE_VLOG_SEGMENT`: Draws a line segment between two points
- `UE_VLOG_SEGMENT_THICK`: Draws a line segment with adjustable thickness
- `UE_VLOG_LOCATION`: Draws a sphere at a location with a given radius
- `UE_VLOG_BOX`: Draws an axis-aligned box centered at a location
- `UE_VLOG_OBOX`: Draws an oriented box with a specified center and rotation matrix
- `UE_VLOG_CONE`: Draws a cone shape defined by origin, direction, length, and angle
- `UE_VLOG_CYLINDER`: Draws a cylinder between two points with a specified radius
- `UE_VLOG_CAPSULE`: Draws a capsule shape with location, half-height, radius, and rotation
- `UE_VLOG_ARROW`: Draws an arrow from a tail location to a head location
- `UE_VLOG_MESH`: Draws a mesh defined by vertices and triangle indices
- `UE_VLOG_CONVEXPOLY`: Draws a convex polygon defined by a set of hull points

All these macros will require specifying an owning Actor, log category, verbosity, color, and shape-specific parameters. Additionally, wrapping your macro with `#if ENABLE_VISUAL_LOG` and `#endif` will ensure that this code is excluded from shipping builds.

As an example, consider the following piece of code that will draw a debug sphere at a specified Actor location:

```
#if ENABLE_VISUAL_LOG
    const FVector LocationToLog = GetActorLocation();
    UE_VLOG_LOCATION(
        this,
        LogPITS,
        Verbose,
        LocationToLog,
        500.f,
        FColor::Green,
        TEXT("My Actor Location")
    );
#endif
```

Once enabled, the visual logger will display a green debug sphere in the level, as shown in *Figure 9.6*:

Figure 9.6 – The UE_VLOG_LOCATION macro in action

In this section, we have examined how Unreal Engine enables the use of its logging system to visualize information within games – an essential aspect of game development. We will now proceed to explore several real-world use cases inside the *Paws in the Shell* project.

Presenting a practical example

As we might expect, Team 33 makes excellent use of logs in its relentless battle against corrupt corporations:

Fernando stormed back into the cavernous hangar of Team 33, his mighty cybernetic legs pounding the ground with relentless force as he cut through the pulsating neon-lit spires of Holo District. The mission had been a crucible of danger – deep within the shadowed underhives, Fernando had shattered the very core of a mecha stronghold, ripping from its grasp vital intelligence on their latest, most insidious behavioral algorithms.

As he landed heavily on the cold steel platform, the mechanical symphony of servos whirring and holographic displays flickering to life surrounded him like a storm. The mechanics, encased in gleaming exosuits that gleamed under the harsh lights, swarmed the cybernetically enhanced flamingo with practiced precision. Their fingers flew over consoles, initiating the critical download process of his mission log. Streams of data cascaded from Fernando's neural interface – every calculated move, every encounter, every minimal yet important anomaly etched in razor-sharp detail. The mechanics' eyes glowed with cold lights as they scoured every bit of information, hunting for any sign of damage within Fernando's cybernetic frame and decrypting the enemy mecha's cryptic behavioral patterns.

"Look here," one mechanic whispered, with a trembling voice tight with urgency, pointing to a moment where a mecha faltered, hesitating before striking. "This... this may be a vulnerability."

Fernando's enhanced optics flickered and dimmed as the download reached its end. Though his body screamed with exhaustion, a fierce spark of satisfaction ignited deep within his core. This mission was only the beginning – now, armed with this precious knowledge, the heroic defenders of Holo District could steel themselves for the brutal battles against the merciless Omnisight Industries minions.

Beneath the cold neon glow and the unyielding steel of the city's heart, Fernando finally rested—ready to rise again when duty called.

In this section, we will be exploring some of the topics presented in this chapter, starting with how I implemented a custom category for the project.

Declaring a custom category

Let's start by opening the *Paws in the Shell* C++ project and heading to the `Public/Utils` folder. You'll find the `PITS_Logs.h` file that contains this single line of code:

```
DECLARE_LOG_CATEGORY_EXTERN(LogPITS, Log, All);
```

As previously mentioned in this chapter, this macro is needed in order to declare the existence of a category without providing its definition, thereby enabling the utilization of the category itself in other files. If you open the corresponding `.cpp` file, you'll find the following line of code:

```
DEFINE_LOG_CATEGORY(LogPITS);
```

This macro is needed to complement the `DECLARE_LOG_CATEGORY_EXTERN` macro, and it will establish the linkage between the declaration and the actual log category. Once declared and defined, the category can be used throughout your log macros. The project has extensively – and perhaps excessively! – employed the `UE_LOG` macro. This approach was adopted to provide clearer explanations of the code presented. As an example, consider the following line of code from the `PITS_BaseCharacter.cpp` file:

```
UE_LOG(
    LogPITS,
    Log,
    TEXT("Taking damage: Original Amount = %f, Effective Amount after Armour =
%f"),
```

```
        DamageAmount,
        EffectiveAmount);
```

As you can see, we are using the `LogPITS` category, and we are displaying a message showing information about damage and armor absorption.

Using UE_VLOG

As an example of using the `UE_VLOG` macro, we are taking a step back to *Chapter 4, Getting the Best out of Pointers*; you may remember that we created an object pool system and now we want to analyze how it is working compared to a classical and non-pooled spawn action. Let's start by opening the `PITS_BaseProjectile.cpp` file and head to the `OnConstruction()` function implementation. You may be aware that this function is called after the Actor is spawned and each time properties change in the Editor. This means we can track when the object is added to the level—handled by an object pool or not. Inside the function, you will find the following line of code:

```
UE_VLOG(
    this,
    LogPITS,
    Log, TEXT("Projectile of type '%s' constructed."),
    *GetNameSafe(this)
);
```

The meaning is quite clear; however, as we will observe shortly, the behavior we record will differ significantly depending on whether the Actor is pooled or not.

Inside the UE Editor, open the **Gym05_ObjectPooling** map and, in the Outliner panel, select the **BP_TrainingTurretActivator** Actor. In the Details panel, tick the **Destroy Pooled Turrets** and **Destroy Weak Pooled Turrets** properties; at the start of the level, only non-object pooled turrets will remain active in the level.

Now, do the following steps:

1. Open the Visual Logger window
2. Hit the **Start** button
3. Disable all the categories by clicking on them, except for the **PITS** one
4. Play the level

The system will begin tracking the construction log for each projectile, resulting in a continuous stream of logs—effectively infinite—generated for every projectile spawned. This logging will persist until the game is terminated. *Figure 9.7* depicts the Visual Logger during this test:

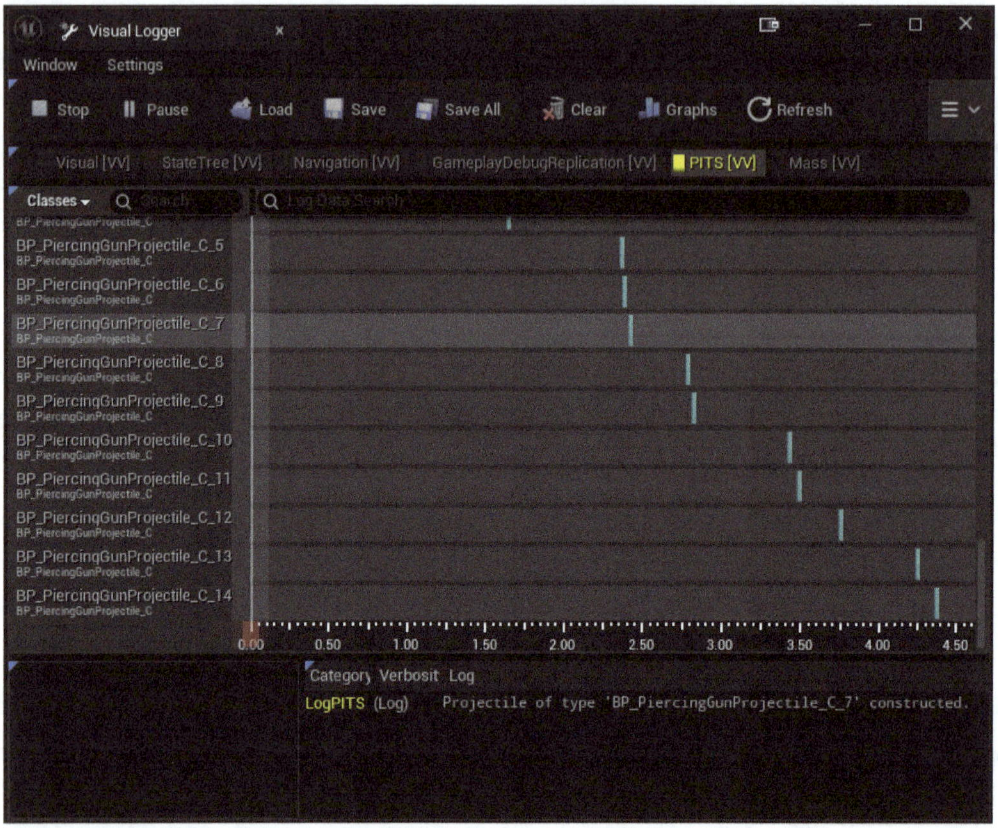

Figure 9.7 – Non-pooled Actors log

Now, clean up the Visual Logger by clicking the **Clear** button and, in the Editor, select again the **BP_TrainingTurretActivator** Actor and untick **Destroy Pooled Turrets** and tick **Destroy Non Pooled Turrets**. Then, repeat the steps to start recording and play the level explained before. You will notice that all projectiles – in this case 100 objects – will be spawned in a single frame and, after that, no other Actors will be spawned, even though the turrets will keep on firing. The Visual Logger with this test is shown in *Figure 9.8*:

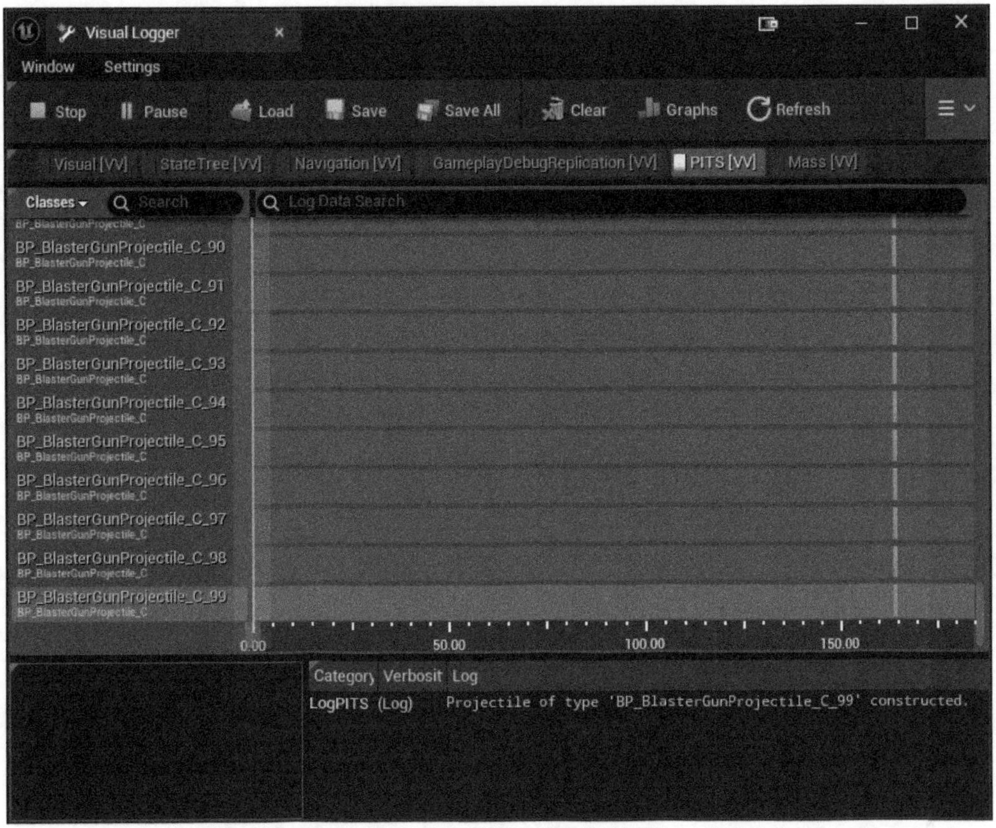

Figure 9.8 – Pooled Actors log

These two examples clearly show how different a mindless spawn is compared with an object pool!

As a side note, this demo level uses State Trees to manage each firing turret. If you are interested in exploring their behavior, you can enable the State Tree category in the Visual Logger to observe the ongoing processes.

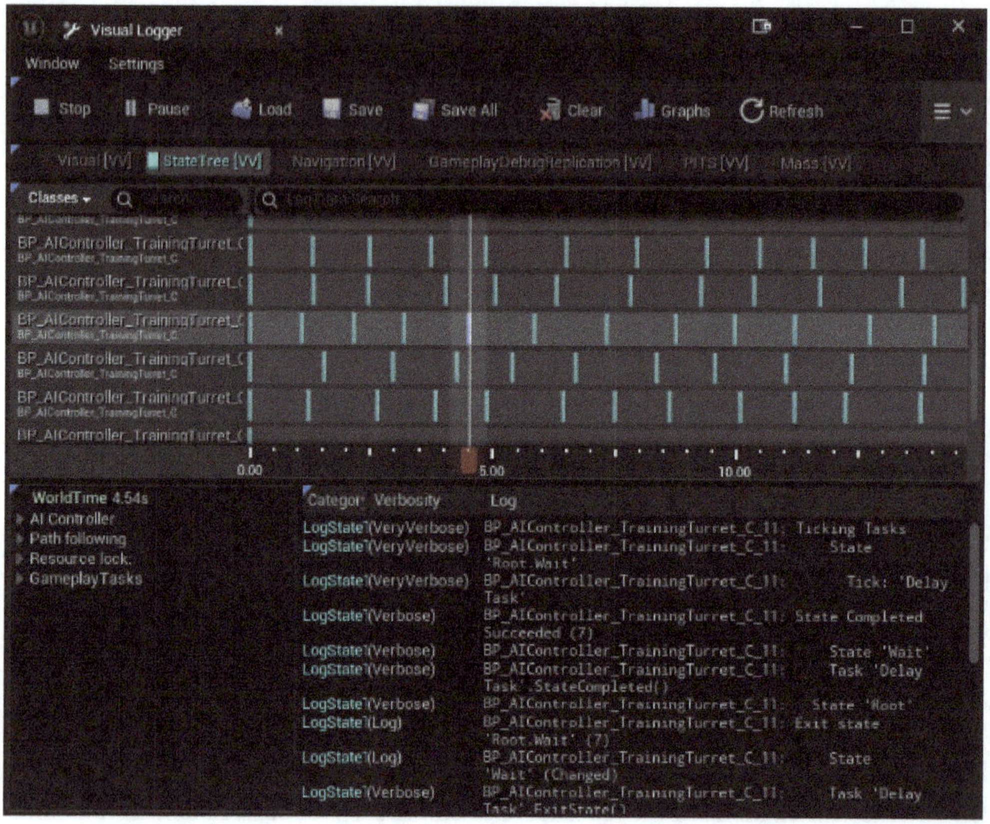

Figure 9.9 – State Trees log

As you've seen from this quick demo, using the Visual Logger can really help you understand and analyze a level while it's running. As usual, it's now time to work a little on your own and write some code.

Develop and self-evaluate

For this chapter, I'd like you to create a simple visual logger for the **Gym03_PointsOfInterest** map. As you'll notice, in this level, the player needs to collect a certain number of credits to clear the level and let the character escape trouble.

Figure 9.10 – The Gym03_PointsOfInterest map

What I am asking you is to create a `PITS_ShortestRouteLogger` C++ class extending `AActor` that will display the quickest path for the player to complete the level. To achieve this, you will need to use the `UE_VLOG_SEGMENT` macro to create a set of segments indicating the correct route. To correctly complete this class, you will need to keep in mind the following points:

- The last segment will need to connect a credit pickup to the exit point that, at the start, will be hidden
- There are two types of pickups, with different values
- There are more credits than needed, so extra credits should not be considered

The task looks pretty simple, but it can get tricky if you don't handle it the right way... Oh, and did I mention you can use Tasks to run heavy computations in the background?

Summary

In this chapter, we have examined the proper methods for logging messages within the UE. Beginning with the humble `Log()` function, we subsequently explored the primary logging macros available and how to use them effectively to maximize their benefits. Next, we have observed that we can benefit from both text-based messages and visually oriented logs. Proper logging is essential for developers as it facilitates efficient debugging, performance monitoring, and maintenance throughout the development lifecycle. In the next chapter, we will be taking a completely different path as we will be considering how to implement additional and reusable features by means of plugins.

Get this book's PDF copy, code bundle, and more

Scan the QR code (or go to `packtpub.com/unlock`). Search for this book by name, confirm the edition, and then follow the steps on the page.

Note: Have your invoice handy. Purchases made directly from the Packt website don't require an invoice.

10

Developing Plugins and Modules

Modularity is a fundamental principle in game development and is absolutely crucial for building scalable and maintainable applications. Through plugins and modules, game programmers will be able to organize their code into well-defined, composable units. Additionally, from a technical standpoint, they significantly optimize development workflows by reducing compilation times through separate compilation units and allowing for conditional loading to improve runtime performance and scalability. This approach streamlines development pipelines and facilitates sharing important features across multiple projects. In this chapter, you will get an overview of the key concepts behind the engine module and plugin system, and I will be presenting a comprehensive guide to creating them efficiently and effectively. In particular, we will be focusing on the following topics:

- Introducing module development
- Designing and developing plugins
- Presenting a practical example

Technical requirements

To get the best out of the following sections, you should have fully understood the previous chapters and have the *Paws in the Shell* project properly set up.

Introducing module development

A **module** in C++ generally refers to a unit of code organization and compilation, typically consisting of a set of related functions, classes, and definitions grouped together to enhance encapsulation and speed up compilation. However, in UE the concept of a module carries a more specific architectural meaning with additional characteristics; modules serve as the core building blocks of the software architecture. Each module operates as an independent code unit that encapsulates dedicated features, editor tools, runtime functionalities, or libraries. This design enforces good code separation by clearly distinguishing public interfaces from private implementations. Modules compile separately and, every time anything changes in your project, only the modules that have changed will need to be recompiled; this means build times will improve greatly. This approach also minimizes unnecessary header inclusions, thereby reducing dependencies and compilation overhead. Additionally, modules provide control over runtime loading and unloading, which helps performance optimization. They also support platform-specific inclusion or exclusion, allowing builds to be tailored for different environments.

Structurally, modules are located within dedicated folders inside the project's `Source` directory or in plugins inside the plugin folder itself. Each module needs to include a `.Build.cs` file that defines its build rules and dependencies. A module code is organized into a `Public` folder, which exposes the module interface, and a `Private` folder, which contains internal logic. Symbols and classes intended for external use are marked with a module-specific API macro to ensure proper linkage.

UE modules can be built as shared libraries (DLLs) to support modular builds or as static libraries for monolithic builds. The UBT manages the dependencies and compilation process based on the module configuration.

For integration into a project, modules must be registered in the main `.uproject` or `.uplugin` files, where properties such as module type—Runtime or Editor—loading phase, and platform restrictions are specified.

Inside your UE project, modules are organized like this:

- A **primary module** that will contain the core gameplay or application code
- Additional modules are added and will be used to organize features, editor expansions or plugins

Creating a module is a five-step process, as described in the following list:

1. Create the module directory structure:
    a. Inside your project's `Source` folder, create a new folder named as your module, for instance `MyAwesomeModule`
    b. Inside the module root folder, create two subfolders: `Public` for your module headers and `Private` for source files

2. Create the build file:
    a. In the module root folder, create a file named `[ModuleName].Build.cs`
    b. Inside this file, define your module dependencies—like `Core`, `CoreUObject`, `Engine` and so on—in the class constructor
3. Define the module class:
    a. Inside the `Public` folder, create the module header file (e.g., `MyAwesomeModule.h`). The module class will need to implement the `IModuleInterface`. Implement the `IModuleInterface` by overriding the `StartUpModule()` and `ShutdownModule()` functions
4. Implement the module class:
    a. Inside the `Private` folder, create the `.cpp` source file (e.g., `MyAwesomeModule.cpp`)
    b. Include the `Modules/ModuleManager.h` file and register the module with the `IMPLEMENT_MODULE(FDefaultModuleImpl, [ModuleName])` macro
5. Update the project to recognize the module:
    a. Add your module as a dependency in your project's primary module `Build.cs` only if your main module uses the new module code
    b. Regenerate your IDE project files to include the new module

After these steps, you will be ready to start implementing your new module, by adding your headers in the `Public` folder and `.cpp` files in the `Private` folder. Just keep in mind you will need to use your module name API – in this case `MYAWESOMEMODULE_API` – for symbols that will be exposed publicly.

It should be noted that, usually, development IDEs with UE integration, will offer module creation. As an example, *Figure 10.1* shows module and plugin options from the **Add** selection inside JetBrains Rider:

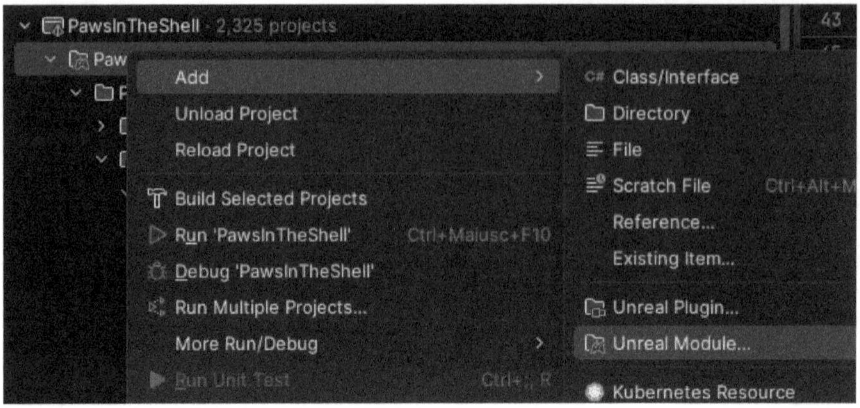

Figure 10.1 – The module creation option

As you have seen in this section, creating a module in Unreal Engine is a straightforward process. Simply follow these steps, and you will be able to successfully set up your module with ease. In the next section, we will take one step further and start checking how to implement a plugin inside the engine.

Designing and implementing plugins

In UE, a **plugin** is an optional package that adds new features or editor tools, often including one or more modules along with assets or content. Plugins can be enabled or disabled per project and can include code, content, or both. The main difference between a plugin and a module is that a module is a code unit – that is, a building block – whereas a plugin is a container that can include one or more modules along with metadata and assets.

> **Note**
>
> At a high level a plugin is simply a collection of modules and assets – there are also content only plugins that supply no code and just `.uasset` files – but we won't be covering that in this section as it's pretty simple if you already understand regular plugins.

A plugin is located in the `Plugins` folder of your project, and it is identified by a `.uplugin` file. Additionally, you will have the option to install a plugin on the editor instead of the project. As previously noted regarding modules, you have the option to create your own plugins using your preferred IDE, provided it supports integration with the engine. However, the UE Editor supports plugin creation straight from the Plugins window, by means of the **Add** button, as shown in *Figure 10.2*:

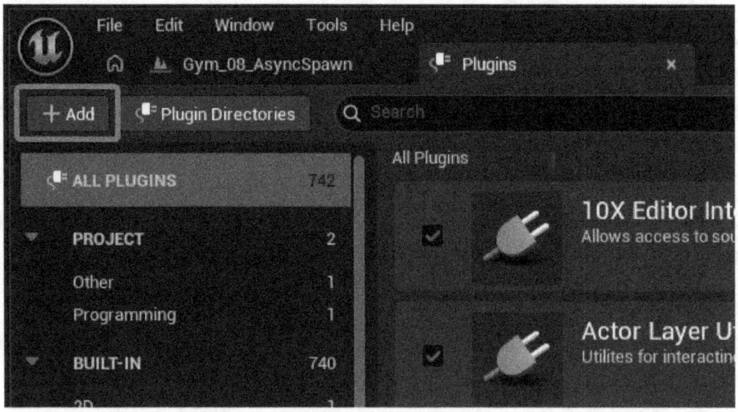

Figure 10.2 – Plugin creation from the Editor

Once the wizard is open, you will have several options for plugin creation, including a **Content Only** – that is, with no code – a **Blueprint Library** or a typical **Blank** plugin:

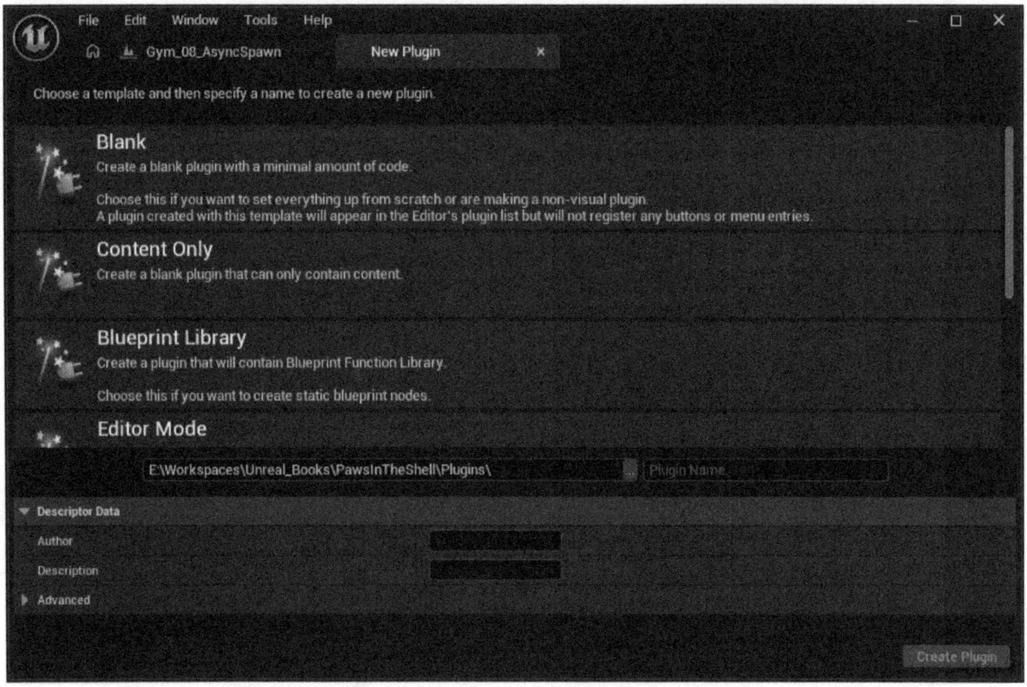

Figure 10.3 – The plugin creation wizard

How should we decide between creating a plugin or a module? Let us explore this in the following subsection.

Choosing between a plugin and a module

When deciding whether to develop a new plugin or add a module to an existing one, the choice ultimately depends on your specific requirements. If the module you are creating is highly specialized for your project and lacks applicability beyond it, integrating it as a module within your project is the most practical approach. On the other hand, if the module offers some features that could be beneficial across multiple projects or serves as a standalone feature, developing it as a separate plugin is highly recommended.

As an example, consider the development of a runtime crafting system. Creating this as an independent plugin offers significant advantages in terms of reusability and ease of sharing across different projects, making its approach preferable. However, if you are developing a specific enemy type for a level, it may be more appropriate to implement its gameplay feature as a dedicated module encapsulating all enemy-related logic.

This will keep gameplay functionality organized and separate from the core game code without needing to create a full plugin.

Implementing plugin API exposure

When developing a plugin, you may take advantage of `MinimalAPI`, a `UCLASS()` specifier that will restrict which symbols are exported from a module. By using it, you will reduce compilation dependencies, especially for classes or interfaces that do not need full DLL export and import visibility. When applied to a class, only the `UClass` pointer – accessible through the `StaticClass()` function – and related functions, will be exported. Class methods, with the exception of the necessary constructors and destructors, won't be exported automatically.

To export class methods explicitly, you will need to mark those methods individually with your plugin full API macro. As an example, consider a plugin with a `MYAWESOMEPLUGIN_API` macro and an Actor class named `AMyActor` that is part of the plugin. To use the `MinimalAPI` specifier, you will be declaring the class as the following code snippet:

```
UCLASS(MinimalAPI)
class MYAWESOMEPLUGIN_API AMyActor : public AActor
{
    GENERATED_BODY()

public:
    AMyActor();
    MYAWESOMEPLUGIN_API void MyExportedAction();
```

```
    void MyInternalAction();
};
```

In this example, only the `AMyActor()` constructor and the `MyExportedAction()` function will be exported; the `MyInternalAction()` function will be used internally and won't be exported. As you may have guessed, using the `MinimalAPI` specifier will give you fine-grained control over symbols exported and will improve binary size and load times while developing your application.

In this section we have explored plugin creation and how to take the best out of them. As usual, in the next section, we will be exploring a real-world scenario, where we will be exploring a plugin used inside the *Paws in the Shell* project.

Presenting a practical example

Let's get started with the new installment on the Team 33 chapter:

In the labyrinthine heart of Holo District, colossal skyscrapers clawed at the smog-choked sky while holographic billboards flickered like restless ghosts. Commander Finn stood still – a frog unlike any other, bearing the weighty mantle of Team 33 leadership.

Tonight, Finn's gaze was locked onto the sanctum of the cyber-med facility. Deep within a cold and sterile chamber, comrade Rae lay motionless upon a cold-steel operating table. Around her, three robotic surgeons moved with surgical precision, their mechanical claws a blur as they fused cutting-edge augmentations into her lithe form.

Finn's amphibian eyes narrowed, a tempest of pride and dread swirling within. Rae was far more than a teammate; she was kin, a bond forged in the crucible of countless missions. These new augmentations promised to improve her agility and senses to near-mythic heights – essential gifts for the perilous missions looming ahead. Yet the procedure was a gamble with fate itself. One minimal misstep, and Rae would be swallowed by the cold, unfeeling maw of the machine. Finn had never dared such enhancements himself – was it caution, or fear, that held him back?

The surgeons exchanged digital code; their electronic voices modulated something almost alien. Though Finn somehow understood the language of technology, he chose to watch silently, vigilant against any sign of disaster. Outside, the city roared with the pulse of a million lives, but here, in this chamber, time seemed to fracture and slow down, hanging heavy with tension.

Then, a soft, definitive beep echoed – a signal that the final implant had been plugged in. Rae's eyes opened, now blazing with intensified light, scrutinizing the room with newfound clarity. She flexed her augmented limbs. A faint, fierce smile curled at the edge of her lips.

Finn stepped forward, his voice steady yet infused with warmth and relief. "Welcome back, my friend. The Pack is now stronger because of you."

Rae's tail flicked with quiet acknowledgment. "I'm ready for the next mission, Commander."

In this section, we will analyze a plugin that has been integrated into the Paws in the Shell project and that will help us in creating some procedurally generated levels.

Presenting the Maze Generator plugin

In my free time, I enjoy exploring various techniques and try to acquire new knowledge by trial and error. Usually, I then share my experiments with free and open-source repositories. Over time, some of these projects often prove valuable in professional contexts. For the *Paws in the Shell* project, I have opted for using a plugin I developed some time ago to generate procedural mazes through a simple but clever algorithm. The original project is called **Maze Generator** and it can be found on GitHub by visiting the following link: `https://github.com/marcosecchi/ue_maze_generator`. The project idea originated after reading a very interesting article on **Wang Tiles**, a mathematical and computational concept used primarily in tiling theory and computer graphics. This concept was originally introduced by mathematician Hao Wang in 1961. Wang tiles have applications in areas such as procedural texture generation, computer graphics, and the study of aperiodic tilings. They are particularly useful for generating large, varied patterns without obvious repetition, which is valuable in game design, simulations, and digital art. The article I was reading is no longer available on the internet, but it is luckily mirrored on Adam Newgas – also known as *Boris the Brave* – website, by visiting this link: `https://www.boristhebrave.com/permanent/24/06/cr31/stagecast/wang/intro.html`.

What impressed me was how easily the **2-edge** tile theory could be applied to maze generation in a game level. Wang Tiles are square tiles with colored edges that are arranged on a rectangular grid in such a way that the colors of adjacent edges must match. These tiles cannot be rotated or reflected and usually fill every cell of the grid. There are two primary styles of matching: edge-matching tiles, which typically create path or maze-like patterns, and corner-matching tiles, which tend to produce patchy or terrain-like designs.

In my case, I opted for the first style and, instead of colors, I focused on walls with open or closed passages. To better understand, consider a room system based on a 2-edge tileset; each room edge can be one of two types – **open** or **closed** – resulting in `2^4 = 16` possible tiles. A "complete" set will include all these combinations, including a room tile with no doors, that is, unreachable. Tiles can be given a unique index by treating open edges as bits:

- **North** = 1
- **East** = 2

- **South** = 4
- **West** = 8

Closed edges are ignored; this means their value is equal to zero.

As an example, consider *Figure 10.4*, which shows a room with a total value of 12:

Figure 10.4 – A Wang Tile room

The room value is given by the straightforward formula:

```
4 (South) + 8 (West) = 12
```

My focus was on creating a system that could generate a maze of interconnected rooms, given a starting grid size. As an additional requirement, every room should be reachable from any point within the maze.

Figure 10.5 shows one such scenario created by the plugin:

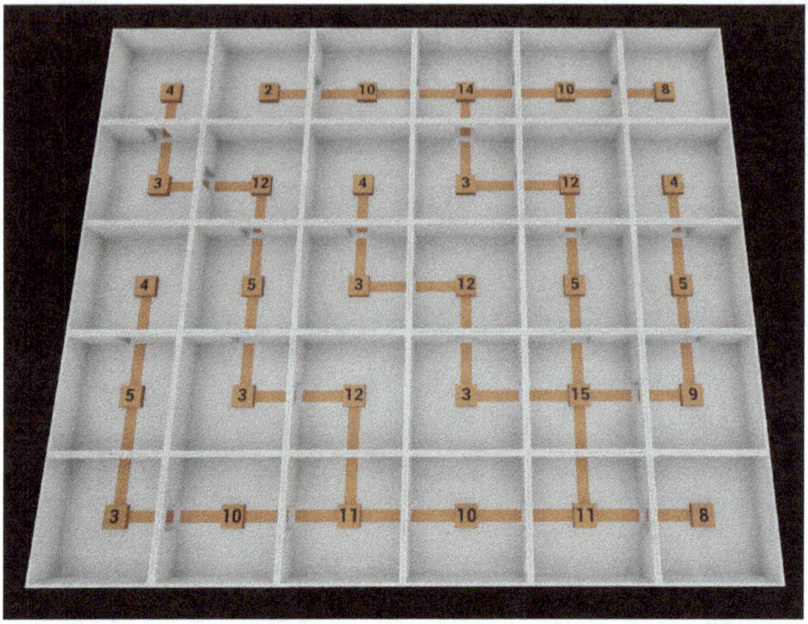

Figure 10.5 – A generated maze

Let's start analyzing the actual organization and implementation of the plugin.

Inspecting the plugin implementation

To better understand how the plugin is organized, open the *Paws in the Shell* source code and look for the `Plugins` folder; you will find a subfolder named `MazeGenerator`. The plugin has been declared inside the `MazeGenerator.uplugin` descriptor file, a JSON file that tells the engine everything it needs to know about the plugin itself, including version, developer info, and modules. At the time of writing this book, the descriptor is as follows:

```
{
    "FileVersion": 3,
    "Version": 1,
    "VersionName": "1.0",
    "FriendlyName": "MazeGenerator",
    "Description": "",
    "Category": "Other",
    "CreatedBy": "Marco Secchi",
    "CreatedByURL": "http://marcosecchi.it",
    "DocsURL": "",
    "MarketplaceURL": "",
```

```
    "CanContainContent": true,
    "IsBetaVersion": true,
    "IsExperimentalVersion": false,
    "Installed": false,
    "Modules": [
        {
            "Name": "MazeGenerator",
            "Type": "Runtime",
            "LoadingPhase": "Default"
        }
    ]
}
```

Inside the Source folder, you will find the `MazeGenerator.Build.cs` file that has been left untouched as I didn't need any additional dependencies. The `Private` and `Public` folders contain plugin declarations and implementations. In particular, we have an enumeration for the directions inside the `MazeDirection.h` file:

```
UENUM(BlueprintType)
enum class EMazeDirection: uint8
{
    North,
    East,
    South,
    West
};
```

Additionally, we have a `MazeGenerationData.h` file to create configurations for the actual generation:

```
USTRUCT(BlueprintType)
struct MAZEGENERATOR_API FMazeGenerationData
{
    GENERATED_BODY()

    UPROPERTY(EditAnywhere, BlueprintReadWrite,
        meta=(UIMin=1, UIMax=33, ClampMin=1, ClampMax=33))
    int32 NumRows;

    UPROPERTY(EditAnywhere, BlueprintReadWrite,
```

```
        meta=(UIMin=1, UIMax=33, ClampMin=1, ClampMax=33))
    int32 NumColumns;

    UPROPERTY(EditAnywhere, BlueprintReadWrite,
        meta=(UIMin=0.f, UIMax=1.f, ClampMin=0.f, ClampMax=1.f))
    float LongPathsSelectionPercentage;

    UPROPERTY(EditAnywhere, BlueprintReadWrite)
    TArray<FIntVector> ExclusionList;
};
```

Finally, the `UMazeGeneratorFunctionLibrary` class includes all the needed code to create a maze based on Wang Tiles. It has been implemented by extending the `UBlueprintFunctionLibrary` class in order to make all its features available inside the Blueprints system. The key component in this context is the `GenerateMaze()` function, which takes an `FMazeGenerationData` parameter and returns a `TMap<FIntVector, int32>` containing the complete maze grid data. This map uses an `FIntVector` as the key to represent each grid element, while the `int32` value indicates which walls have entrances and which do not.

All other functions are helpers that will ease the creation process. This process will connect each room to at least another one, making the full maze visitable. It will start by creating a map with all elements in the grid. Each tile in the map will start with a value of zero, that is, with no openings. From this map, we will exclude all coordinates that should be omitted from the final maze. This additional step allows for the generation of maps with missing tiles, resulting in shapes that are not perfectly rectangular. An additional array, called `VisitedList`, will include all tiles that have already been considered during the generation phase. A random position, or cell, is selected as the starting point for the generation, and it is added to the `VisitedList` array. Next, we will start the generation phase by repeating the following steps in a loop:

1. Select a cell that has already been visited from the `VisitedList` array
2. Create a list of all adjacent empty cells that can be moved to
3. If this list contains at least one cell, then:
    a. Randomly select one of the adjacent cells

   b. Move to the selected empty cell, creating a path as you go; this means adding the corresponding number for the selected direction to the tile value
   c. Add this cell to the end of the `VisitedList` array
4. Otherwise, if there are no empty adjacent cells:
   a. Remove the current cell from the `VisitedList` array

When the `VisitedList` array is empty, the maze is complete; the result will be a fully connected environment. The returned map, being so generic, can be used with any system you will be implementing. As an example, *Figure 10.6* shows a road system created by using models from the *City Roads* set by Kenney:

Figure 10.6 – A road maze

Let's now focus on how this plugin has been used inside the *Paws in the Shell* project.

Using the plugin

The plugin has been put to good use by creating a Blueprint that will generate procedural maps at runtime. To take a peek at a random city generation, open the **Gym_10_LevelGeneration** map and hit the Play button. You will be getting something similar to *Figure 10.7*:

Figure 10.7 – A generated map

As you can see, the floating platforms are just placeholders but consider the possibilities in using a set of custom HoloCity District Blueprints!

The generation is handled by the **BP_MazeGenerator** Blueprint, so open it up to inspect it. This Blueprint has some configuration properties to consider:

- Spacing: To properly position each tile in the grid
- Tile Classes: to list all possible tiles that can be spawned, with each of them solving connections internally
- Data: An `FMazeGenerationData` structure to set the maze shape

The generation process is simple and straightforward. Just open up the Event Graph panel and you will see a single call to the **Generate Maze** function library when the game starts:

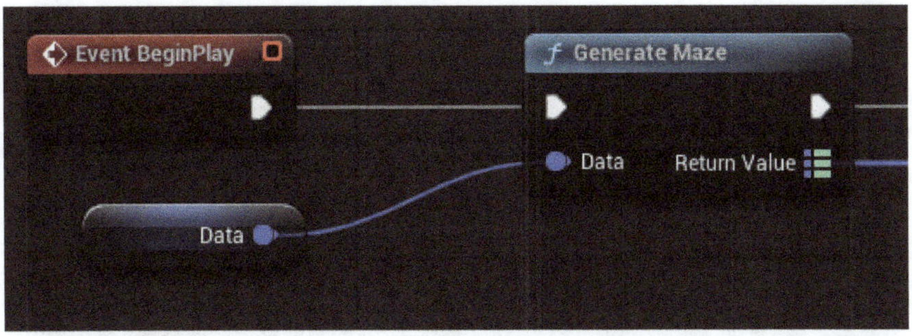

Figure 10.8 – The generate maze node

After this call, it's all just a matter of looping through the map and instantiating random tiles from the **Tile Classes** array. The only thing worth mentioning is that we are initializing each tile with the corresponding value from the generated map:

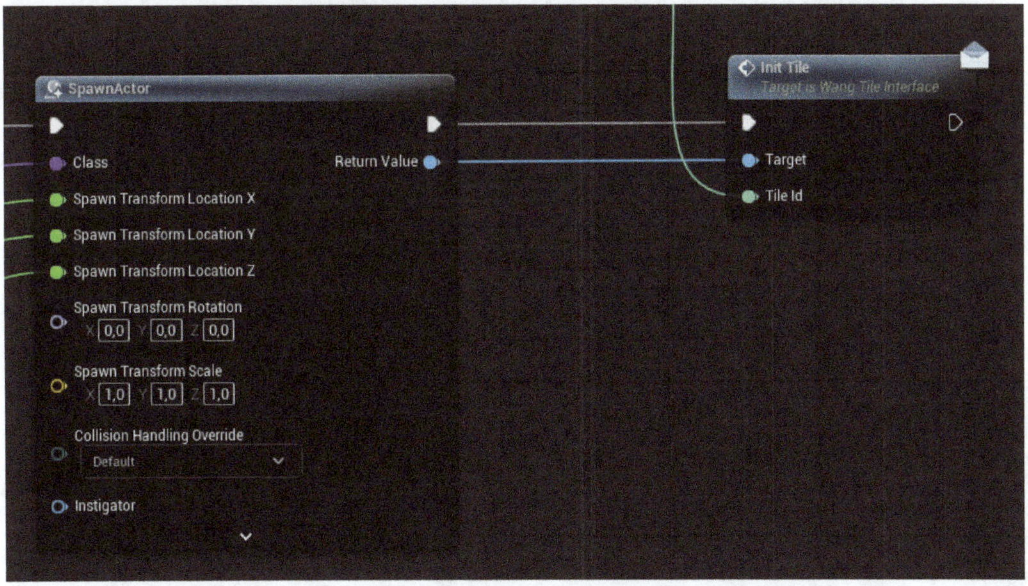

Figure 10.9 – The tile initialization

This initialization is achieved through the **WangTileInterface**, which can be found inside the `Blueprints/Interfaces` folder. The **BP_TileBase** implementing this interface will be responsible for setting the correct appearance of the tile.

Figure 10.10 – The base tile

When initialized, it will check every direction with the passed tile value and destroy any connection that should not be activated. As an example, consider the following block of code, that will check the connection for the **East** direction:

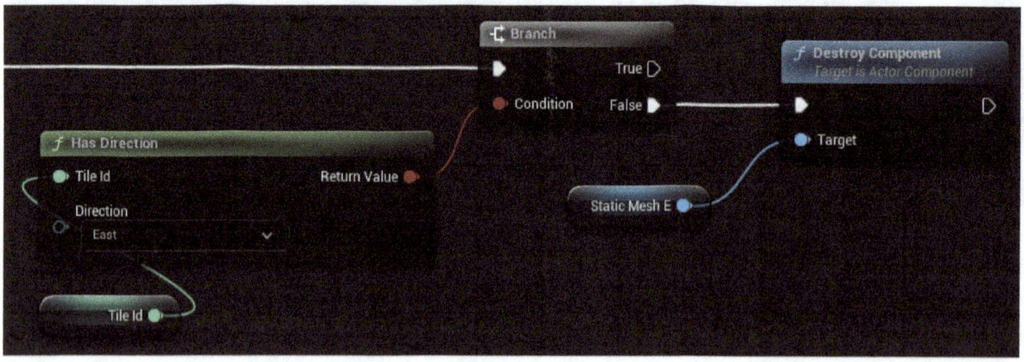

Figure 10.11 – The Check Connection call

If there is no connection, the corresponding StaticMesh Component will be destroyed, effectively removing the connection. The **Has Direction** node has been implemented in the

`UMazeGeneratorFunctionLibrary` class and is a simple bitwise check with each possible direction:

```
bool UMazeGeneratorFunctionLibrary::HasDirection(
    const int32 TileId, EMazeDirection const Direction)
{
    switch (Direction)
    {
        case EMazeDirection::North:
            return (TileId & 1) == 1;
        case EMazeDirection::East:
            return (TileId & 2) == 2;
        case EMazeDirection::South:
            return (TileId & 4) == 4;
        case EMazeDirection::West:
            return (TileId & 8) == 8;
        default:
            return false;
    }
}
```

This wraps up the analysis of the Maze Generator plugin and how it's been used in the *Paws in the Shell* project. By now, I'm guessing you're pretty comfortable with C++ inside UE, so it's time to start creating your own plugin!

Develop and self-evaluate

The task I'm asking you to do in this chapter is pretty straightforward. Going back to *Chapter 4, Getting the Best out of Pointers*, and looking at the object pool Subsystem, I think it would be really valuable if it could be reusable and used in other projects too. So, why don't you create a dedicated plugin for object pooling? This will make it easier to manage and share across multiple projects. Begin by creating an empty plugin and start refactoring the existing project code to migrate the feature into it. It is likely that you have already implemented additional features as outlined in the Develop and self-evaluate subsection of that chapter, resulting in a fully developed pooling system ready for use in your own games.

Summary

In this chapter, we have covered modules and plugin development. Beginning with the declaration of a module, we have examined its significance in game development to enable better code organization, modularity, and reusability across projects. Next, we have considered plugins and how to get the best out of them in UE. Finally, as usual, we've explored a real example of plugin development and how to use that plugin within a project. In the next – and last – chapter of this book, we will be testing things out; something a true developer cannot miss!

11

Testing Your Application

Testing UE applications is essential for ensuring code reliability, functionality, and overall product quality. UE offers developers a suite of testing tools designed to verify that game systems perform as intended throughout the lifecycle of development and CI processes. Within this extensive framework, advanced features are dedicated to validating specific gameplay systems in a controlled environment, simulating real-world use cases to identify issues early. These tests typically involve configuring game states, executing sequences, and verifying outcomes, making them vital for thorough feature validation.

Additionally, dedicated quality functionalities are built upon the UAT framework to facilitate the creation and management of tests in C++. They provide reusable test fixtures and commands that automate setup and teardown procedures, simplifying the development of asynchronous and state-dependent tests. Integrating these methodologies into your project will enhance test development efficiency and help maintain clean, consistent code standards.

In particular, this chapter will focus on the following topics:

- Introducing Unreal Engine testing features
- Working with Functional Tests
- Working with Code Quality Tests
- Presenting a practical example

Technical requirements

To get the best out of the following sections, you should have fully understood the previous chapters and have the *Paws in the Shell* project properly set up.

Introducing Unreal Engine testing features

As we already mentioned in *Chapter 1, Analyzing the Unreal Engine Build Pipeline*, UE has a fully-fledged, multi-layered testing ecosystem designed to ensure project stability throughout the entire development lifecycle. The core system is the **Automation Test Framework**, a suite that allows developers to verify that gameplay systems, core engine features, and assets are functioning correctly without manual intervention. This suite is developed entirely in C++, operating independently of the `UObject` environment and the Reflection System. This means it is not inherently accessible to Blueprints. The primary user interface, known as the **Session Frontend**, can be opened by selecting **Tools** | **Session Frontend** from the main menu.

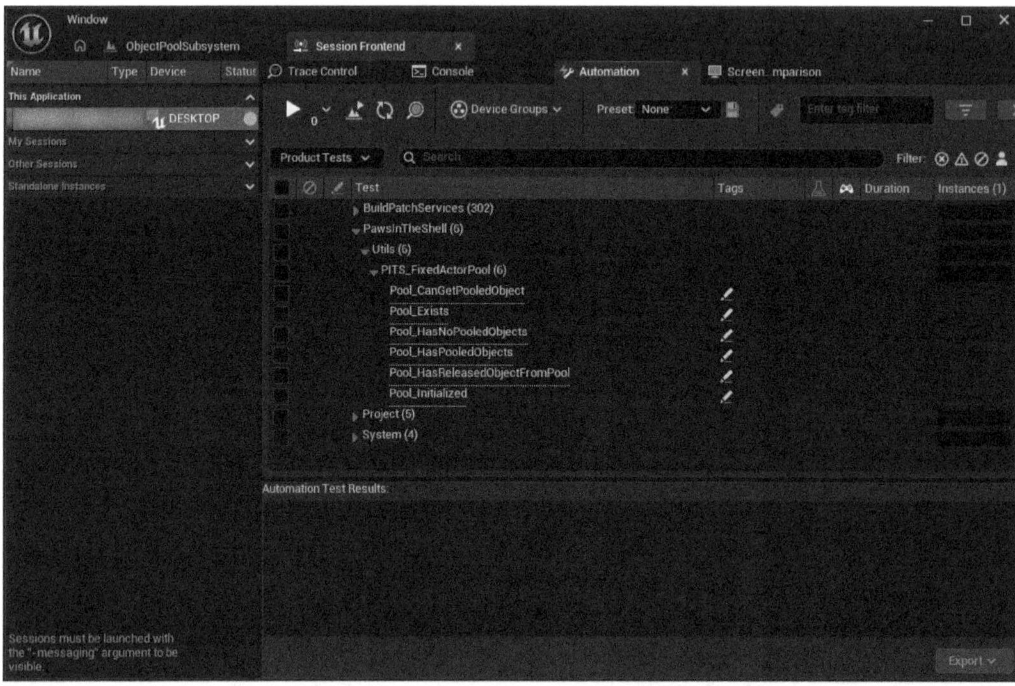

Figure 11.1 – The Session Frontend window

This interface enables users to select, execute, and review the outcomes of your project tests and the engine.

There are many types of tests you can run with this system, for instance **smoke** tests are designed as low-level assessments to verify fundamental system stability. Their primary purpose is to act as minimum acceptance checks to ensure that the most basic and critical parts of a system are stable before more complex testing begins. Their main characteristic is that they should run very fast – usually within a second – and should be run frequently, usually when starting the application to catch immediate regressions.

Inside the Session Frontend window, you can select the **Screenshot Comparison Tool** browser that will allow you to quickly compare screenshots captured within the Unreal Engine Editor. Screenshots generated through automation tests can be viewed using the Unreal Session Frontend tool, which maintains a history of screenshots, making it easy to identify clear rendering errors between different builds. To capture screenshots during your automation tests, you will be using a **Functional Screenshot Test** Actor, that can be placed on your level and used to capture a screenshot to be inspected later.

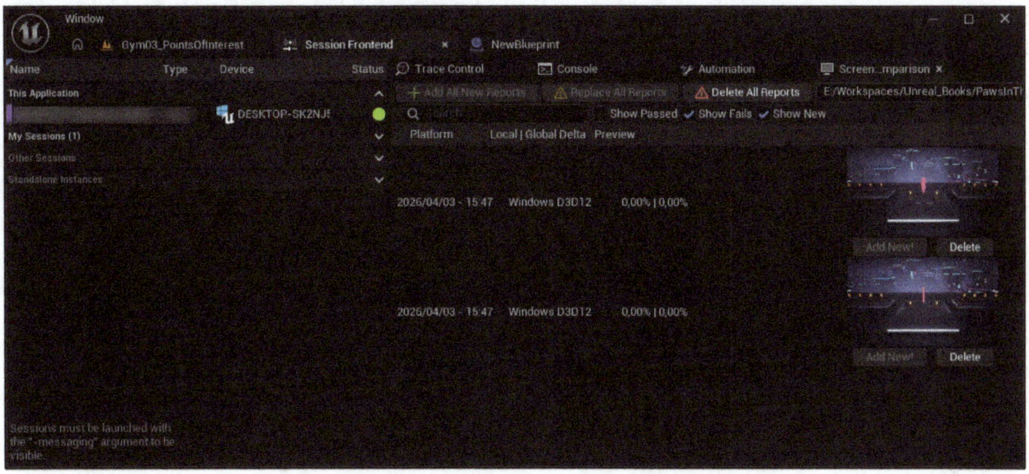

Figure 11.2 – The Screenshot Comparison Tool

Another pretty useful feature is exposed by **latent commands**, which are specialized objects designed to manage actions that span multiple frames. Standard automation tests typically execute as a single blocking function call and, as such, are unable to wait for asynchronous events, such as a map finishing loading or a character completing a montage animation. Latent commands address this limitation by queuing tasks that the engine will process over time; this is usually achieved through the `Update()` function, which is invoked once per frame. This function determines the command progress: if it returns `false`, the test pauses and will wait until the next frame to retry; if it returns `true`, the command is deemed complete, and the test will advance to the next command. These commands are stacked sequentially within a test and are executed in the order they were added.

If you plan to use **Behavior-Driven Development** (**BDD**), you can benefit from **Automation Spec**. In this case, instead of following a linear execution, you will organize expectations in a hierarchical, human-readable structure using a *given/when/then* approach.

To manage more complex user interactions, **Automation Driver** offers a platform-independent API that can simulate mouse movements, clicks, and keyboard inputs. This capability is pretty useful when testing UI workflows and HUD responsiveness without depending on manual playtesting. Used alongside Automation Spec and the Screenshot Comparison tool, you will be able to effectively prevent both logical errors and unintended changes in visual quality.

If you are developing a multiplayer game, **Network Emulation** is the right thing for you. As gameplay logic must remain stable under real-world conditions, Network Emulation will let you simulate latency and packet loss directly within the Editor or via command-line arguments. This way you will ensure that replicated events will behave correctly on high-latency connections.

If you need direct validation of gameplay logic within a level, you will most probably use the **Functional Testing** module; this will let you, as a developer, but also designers, script automated scenarios – such as verifying a weapon spawning system or objective completion – using either C++ or Blueprints.

Another way to improve your development pipeline is by using the **Code Quality Test (CQTest)** module; this module has been developed to extend the engine's automation framework by providing streamlined test fixtures and robust before-and-after actions that automatically reset state between executions.

A final mention to this long list of features goes to the **Gauntlet Automation Framework**. This framework is the engine platform-independent test orchestrator designed to automate the entire lifecycle of a game session across various devices and configurations. It will let you streamline the process by taking a build, deploying it to target devices such as PC, console, or mobile, launching the application, and monitoring its execution. It is also built to manage complex multi-process sessions; as an example, it will let you launch a dedicated server alongside multiple clients to test multiplayer stability. Gauntlet architecture consists of two parts: a set of C# scripts within the UAT that handle device reservation, installation, and log retrieval, and an optional C++ game-side plugin that acts as a `GauntletTestController` object to control the game by simulating actions and reporting results back to the orchestrator. Additionally, it will validate builds by capturing logs, screenshots, and performance data like Unreal Insights traces; this way you will avoid crashes or performance regressions in your game.

> **Note**
>
> Gauntlet Automation Framework is not a test framework and will not replace all other aforementioned tools. Instead, it will provide a way to run your tests automatically on real hardware.

As you have seen in this non-exhaustive section, the engine ecosystem offers a fully-fledged range of testing tools designed to meet the diverse needs of developers. Unfortunately, there is not enough space in this book to cover them all, so we will be focusing on a couple of them that have been used in the *Paws in the Shell* project. We will start by inspecting how the Functional Testing module is set up and used.

Working with Functional Tests

When developing complex game systems within UE, Functional Testing acts as an intermediary between low-level unit verification and manual QA processes. Conventional Automation Tests are usually well-suited for validating isolated C++ logic and core engine modules; on the other hand, Functional Testing constitutes a gameplay-focused framework aimed at assessing the interaction of multiple systems – such as game mechanics, AI, and physics – within a dynamic, live environment.

As a developer, you will be able to script reproducible, level-based scenarios that will emulate authentic player behavior. This means you will be shifting the evaluative emphasis from verifying if a function returns the correct value to determining if a gameplay feature is operating as intended within the context of a game world. As an example, you will be able to inject movement commands through the engine Enhanced Input System to validate traversal mechanics or monitor state transitions during combat sequences and, as such, you will be reducing the reliance on manual regression testing.

Functional Testing can be implemented both in C++ and in Blueprints; in this section we will be focusing on C++ implementation. To start using functional tests in C++, you will be declaring the `FunctionalTesting` module inside your `.Build.cs` project or plugin file, usually inside the `PrivateDependencyModuleNames` declaration array.

When creating a functional test, you will be extending the `AFunctionalTest` class that, being a child class of `AActor`, can be placed in a level to drive the test logic. This class can then be extended both in C++ and in Blueprint, giving you the choice over its implementation. When implementing a C++ functional test, first of all you will be using the `PrepareTest()` function to set up all needed elements that will be used during the test itself. For complex tests that require a setup time longer than a single frame, you will be provided with the `IsReady()`

function that is called every frame; being a `BlueprintNativeEvent`-declared function – that is, implementable both in C++ and in Blueprints – when testing in C++, you will be using the `IsReady_Implementation()` function. To initiate the test, you will be using the `StartTest()` function.

Inside your test class, you will be calling `FinishTest()` every time the test should succeed or fail. As an example, consider the following code snippet:

```
FinishTest(
    EFunctionalTestResult::Succeeded,
    TEXT("Projectile has been correctly spawned"));
```

This will notify the system that the test has succeeded, and everything is working as expected. On the other hand, should you make the test fail, you will be using something like the following piece of code:

```
FinishTest(
    EFunctionalTestResult::Failed,
    TEXT("Projectile has not been spawned"));
```

> **Note**
>
> When implementing your tests in Blueprints, you will be using the **Event Prepare Test** and **Event Start Test** nodes that correspond to the C++ aforementioned functions. Additionally, you will be able to override the **IsReady** function to check when the tests should start.

Another handy function is `RegisterAutoDestroyActor()`, which will let you mark an Actor for destruction after the test is finished; this will reduce manual cleanup and make your code cleaner and easier to understand.

To start functional tests, you will need to add your `AFunctionalTest`–based implementations to a test level and open the **Session Frontend** window. You will find your tests in the **Automation** panel by selecting the **Product Tests** option in the panel drop-down menu.

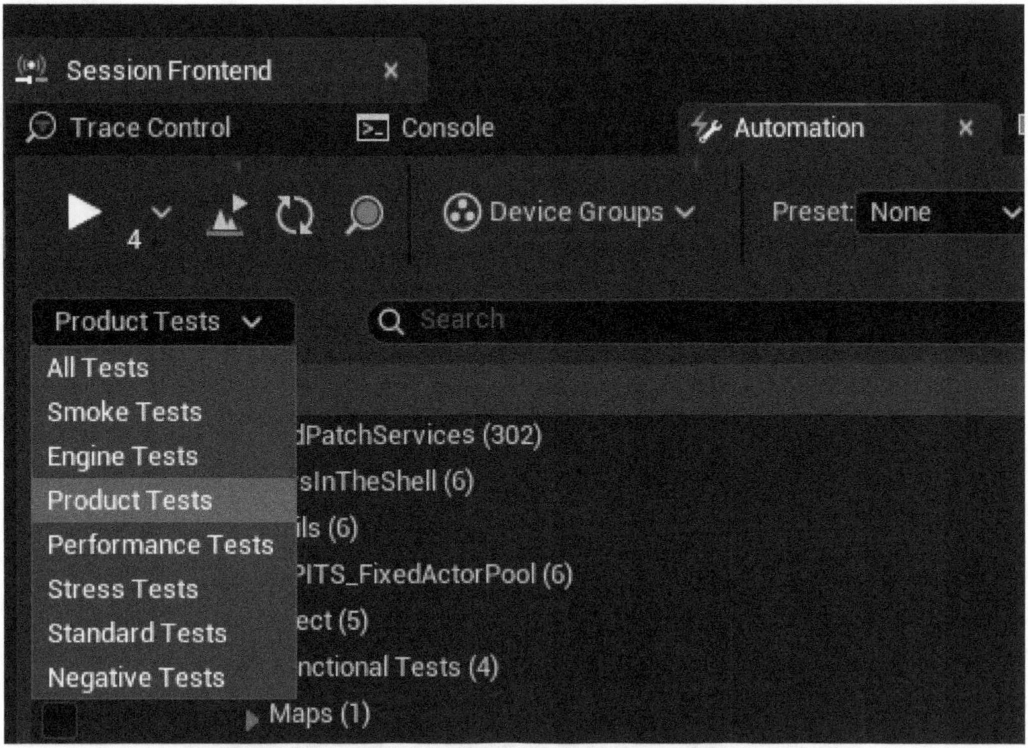

Figure 11.3 – Selecting the Product Tests

By clicking the **Start/Stop tests** button, you will initiate the testing phase; every level that includes at least one Functional Test will be opened, and the tests will be run.

One additional point worth mentioning is the instance editable test properties. Once added to a level, you will be provided with a set of very useful properties – including test ownership, tag, and log handling – that will simplify your testing processes. A couple of them are pretty important. The first property is the **Observation Point** property, which will let you choose a level Actor to view the test from.

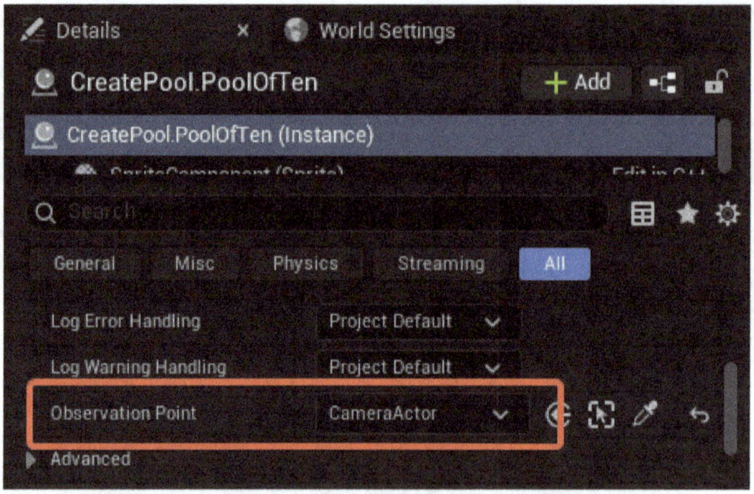

Figure 11.4 – The Observation Point property

This Actor will usually be a Camera Actor that will provide a handy way to observe the test when it is running, as depicted in *Figure 11.5*:

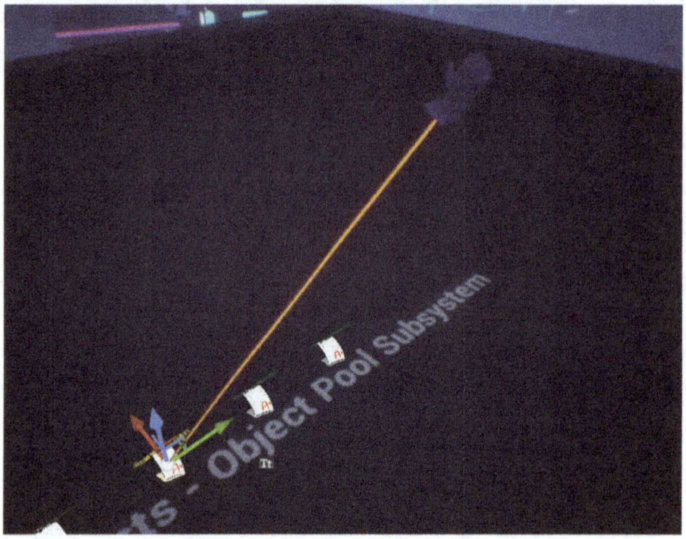

Figure 11.5 – The camera Observation Point

The second item is not a single property but rather a section within your Details panel. The **Timeout** section allows you to manage the timing of each test and address situations where a test may be taking too long, such as in cases of infinite loops.

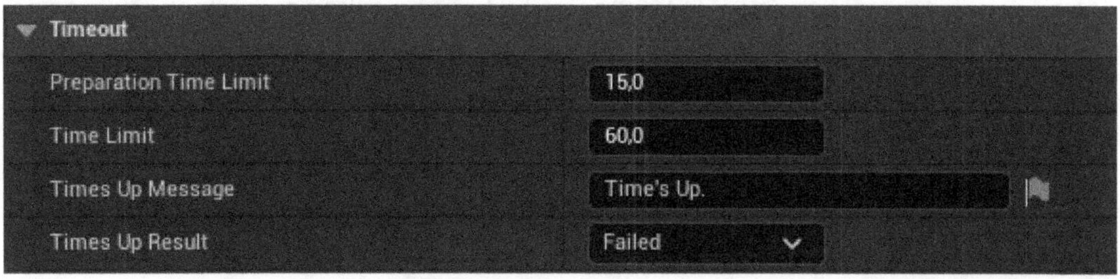

Figure 11.6 – The Timeout section

In this section, you have been introduced to Functional Testing, an in-engine feature that offers a scalable approach to validating complex gameplay elements. When used correctly, it will help minimize the risk of introducing new issues or inadvertently removing existing functionality as the project evolves. In the next section, I will present you with another useful testing option I am using in my everyday job and, obviously, in the *Paws in the Shell* project.

Working with Code Quality Tests

As mentioned earlier in this chapter, CQTest is an advanced testing feature that has been designed to optimize development of C++ automation tests. It is basically a high-level framework that will let you streamline the testing lifecycle by providing robust test fixtures and standardized automation commands. Unlike conventional automation tests, CQTest emphasizes developer productivity and test reliability by supporting standardized before-and-after actions; therefore, it will ensure a clean testing environment for each execution, with automatic state resets that prevent side effects between test runs. CQTest has been released as a C++ module and, as such, can be seamlessly integrated into any project's build dependencies, enabling smooth incorporation within existing development workflows. What's more, it leverages specialized plugins – such as the **Code Quality** and **Enhanced Input Code Quality** test plugins – offering a fully-fledged suite of pre-built tests to validate essential engine functionalities and input systems.

To start using CQTest in C++, you will be declaring the `CQTest` module inside your `.Build.cs` project or plugin file, usually inside the `PrivateDependencyModuleNames` declaration array. Then, you will usually create a `.cpp` in your project's `Private` folder with the following declaration:

```
#include "CQTest.h"
```

A test is declared through the TEST_CLASS() macro, where you will be declaring the class name and the test directory. As an example, you may use the following declaration to create a test:

```
TEST_CLASS(MyAwesomeClass, "My.Test.Directory")
{
    // Implement test setup and teardown
    // Implement tests
}
```

Note

If you need simple standalone tests that do not require a persistent state or complex setup, you can take advantage of the TEST() macro instead of TEST_CLASS().

Inside the test class, you will be adding your tests through the TEST_METHOD() macro declaring the test name, as shown in the following code snippet:

```
TEST_METHOD(MyAwesomeTest)
{
    // Implement test
}
```

If you need to categorize and filter your tests inside the engine automation ecosystem, you can take advantage of the TEST_METHOD_WITH_TAGS() macro. Inside your test methods, you will be using the ASSERT_THAT() macro that will make your test succeed. As an example, consider the following piece of code that checks if an Actor pointer has been properly initialized:

```
ASSERT_THAT(IsTrue(MyActor != nullptr));
```

Finally, within your test framework, you will be using BEFORE_EACH() to execute code prior to each individual test, and AFTER_EACH() to run code following each test. Additionally, you can take advantage of BEFORE_ALL() and AFTER_ALL() to perform setup and teardown operations that apply to all test methods collectively.

Note

As a best practice, always ensure that spawned actors or modified global states are properly cleaned inside the AFTER_EACH() macro, in order to prevent wrong results in your tests.

To start CQTests, you will once again need to open the **Session Frontend** window and find your tests in the **Automation** panel by selecting the **Product Tests** option in the panel drop-down menu. Tests will be categorized through the test directory you have been declaring in your `TEST_CLASS()` macro.

Now that you have a good grip on how to set up CQTests, let's start checking how they are used in a real-world implementation. As always, we will be considering the *Paws in the Shell* project.

Presenting a practical example

Team 33 seems to be preparing for the last and final mission.

Beneath the relentless glare of pulsating neon veins, Holo District throbbed with restless and almost sinister energy. Barbara – an eerie blend of organic grace and cold cybernetic precision – hummed with a quiet menace. Her wings flickered in excitement with iridescent circuits, casting fractured shadows, while her eyes glowed with cryptic data streams visible only to her.

She moved like a ghost within the simulation chamber high above the city's darkened streets. Inside, virtual enemies flickered into existence and vanished like phantoms – Omnisight Industries' elite security drones, cold and unyielding, programmed to predict and crush any resistance. Barbara weaved through the digital carnage, each strike a calculated blade, every dodge a whispered promise of destruction. Her movements were surgical, merciless, honed by countless repetitions.

The mission ahead was stark and unforgiving: The Pack was to infiltrate Omnisight Industries' fortress-like stronghold, extract the forbidden data on their latest AI constructs, and disappear into the shadows without a trace. Failure meant capture or something far worse. But Barbara's endless drills were more than mere preparation; they were a ritual of survival, a deadly dance where every simulated kill sharpened her instincts.

Barbara's wings buzzed with mounting urgency, her systems beating in perfect harmony with the city's pulsing heartbeat. The last test was no longer distant – it loomed like a storm on the horizon. In the suffocating shadows of Holo City, Team 33's final mission was about to start.

In this section we will be checking some tests implemented in the *Paws in the Shell* project; as previously mentioned, we will be analyzing Functional testing and CQ Testing. The following subsections will primarily focus on our cherished object pooling system, as it enables us to examine both creation policies and in-game logic. We will be starting with how Functional Testing has been implemented.

Inspecting Functional Tests

The functional test example we are taking into consideration is object pooling; in particular, we will be checking if the `PITS_ObjectPoolSubsystem` class has been properly set up and initialized. Tests are located in the `Tests/FunctionalTesting/Subsystems` folder of the project source code, so start your IDE and open the `PITS_ObjectPoolSubsystem_CreatePool_FunctionalTest.h` file. You will find the following property declarations:

```
UPROPERTY()
TObjectPtr<UPITS_ObjectPoolSubsystem> PoolSubsystem;

UPROPERTY(EditAnywhere)
int32 PoolSize = 10;

UPROPERTY(EditAnywhere)
TSubclassOf<AActor> SpawnableClass;
```

As you can see, we will need a reference to the Subsystem, the pool size and the Actor class we will be using to create an actual pool. In addition, you will find the following two function overrides:

```
virtual void PrepareTest() override;
virtual void StartTest() override;
```

If you open the corresponding `.cpp` file, you will see that the `PrepareTest()` function is actually quite straightforward as it will just retrieve the Subsystem:

```
PoolSubsystem = GetWorld()->GetSubsystem<UPITS_ObjectPoolSubsystem>();
```

Tests are obviously run inside the `StartTest()` function implementation. First of all, the test will fail if the `Subsystem` property or the `SpawnableClass` property is null, as shown in the following code snippet:

```
if (PoolSubsystem == nullptr)
{
    FinishTest(
        EFunctionalTestResult::Failed,
        TEXT("UPITS_ObjectPoolSubsystem is null"));
    return;
}

if (SpawnableClass == nullptr)
{
    FinishTest(
```

```
        EFunctionalTestResult::Failed,
        TEXT("SpawnableClass is null"));
    return;
}
```

Next, we create the actual pool after cleaning up any previous pool creations with the same class:

```
PoolSubsystem->CleanupObjectPool(SpawnableClass);
PoolSubsystem->CreateObjectPool(SpawnableClass, PoolSize);
```

The next step is to check if the pool size is actually correct and if at least one pooled object has been created.

```
if (PoolSubsystem->GetPoolSize(SpawnableClass) != PoolSize)
{
    FinishTest(
        EFunctionalTestResult::Failed,
        TEXT("Pool size does not match expected value"));
    return;
}
if (PoolSubsystem->GetPoolSize(SpawnableClass) == 0)
{
    FinishTest(
        EFunctionalTestResult::Failed,
        TEXT("Pool size should have at least one object"));
    return;
}
```

The second check is necessary as we are working with a fixed pool size, and we don't want to create empty pools that won't be usable at all. A lazily initialized pool – that is, a pool that can grow at runtime – won't obviously necessitate this check.

If all these checks are passed, it means the test has succeeded and so we can finish the test with a `Succeeded` result:

```
FinishTest(
    EFunctionalTestResult::Succeeded,
    TEXT("Pool subsystem functional test passed"));
```

Please note that, just before finishing the test, we execute a cleanup on the Subsystem for the next tests:

```
PoolSubsystem->CleanupObjectPool(SpawnableClass);
```

It should be noted that the `GetPoolSize()` and `CleanupObjectPool()` from the `PITS_ObjectPoolSubsystem` class have been created for testing purposes only. This means they should not be available publicly. If you open the `PITS_ObjectPoolSubsystem.h` file, you will find the actual declarations wrapped within an `#if` directive, as shown in the following code snippet:

```
#if WITH_DEV_AUTOMATION_TESTS
public:
    int32 GetPoolSize(
        const TSubclassOf<AActor> SpawnableClass) const;

    void CleanupObjectPool(
        TSubclassOf<AActor> SpawnableClass);
#endif
```

This will ensure the function will be available only when performing automation tests. Space for this chapter is a bit limited, but if you are curious, you can check all other functional tests available in the project.

To check where the tests are actually used, you will need to open the UE Editor and open the **ObjectPoolSubsystem** map located in the `Tests/FunctionalTests` folder.

Figure 11.7 – The Functional Tests map

You will be finding a set of test Actors whose names have been set using dot notation; by using this convention your tests will be categorized once displayed inside the Session Frontend tool.

Now, let's consider a CQ Test in the next subsection.

Inspecting CQ Tests

For the CQ Tests, we will also consider object pooling, with a primary focus on the `UPITS_FixedActorPool` class. These tests are located in the `Private/Tests/CQTesting/Utils` folder. Open the `PITS_FixedActorPool_Tests.cpp` file and you will find the `TEST_CLASS()` declaration:

```
TEST_CLASS(PITS_FixedActorPool, "PawsInTheShell.Utils")
{
    // Execute tests
}
```

We will be using just two properties – a pool reference and the pool size – to run the test:

```
TObjectPtr<UPITS_FixedActorPool> TestPool = nullptr;
int32 PoolSize = 5;
```

Before each test, we will be creating the actual pool and after each test we will destroy it as shown in the following code snippet:

```
BEFORE_EACH()
{
    UWorld* World = GWorld;
    TestPool = NewObject<UPITS_FixedActorPool>(World);
}

AFTER_EACH()
{
    if (TestPool)
    {
        TestPool->ConditionalBeginDestroy();
        TestPool = nullptr;
    }
}
```

Next, you will find a list of all the tests that will be run through the `TEST_METHOD()` macro. As an example, the following test simply checks that the pool has been properly initialized with the requested pool size:

```
TEST_METHOD(Pool_Initialized)
{
    TestPool->InitializePool(
        AActor::StaticClass(),
        PoolSize);
    ASSERT_THAT(
        IsTrue(TestPool->GetPoolSize() == PoolSize));
}
```

The following block of code checks if a pooled object can actually be retrieved:

```
TEST_METHOD(Pool_CanGetPooledObject)
{
    TestPool->InitializePool(
        AActor::StaticClass(),
        PoolSize);
    const AActor* Actor = TestPool->GetObjectFromPool();
```

```
    ASSERT_THAT(IsTrue(Actor != nullptr));
}
```

The following test checks object availability once the pool has been depleted:

```
TEST_METHOD(Pool_HasNoPooledObjects)
{
    TestPool->InitializePool(
        AActor::StaticClass(),
        PoolSize);
    for (int32 i = 0; i < PoolSize; i++)
    {
        TestPool->GetObjectFromPool();
    }
    ASSERT_THAT(
        IsFalse(TestPool->HasAvailableObjectsInPool()));
}
```

There are some other tests created, and I highly recommend exploring all of them in order to gain a comprehensive understanding of the system functionality. As you can see, tests are quite straightforward and fast, but they cover most of the potential issues that may arise.

In the next subsection, we will be running the tests through the Session Frontend tool to check whether everything is behaving as expected.

Running the tests

To run the test, we need to get back to the UE Editor, open the Session Frontend window and select the **Automation** tab. From the drop-down menu, select **Product Tests** in order to show the project tests. Functional Tests can be found inside the **Project** | **Functional Tests** | **Tests** section, while CQ Tests will be categorized inside the **PawsInTheShell** section. To run tests you will just need to select those you need to check and hit the **Start/Stop tests** button. Tests that succeed will display a satisfying green bar while failed tests will show a red bar. Tests that have logged warnings will be displayed as yellow.

As you can see from *Figure 11.8* all tests have succeeded except for the first one that displays a red bar:

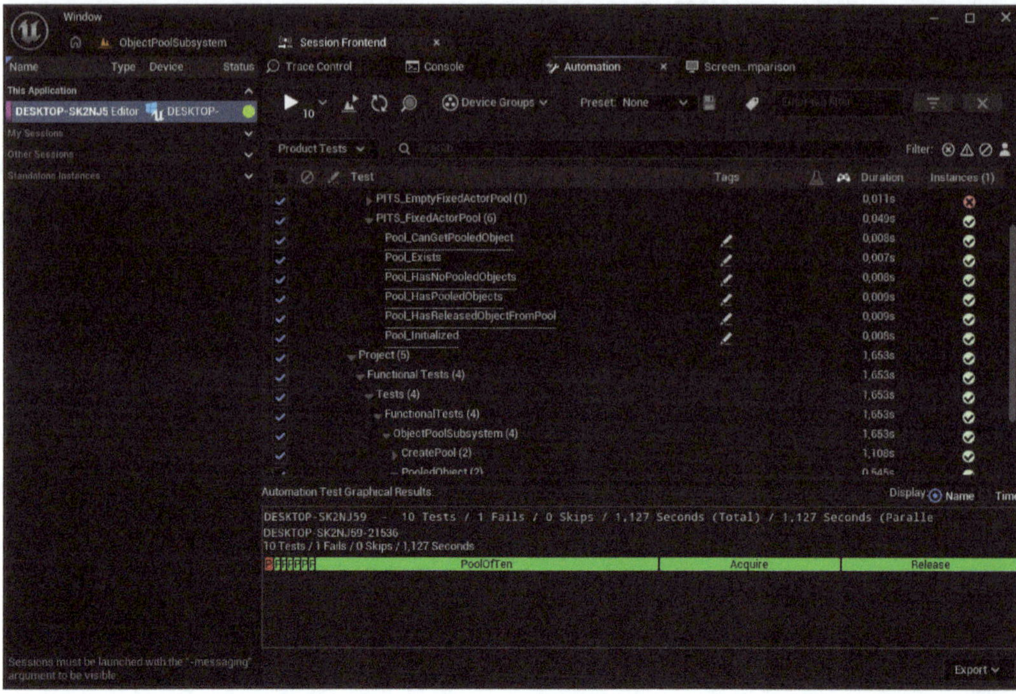

Figure 11.8 – Test results

The length of each bar corresponds to the time required to complete it; you will notice that CQ Tests are relatively quick, whereas Functional Tests take significantly longer. This is because Functional tests need to open maps and properly initialize the scene.

After running some tests, you might have seen a few fail – that's because I have hidden some sneaky little bugs for you to find. Now it's your turn to track them down!

Develop and self-evaluate

As mentioned, there are some bugs inside the object pooling system; by running the tests you will notice some of them will actually fail. These tests are failing because we are requiring an object pool to have at least a pooled object; as mentioned earlier in this chapter, a fixed pool with no object would simply be useless!

Figure 11.9 – The failing tests result

The first test to fail can be found in the `PITS_EmptyFixedActorPool_test.cpp` file:

```
TEST_METHOD(Pool_HasAtLeastOneObject)
{
    TestPool->InitializePool(
        AActor::StaticClass(), PoolSize);
    ASSERT_THAT(IsTrue(TestPool->GetPoolSize() != 0));
}
```

After pool initialization, it requests at least one object to be available inside the pool.

The second test that is failing is related to the first one and can be found inside the already mentioned `UPITS_ObjectPoolSubsystem_CreatePool_FunctionalTest` class; in this case, we are requiring at least a pooled object in the Subsystem pool map. With these bugs in the project, it's time to fix them and get a full green test bar!

Continuing the project

The *Paws in the Shell* project is definitely still a work in progress! There's a lot to add, from smarter enemy AI and gameplay levels to a fully completed mission system. If you enjoyed coding your logic as much as I enjoyed coming up with tasks for you, I definitely recommend trying to add your own features and turn it into a fully featured, publishable game.

On my own side, I will keep implementing the game by working on this repository: `https://github.com/marcosecchi/PawsInTheShell`.

Just check it from time to time in order to take a peek at how things are progressing.

Summary

In this last chapter, we have been considering different ways to test your own application; as you have seen, UE offers a full set of tools and features that give you the power to make your project smooth and efficient before reaching your audience. Due to space constraints, we have limited our examination to Functional Testing and CQ Tests, which have been used within the *Paws in the Shell project*. Becoming proficient with these testing tools is essential to delivering a polished and reliable application.

I truly hope that by now your coding skills have reached an expert level and that you feel confident using them to solve tricky problems with creativity and accuracy!

Epilogue

As the neon lights of Holo District flickered, a fragile calm settled over the darkened skyline. Team 33 stood vigilant – silent guardians in a world where shadows hid both danger and hope. Their last mission against OmniSight Industries had not ended in a grand victory or a decisive defeat; instead, it was an ongoing war fought in the cracks of the city's steel and circuitry.

Though scars marked their bodies and memories, Team 33 remained unbroken. Each mission had forged them into more than soldiers – they were now a pack bound by loyalty, resilience, and the unyielding will to protect the people of Holo District from the cold grip of corporate tyranny.

In the heart of the city, whispers of rebellion stirred among the citizens, inspired by the courage of those who refused to bow. The fight was far from over, but as long as the four guardians stood vigilant, Holo District had a chance to reclaim its soul from the machines that sought to own it.

And so, beneath the flickering city glows, hope endured – fueled by those who dared to stand against darkness, ready to write the next chapter of resistance.

Wishing you fun with your code!

Get this book's PDF copy, code bundle, and more

12

Unlock Your Exclusive Benefits

Your copy of this book includes the following exclusive benefits:

Complete Code Bundle

Download the full source code for this book's examples and projects.

DRM-Free PDF Version

Download DRM-free PDF and ePub copies of this book.

7-Day Packt Library Access

Get 7-day unlimited access to 8,000+ books and videos. No credit card required.

Available for first-time Packt+ trial users only.

Next-Gen Reader Access

Read this book on Packt Reader with progress sync, dark mode and note-taking.

Follow the guide below to unlock them. The process takes only a few minutes and needs to be completed once.

Unlock this Book's Free Benefits in 3 Easy Steps

Step 1

Keep your purchase invoice ready for *Step 3*. If you have a physical copy, scan it using your phone and save it as a PDF, JPG, or PNG.

For more help on finding your invoice, visit `https://www.packtpub.com/en-us/unlock?step=1`.

> **Note**
>
> If you bought this book directly from Packt, no invoice is required. After *Step 2*, you can access your exclusive content right away.

Step 2

Scan the QR code or go to `packtpub.com/unlock`.

On the page that opens (similar to *Figure 12.1* on desktop), search for this book by name and select the correct edition.

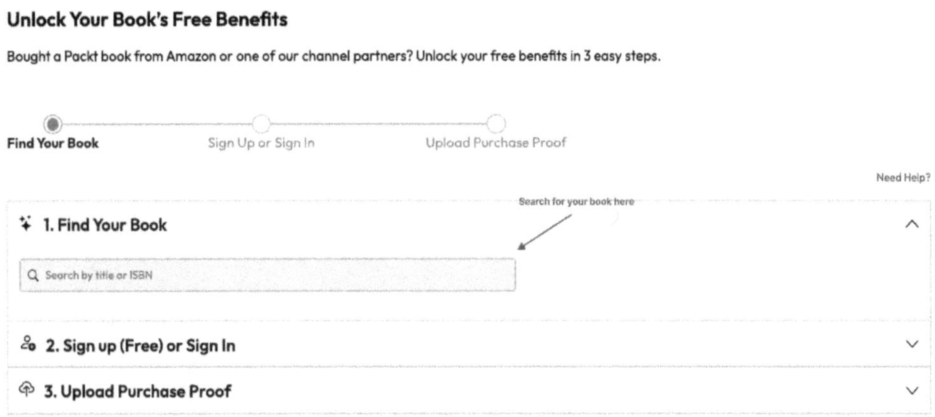

Figure 12.1: Packt unlock landing page on desktop

Step 3

After selecting your book, sign in to your Packt account or create one for free. Then upload your invoice (PDF, PNG, or JPG, up to 10 MB). Follow the on-screen instructions to finish the process.

Need Help

If you get stuck and need help, visit `https://www.packtpub.com/unlock-benefits/help` for a detailed FAQ on how to find your invoices and more. This QR code will take you to the help page.

Note

If you are still facing issues, reach out to `customercare@packt.com`.

Other Books You May Enjoy

If you enjoyed this book, you may be interested in these other books by Packt:

Unreal Engine 5 Game Development with C++ Scripting

Zhenyu George Li

ISBN: 9781804613931

- Develop coding skills in Microsoft Visual Studio and the Unreal Engine editor
- Discover C++ programming for Unreal Engine C++ scripting
- Understand object-oriented programming concepts and C++-specific syntax
- Explore NPC controls, collisions, interactions, navigation, UI, and the multiplayer mechanism
- Use the predefined Unreal Engine classes and the programming mechanism
- Write code to solve practical problems and accomplish tasks
- Implement solutions and methods used in game development

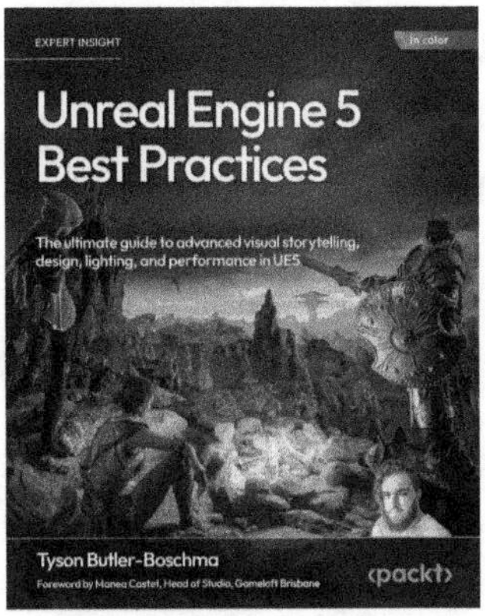

Unreal Engine 5 Best Practices

Tyson Butler-Boschma

ISBN: 9781836205654

- Explore advanced lighting techniques to create dynamic, realistic lighting using Lumen
- Build and edit assets directly inside Unreal with its built-in modeling tools
- Craft compelling cinematic sequences with cameras and storytelling
- Design stunning, immersive worlds through layout and composition design
- Add destruction and realism with Chaos integration
- Profile and boost efficiency across your projects
- Solve real-world development challenges with tested UE5 strategies

Packt is searching for authors like you

If you're interested in becoming an author for Packt, please visit `authors.packt.com` and apply today. We have worked with thousands of developers and tech professionals, just like you, to help them share their insight with the global tech community. You can make a general application, apply for a specific hot topic that we are recruiting an author for, or submit your own idea.

Share your thoughts

Now that you've finished *Mastering Unreal Engine 5 Game Development with C++ Scripting*, we'd love to hear your thoughts! Scan the QR code below to go straight to the Amazon review page for this book and share your feedback or leave a review on the site that you purchased it from.

https://packt.link/r/180666593X

Your review is important to us and the tech community and will help us make sure we're delivering excellent quality content.

Index

Symbols

A

B

C

D

U

www.ingramcontent.com/pod-product-compliance
Lightning Source LLC
LaVergne TN
LVHW060031210926
848481LV00013B/3835
9781806665938